ON EXPERIENCE, NATURE,
AND FREEDOM

The Library of Liberal Arts
OSKAR PIEST, FOUNDER

ON EXPERIENCE, NATURE, AND FREEDOM

Representative Selections

JOHN DEWEY

Edited, with an introduction, by
RICHARD J. BERNSTEIN
Department of Philosophy, Haverford College

· ·

The Library of Liberal Arts
published by
THE BOBBS-MERRILL COMPANY, INC.
INDIANAPOLIS · NEW YORK

John Dewey: 1859-1952

PREFACE

The primary purpose of this collection of John Dewey's writings is to lay bare the outlines of his comprehensive theory of experience and nature. In the Introduction, I argue that beginning roughly with the publication of *Experience and Nature* in 1925, Dewey self-consciously turned to a more careful clarification and justification of the central themes of his philosophy. All except two of the selections appeared after 1925. The two earlier articles ("The Need for a Recovery of Philosophy" and "The Subject Matter of Metaphysical Inquiry") help to bring the mature phase of Dewey's philosophic career into clearer focus.

Consequently these selections provide a general introduction to Dewey's philosophy and exhibit the variety of his investigations. Several extremely important articles for appreciating and evaluating Dewey which are now to be found only in scattered out-of-print books and journals are reprinted here. The selections have been arranged so as to lead the reader from the more intimate and concrete to the more comprehensive features of Dewey's thought, unfolding the themes of experience, nature, and freedom. The introductory comment for each selection clarifies its context and suggests some key connections with other selections.

The Introduction, as well as the final choice of selections, has benefited from the acute sympathetic criticism of Professor Charles W. Hendel and Professor John E. Smith. It was they who first taught me to appreciate that Dewey was attempting to say something original and important. I am also indebted to Mr. Oskar Piest, who has not only given me valuable editorial advice, but has actively participated in shaping the character of this volume. Miss Suzanne Boorsch has graciously assisted in reading proof and compiling the Index. Finally, it was my wife, Carol, who originally suggested compiling this collection and has cheerfully aided in its publication.

R. J. B.

ACKNOWLEDGMENTS

For permission to reprint the essays in the present volume, grateful acknowledgment is made to:

Macmillan Company for "From Absolutism to Experimentalism," in *Contemporary American Philosophy,* II, 1930.

Henry Holt and Company for "The Need for a Recovery of Philosophy," in *Creative Intelligence: Essays in the Pragmatic Attitude,* 1917; and "The Pattern of Inquiry," in *Logic: The Theory of Inquiry,* 1938.

Columbia University Press for "An Empirical Survey of Empiricisms," in *Studies in the History of Ideas,* III, 1935.

University of California Press for "Context and Thought," in *University of California Publications in Philosophy,* XII, 1931.

New York University Press for "Time and Individuality," in *Time and its Mysteries,* II, 1940.

The *Philosophical Review* for "Nature in Experience," XLIX, 1940.

Mrs. John Dewey and the *Journal of Philosophy* for "The Subject Matter of Metaphysical Inquiry," XII, 1915; and "Peirce's Theory of Quality," XXXII, 1935.

Mrs. John Dewey, Mrs. Albert G. A. Balz, and the *Journal of Philosophy* for "A Letter in Reply to Mr. Albert G. A. Balz," XLVI, 1949.

G. P. Putnam's Sons for "Having an Experience," in *Art as Experience,* 1934.

Mrs. John Dewey and G. P. Putnam's Sons for "Qualitative Thought" and "Philosophies of Freedom," in *Philosophy and Civilization,* 1931, 1958.

CONTENTS

· · · · · · · · · · · · · · · · ·

EXPERIENCE, NATURE, AND FREEDOM

INTRODUCTION

I. THE DEWEY LEGEND

It is less than a decade since the death of John Dewey in 1952, and a hundred years since his birth in 1859. His active philosophic career ranged over a period of sixty-five years, and the story of his development and shifts of interest is the history not only of a single man, but of a whole era of intellectual endeavor. Yet when one asks what exactly was the contribution of America's most influential philosopher, what there is that is distinctive and of lasting value in his philosophy, a number of clichés are evoked which cloud clear understanding. Even more misleading is the emergence of the Dewey legend.

Recently Dewey's philosophy, or rather a caricature of it, has been attacked from a number of directions. The influence of his educational philosophy has been cited as a primary cause for the slackness and waste in American education. It is commonly assumed that he believed that the function of education is to cater to the needs of the child and to adjust him to his environment. Dewey has been accused of promulgating the adjustment ethic which is perniciously affecting so many forms of American social life. His pragmatism or instrumentalism is represented as the shallow and anti-intellectual doctrine that something is only meaningful, true, or valuable if it is a means to a practical end. With the recent popularity of neo-orthodox theology, another charge has been leveled: that for Dewey man is a *homo faber,* a technological animal who is constantly making and doing, preparing for a future that never seems to come. Dewey, these critics claim, neglects the more profound personal experiences of human life. These various attacks on Dewey have given rise to the legend that Dewey was a muddle-headed thinker whose social and educational views have misled America, and whose philosophy when stripped down to fundamentals is essentially anti-intellectual.

① All this is a gross distortion of what Dewey actually believed, and it is a dangerous one. It is dangerous because frequently the attack on Dewey cloaks an attack on the role of intelligence in a democratic society. It was Dewey's fundamental belief, one may even say his first principle, that with the proper use of intelligence, men could come to grips with the complex, pressing problems in the contemporary world. Men could lead, if not the good life of the classical philosophers, at least better, more valuable, and humane lives. Dewey was no sentimentalist. His faith in intelligence was not based on a naïve optimism about human nature. Contrary to what many philosophers have believed, Dewey argued that man is *not* naturally intelligent or rational. Intelligence is not a faculty of the mind which can be exercised at will. It consists of a set of habits and dispositions which, like a tender plant, need to be carefully and deliberately cultivated, for otherwise it will wither away. The encouragement and use of intelligence by all men in all spheres of life is the perpetual task of a creative democracy.

fundamental belief in intelligence

There is no short cut to making the ideal of intelligence effective. It requires constant attention and patience. Recently there has been an increasing disillusionment and impatience with this ideal of intelligence. And the Dewey legend has been a vehicle for mocking this ideal and ridiculing the effectiveness of intelligence. Before it had become fashionable to despair at the potency of reason, Dewey warned that the right response to contemporary challenges to intelligence is not despair or escapism, but greater persistence and effort in making the ideal a concrete reality.

② The best critic of the Dewey legend in all its variations is certainly Dewey himself, and the selections in this anthology will disclose this. Consider, for example, the issue of Dewey's educational philosophy. Dewey never advocated that education ought simply to cater to the needs and whims of the child. In one of his earliest monographs on education, *The*

Child and the Curriculum (1902), he criticized the child-orientated theory of education by acutely noting that it harbors a formal and empty concept of development. The child is expected to "work things out for himself" [1] without receiving the proper guidance. Advocating complete freedom of the child reflects a "sentimental idealization of the child's naïve caprices and performances" [2] and inevitably results in "indulgence and spoiling." [3] Both critics and defenders of Dewey have often neglected his critique of the laissez-faire approach to education. This critique is developed and explained throughout Dewey's writings. He tells us that "doing as one pleases signifies a release from truly *intellectual* initiative and independence," [4] and that when unlimited free expression is allowed, children "gradually tend to become listless and finally bored, while there is an absence of cumulative, progressive development of power and of actual achievement in results." [5] In opposition to this view, Dewey argues for the necessity of deliberate guidance, direction, and order. Education is, or ought to be, a continuous process of reconstruction in which there is progressive movement away from the child's immature immediate experience to experience which becomes more pregnant with meaning, more systematic and ordered. This can only be accomplished with the intelligent guidance of the teacher.

The kernel of Dewey's educational philosophy is reminiscent of the practice of another educator, Socrates. We can see this most clearly in the early dialogues of Plato where Socrates is usually engaged in conversation with the youths of Athens. Sensitive to the differences of his interlocutors, and alert to their potentialities and limitations, Socrates skillfully draws

[1] *The Child and the Curriculum,* with *The School and Society* (Chicago: University of Chicago Phoenix Books), p. 18.
[2] *Ibid.,* p. 17.
[3] *Ibid.,* p. 15.
[4] *Construction and Criticism* (New York: 1930), p. 11.
[5] "Individuality and Experience," *Journal of the Barnes Foundation,* II (1926), p. 1.

upon their natural interests and gradually introduces them to the subtleties of philosophic analysis. In the *Lysis,* the conversation moves from a discussion of chariots, home life, and friends to an examination of the more abstract and complex subject, the nature of friendship. Socrates is always in control of the dialogue and uses what is familar and interesting to Lysis and Menexenus in order to develop their intellectual capacities and lead them to more systematic and deliberate thinking. What cannot be neglected in Dewey's educational philosophy and is usually neglected, is his insistence on clear objectives and skillful guidance in fostering the art of critical thinking, the most difficult of all arts. Though there is a widespread belief that American education has suffered from Dewey's influence, it would be more accurate to say that insofar as it has failed to develop the tough-minded habits of intelligence, it has failed to be influenced by what is most basic for Dewey.

Another dogma which has become part of the legend is that the *summum bonum* for Dewey is adjustment to the existing social environment. To interpret Dewey as advocating the adaptation of oneself to prevailing social conditions is to miss the point of everything he said and did. The dogma will be found challenged on almost every page of the present collection of his writings. Dewey's emphasis is always on reconstructing or readjusting the environment for the purpose of making it and consequently one's own experience into something more ideal and valuable. It is an irony of history that an adjustment ethic should be attributed to Dewey, for one of the concerns constantly manifest in his writings is that modern technological society is creating a more docile, passive individual. This, he claimed, is the greatest threat to a democratic society because it is conducive to a lack of individuality and to greater mediocrity. Long before the recent wave of sociologically orientated literature, Dewey warned that the natural tendency of existing social institutions is to mold man into a passively adaptable creature who loses his freedom and individuality.

Dewey's concern with the social and the public aspects of experience has been the target of a number of attacks. It has been taken as evidence of a failure to be seriously interested in the personal and private aspects of experience. But it would not be an exaggeration to say that Dewey's analyses of social phenomena are unintelligible unless we appreciate his end-in-view of a society of creative *individuals.* The belief that freedom, individuality, and creativity are natural endowments of man which are released when external restrictions are removed is based on a faulty conception of human nature. Herein too lies the essential reason for Dewey's criticism of classical liberalism which, although it served an important historical function, is no longer adequate for the contemporary world precisely because it underestimates the tremendous formative influence of the specific social environment. As Dewey tells us in "Philosophies of Freedom," "mere elimination of obstructions is not enough to secure rights and achieve freedom." Man's freedom is not a fact, it is a possibility. "But like all other possibilities, this possibility has to be actualized; and like all others, it can only be actualized through interaction with objective conditions." If man is to achieve genuine freedom and individuality, it is necessary to counter the natural tendency of a technological society. Present social institutions must be reconstructed so that they will encourage the realization of creative individuality. How this is to be achieved cannot be answered in a wholesale manner, for it is a matter of specific reforms in particular situations.

We see, then, that adapting ourselves to the existing social environment where this entails simply accepting the current values that are ingredient in it would be the very antithesis of Dewey's proposal. On the contrary, we must attempt continually to reform and rebuild social institutions so that our ideal values become concretely realized. The relevance of this view of social reform to education should be clear. We frequently speak of the failures of a generation and the hope that the younger generation will do a better job. This is an idle and fanciful hope unless we take the concrete steps to reform the educational process so that those dispositions which are essential for leading more creatively intelligent lives are encouraged. When Dewey spoke of the school as a society, he did not mean that the school should mirror the prevailing values of the society, but that the school society should approximate a more ideal society. If from a very early age the child receives the type of training which provides him with the instruments of "effective self-direction" [6] in the life of the school, then we will have the best guarantee for effective reform of other social institutions.

The temptation to think that when a philosopher emphasizes the role of society he is probably undervaluing the claims and rights of the individual, reveals a separation in one's thinking between the individual and society. Dewey challenges this separation: individual-and-society is a unified organic interaction in which the quality and significance of one aspect is dependent on the other. Dewey's concern with social institutions is founded therefore on the principle that creative individuals do not arise spontaneously, but only when the society that is the medium of their activity fosters their development.

The confusions surrounding Dewey's theory of education and social reconstruction which have become part of the legend are furthered by other misconceptions concerning his instrumentalism or pragmatism. We shall discuss the context and significance of Dewey's instrumentalism later when we examine his philosophic development, but at this time we can remove the main obstacle in the way of a clear-sighted approach to his position. It was perhaps a mistake for Dewey to commit himself to the labels "pragmatic" and "practical," since they have given rise to so much confusion. He preferred to characterize his position as instrumentalism before "pragmatic" became popular, and then when the latter term evoked so much misunderstanding, he did abandon it. For "pragmatism" is now a word in our common language which has

[6] *The School and Society*, p. 29.

come to stand for the doctrine that something is meaningful or true only if it works or has some grossly practical consequences. Dewey explicitly repudiated any position which even resembles this popular conception of pragmatism. As he himself once said,

> It is easier to start a legend than to prevent its continued circulation. No misconception of the instrumental logic has been more persistent than the belief that it makes knowledge merely a means to a practical end, or to the satisfaction of practical needs—practical being taken to signify some quite definite utilities of a material or bread-and-butter type. Habitual associations aroused by the word "pragmatic" have been stronger than the most explicit and emphatic statements which any pragmatist has been able to make.[7]

Yet we have to ask, What does Dewey himself mean by "pragmatic?" In the same article he declares that "pragmatic" is used to call attention to the need to refer to *consequences* for the final meaning and test of all thinking. These consequences are not necessarily "practical" in the common-sense meaning of this term; they may be "aesthetic, or moral, or political, or religious in quality." [8]

Dewey's instrumentalism has been compared also with the verifiability criterion of empirical meaning of the logical positivists. His instrumentalism is actually a far richer and more liberal position. The positivists, at least in their early days, gave an epistemological priority to a special type of consequence, that which is directly observable. From Dewey's perspective, the doctrine of strict verifiability presupposes an emasculated and faulty conception of experience which has been uncritically taken over from the British empiricist tradition. He argues, as seen throughout the following selections, and especially in "Qualitative Thought," that experience can be pervaded with innumerable shades of quality, and contains far more than is recognized in the philosophy of the positivists.

[7] "An Added Note as to the 'Practical,'" in *Essays in Experimental Logic* (New York: 1916), p. 330.
[8] *Ibid.*, p. 330.

It is the obsessive concern of modern philosophy with epistemology which is responsible for assigning a privileged status to sense perception while neglecting the multifarious qualitative diversity of experience that surrounds and includes sense perception. Instrumentalism cannot be classified with those empiricisms which strip experience of its concrete richness and confuse it with a bloodless abstraction. Instrumentalism, by calling attention to the qualitative variety of experience and emphasizing the role of future experiential consequences in understanding and evaluating an idea or hypothesis, introduces a new and transforming dimension to the empirical tradition.

When we appreciate the greater adequacy of Dewey's analysis of experience, especially as it is discussed in his later philosophy, we also detect the mistake of those who claim that Dewey thinks of man as a technological animal, a restless creature who is always doing and making for a goal which is never achieved. Dewey does insist that knowing is not simply something that goes on in our heads, but involves an active manipulation of the environment. In this respect he is developing an insight of Kant, who had realized that a revolution occurred in science when it became genuinely experimental, rather than a collection of random observations. When nature is approached with a rational plan and actively constrained to give answers to specific questions, man achieves scientific knowledge. So too, in analyzing moral situations, Dewey emphasizes the role of action. In moral situations a decisive action is demanded which cannot be avoided, the problem being to make the wisest decision and to pursue the best course of activity. Thus Dewey emphasizes activity in both scientific and moral inquiry. But he carefully noted and analyzed the consummations and fulfillments within experience. Dewey was sensitive to the criticism that in working out his instrumentalism he had emphasized the moment of conflict, and in his more mature writings, he paid closer attention to the consummatory phase of experience.

There are experiences which are organically integrated and

aesthetically coherent. In Dewey's terminology such vital experiences are "funded" with meaning and value. These fulfillments are the source of what is most valuable in human life. Experience, Dewey insisted, ought to become more vital, aesthetic, and pregnant with meaning. As long as man is alive, of course, there will be new conflicts and problems which demand action and solutions, but it is just as true and as fundamental that man's life consists of consummations in which conflicts are reconciled and overcome, in which our endeavors are fulfilled. By the use of intelligence we can bring into existence and secure the precarious values which make life worth living. Thus knowledge is instrumental in two basic ways: it is instrumental to gaining intellectual and practical control of a troubling situation, and it is also instrumental to the enrichment of the immediate significance of subsequent experiences." [9]

We have discussed the popular confusions which make up the Dewey legend. There is, however, a more fundamental distortion which needs to be corrected, and the primary purpose of this collection of writings is to correct this. When the name of John Dewey is mentioned, it is usually in connection with his educational and social philosophy or his instrumental theory of knowledge. This is the aspect of his philosophy which has received the greatest attention from both followers and critics, but to understand even this aspect of his work, it is indispensable to understand his comprehensive theory of experience and nature—the heart of Dewey's philosophy.

Dewey rebelled against traditional philosophy and metaphysics (like many philosophers before him), but the rebellion was not tantamount to a complete rejection. He did not believe that the philosophic tradition was valueless, nor did he give up its philosophic ideal of comprehensiveness and generality. Unless philosophy looks beyond the specific and the "piecemeal" and attempts to suggest a comprehensive perspective for understanding man and the universe, it is deficient. It is a perennial task of philosophy to enlarge men's

[9] "Introduction," *Essays in Experimental Logic,* p. 17.

vision. Dewey, like Charles S. Peirce and William James, attempted to combine a new method for dealing with specific problems within a comprehensive theory of experience and nature. It is an interesting commentary on the philosophic scene of the past half century that only the negative aspect of this rebellion has caught the attention of philosophers, while the speculative interests of all three, Peirce, James, and Dewey, and their attempts to reconstruct metaphysics and place it on a new foundation have been almost totally ignored. This lack of balance has led unfortunately to a myopic view of their philosophies.

Metaphysics

Especially in his later philosophy, Dewey became increasingly concerned with formulating what he called a naturalistic metaphysics. Such a metaphysics makes no claim to reveal a reality which is beyond all experience and is known only in an *a priori* fashion. It is an *a posteriori* metaphysics, descriptive and hypothetical. Its objective is to describe and exhibit the interrelations of the generic traits of existence. It differs from a scientific account of existence because of its generality, not because of the uniqueness of its subject matter or its method of investigation. In 1915 (see "The Subject Matter of Metaphysical Inquiry") Dewey outlined a program for a naturalistic metaphysics which is carried out in a number of selections presented here.

Though Dewey explicitly turned to the study of the generic traits of existence in *Experience and Nature,* his interest in a descriptive metaphysics grew out of his concern with specific problems and felt difficulties. In dealing with these problems he was forced to examine the fundamental categories of experience and nature. Gradually, out of these specific discussions, a coherent comprehensive point of view emerged which in turn sheds new light on the whole of Dewey's philosophic investigations. If we are to understand the mature theory of generic traits, we must examine the contexts in which it was progressively developed. We must retrace Dewey's own philosophic development to gain a clear insight into its genesis, structure, and significance.

II. DEWEY'S PHILOSOPHIC DEVELOPMENT

We can detect three continuous phases in Dewey's philosophic development, each lasting approximately two decades. The first may be described as his formative years and lasted from his earliest publications in 1882 until the appearance of the *Studies in Logical Theory* in 1903. This period is usually slighted in discussions of Dewey, though he wrote or collaborated in writing some half-dozen books and was a prolific writer of articles. Most of his later ideas are found here in an embryonic form. We shall try to dispel some of the ignorance about this early phase in order to see how it helps us to understand his later work.

The second phase, which is the most popularly discussed, lasted from about 1903 until 1925. The *Studies in Logical Theory* marked the culmination of Dewey's earlier explorations and the explicit introduction of his instrumental logic. Shortly after its publication, Dewey moved from the University of Chicago to Columbia University, where he encountered a fresh and challenging intellectual climate which further contributed to the new stage of development. During the following two decades, he developed his instrumental theory of knowledge and valuation as well as his educational and social philosophy. This is the time, too, when he exerted an enormous influence in American thinking.

The third phase can be dated roughly from the publication of *Experience and Nature* in 1925. The distinctive characteristics of this third stage are little known or appreciated. There is a widespread belief that during his later years Dewey only said in a more elaborate way what he had been saying all along. Yet this is Dewey's most interesting and important period. He returns to earlier ideas, re-examines them, and critically analyzes the presuppositions of his position. Interrelations among the various aspects of his philosophy are made more explicit, and there is the emergence of a coherent and comprehensive point of view. It is during this time that Dewey's most important books were published, including *Experience and Nature* (1925), *The Quest for Certainty* (1929), *Art as Experience* (1934), and *Logic: The Theory of Inquiry* (1938), as well as a number of significant articles that are included here.

By dividing Dewey's development into three stages, we do not intend to suggest that they are sharply divorced, or that he consciously entered into new phases. There are, however, fundamental shifts of emphases which enable one to discriminate different though continuous stages. Dewey's progress may be characterized by his own favorite category of the organic in which there are "stages of development." The incipient form of a later stage is found in the preceding one, and the later stage clarifies the strengths and weaknesses of the earlier one. Let us turn to the distinctive traits of each stage.

1. *The Formative Years*

In 1884, John Dewey, a bold young philosopher of twenty-five who had recently discovered Hegel, wrote:

> Experience is realistic, not abstract. Psychical life is the fullest manifestation of this experience. The New Psychology is content to get its logic from this experience, and not do violence to the sanctity and integrity of the latter by forcing it to conform to certain preconceived abstract ideas. It wants the logic of fact, of process, of life.[10]

This passage, with its suspicion of *a priori* categories and its emphasis on concrete fact, echoes the neo-Hegelianism which Dewey had learned from his teacher and later colleague at the University of Michigan, G. S. Morris. It also announces the dominant theme of Dewey's philosophic endeavor: to develop a logic from experience and not to force experience into artificial categories. And it is prophetic of Dewey's eventual rejection of Hegel, who in the final analysis does violence to the "sanctity and integrity" of experience.

[10] "The New Psychology," *Andover Review*, II (1884), 288.

The young Dewey was ripe for Hegel. In his autobiographical sketch ("From Absolutism to Experimentalism"), he has recorded an intimate account of his infatuation with Hegel's organic unity.

> It supplied a demand for unification that was doubtless an intense emotional craving, and yet a hunger that only an intellectualized subject matter could satisfy. . . . Hegel's synthesis of subject and object, matter and spirit, the divine and the human, was, however, no mere intellectual formula; it operated as an immense release, a liberation. Hegel's treatment of human culture, of institutions and the arts, involved the same dissolution of hard-and-fast dividing walls, and had a real attraction for me.

What attracted Dewey to Hegel was not the technicalities of dialectic, or even a specific doctrine: it was the elevation of the organic into a cosmic philosophic category. In almost everything that Dewey wrote during the first decade after his discovery of Hegel, whether in the field of psychology, ethics, or social philosophy, he argued that by the application of the organic, the false philosophic dualisms would be destroyed and progress would certainly follow. His work was mainly programmatic, for he failed to give a clear analysis of what he meant by the organic, though it is possible to grasp the drift of what he intended.

The category of the organic would overcome the radical dualisms which have plagued philosophy, including mind-body, thought-reality, and subject-object. An organic unity is a whole in which there is differentiation without segmentation, for the distinctions within it are functional in character. The category also focuses attention on the necessity of understanding the genesis and development of an idea or an institution in order to know its nature. And finally, only the organic adequately represents experience in its specificity and concreteness.

Dewey's native suspicion of the dualistic tendency in philosophy was reinforced by Hegel, who had criticized severely all varieties of philosophic dualisms. A mistrust of dualisms stood in the foreground of Dewey's philosophy throughout his life. He believed that the dualistic strain in modern philosophy resulted from a neglect of the context in which distinctions are instituted, and from a failure to appreciate the organic character of experience. This neglect of the context with its subsequent distortion of reality is the most pervasive fallacy in philosophic thinking. Dewey, then, reacted against the same tendency in philosophy that had aroused Bergson, James, and Whitehead, and that is epitomized in Whitehead's expression, "the fallacy of misplaced concreteness."

Dewey's interest during these early days was not restricted to exploring neo-Hegelianism. From the very beginning of his career, he displayed a strong interest in science and its methodology, especially the biological and the rising social sciences. The latter part of the nineteenth century was alive with the implications of Darwin's theory of evolution. (*The Origin of Species* was published in 1859, the year of Dewey's birth.) Unlike the social Darwinians who attempted directly to project the biological categories of the theory of evolution on the entire universe, Dewey was influenced by Darwin in a more subtle manner. The import of the theory of evolution, according to Dewey, was that it showed that scientific method could be extended to the study of man as a biological and social creature. It paved the way for a new psychology which could rid itself of introspectionist terminology and make new progress from a biological perspective. It was the biological strand in William James's *Principles of Psychology* that influenced Dewey more than James's pragmatic writings. As a result of Darwin's contribution, Dewey also came to realize that many of Hegel's insights could be freed from the obscure Hegelian terminology and expressed in a language more congenial to a scientific viewpoint.

We must recall that this was a time when the boundaries between philosophy and psychology were not clearly demarcated. Dewey was more than a sympathetic observer of the development of psychology as a science: he was an active contributor. One of his most suggestive articles is "The Reflex

Arc Concept in Psychology" (1896).[11] It is an excellent example of how ideas which Dewey absorbed from Hegel are
transformed and recast into a scientific context. Dewey objected to the prevailing concept of the reflex arc as consisting
of three independent and discrete existences: sensory stimulus,
psychical reception, and motor response. This description presupposes that "physical stuff" and "psychical stuff" are connected in a mechanical way, and harbors all the problems of
the old metaphysical dualism of mind and body. The result is
a disjointed psychology which fails to explain what it is intended to explain. In place of this misleading analysis, Dewey
argues that the reflex arc must be described as an organic
circuit or co-ordination in which a temporary conflict arises—a
break within the continuity of our experience—which needs
to be overcome through a reconstruction of the situation. This
conflict generates an awareness of the distinction between
sensory stimulus and motor response. The "stimulus" represents the conditions to be met in order to successfully complete the co-ordination, and the "response" respresents the
means or instruments for accomplishing this end. "Stimulus-
response" does not name discrete existences: it is a functional
distinction within a unified co-ordination. One and the same
occurrence may be both stimulus and response, depending on
its specific role within the developing organic situation.

In this analysis of the reflex arc concept, the cosmic category
of the organic which is so prominent in Dewey's early Hegelian writings is given a naturalistic and specific interpretation.
The instrumental logic which Dewey was soon to elaborate is
foreshadowed in this description of an experience in which
there is a conflict to be overcome through a reconstruction of
the situation. The distinction between structure and function
which is central to the instrumental logic is here anticipated.
"Function" designates the process, the dynamic transition in

11 *Psychological Review*, III (1896), 357-70. Cf. Professor Charles W.
Hendel's excellent discussion of this article in his lecture "The New
Empiricism and the Philosophical Tradition" in *John Dewey and the
Experimental Spirit in Philosophy* (New York: 1959).

the evolving co-ordination. The distinctions *within* a function "are structural, contemporaneous, and distributive. . . . Co-incident, simultaneous, and correspondent *within* doing is the distinction of doer and deed; *within* the function of thought, of thinking and the material thought upon; within the function of striving, of obstacle and aim, of means and end." [12] "Function" and "structure" are therefore mutually dependent; we cannot understand one without an appeal to the other. Even the terminology which is familar to his later work is already present in this pioneering article on the reflex arc: "conflict," "problem," "instrumental," and "reconstruction." And finally the analysis of experience as an organic interaction which is something more than a conglomeration of independent entities and something less than the all-encompassing Absolute, is the heart of Dewey's mature philosophy of experience.

Experience

It was at the time when Dewey was becoming increasingly dissatisfied with the sterility of Hegelian dialectic and more concerned with a scientific approach to problems that he accepted an appointment at the University of Chicago, where he started the famous Laboratory School. In 1894, Dewey became head of what was then the Department of Philosophy, Psychology, and Pedagogy. Believing that ideas should be developed from experience and tested in experience, Dewey now had an excellent opportunity to carry out his program. The experimental elementary school was designed to test and develop educational and psychological hypotheses. The theory of education as a deliberate and continuous reconstruction of experience was elaborated in connection with Dewey's firsthand experience at the Laboratory School. Moreover, Chicago, which was a rapidly growing urban center experiencing the social problems of an expanding industrial community, presented fresh challenges to relate philosophy to social affairs. Dewey discovered further opportunities in Chicago for testing

[12] "Thought and Its Subject-Matter" in *Essays in Experimental Logic*, p. 95.

his conviction that the concrete realization of philosophic criticism is social reform.

As Dewey became more concerned with the application of scientific method to social phenomena, he felt a striking disparity between the actual character of scientific inquiry and knowledge, and what philosophers said about knowledge in their epistemological studies. The mark of true knowledge, according to one dominant philosophic tradition, is supposed to be its absolute certainty, yet a distinguishing feature of scientific knowledge is its hypothetical character. Knowing is supposed to be something that goes on in one's mind, yet experimental science shows the importance of active manipulation of external phenomena in achieving knowledge. According to some empirical epistemologies, the test of legitimacy is to be found in the origins of an idea, but the ultimate test of scientific knowledge lies in future consequences and inquiries. Something was clearly wrong in this divorce between philosophic theories of knowledge and the actual knowledge that we possess. If philosophy is to take account of our actual knowledge and not spin idle fancies, then a new analysis of inquiry is demanded, and this is the project which Dewey turned to in the *Studies in Logical Theory*.

For the contemporary reader who is unacquainted with the context in which the *Studies* were written, the book presents difficulties. It is like a geological specimen in which three strata corresponding to the various plateaus in Dewey's thinking during the twenty years prior to its publication are intermixed. The language of Hegel and idealism is expressive of the oldest and deepest substratum. The theory of organic coordination of "The Reflex Arc Concept" forms the next stratum. The psychological doctrine described there is reflected in his analysis of thinking as an instrumental response to a specific stimulus. And lastly the most recent stratum consists of the new pragmatic elements in which the testing and verifying of hypotheses by experiential consequences is emphasized. It is because these various strata are not clearly distinguished that the *Studies* is at first confusing to the reader. And when this book appeared, it immediately evoked a great deal of discussion and criticism. Dewey was forced to clarify, explicate, and defend his position, a task which occupied him for the rest of his life.

Dewey, then, entered the twentieth century with new and exciting ideas. They were tentatively worked out and loosely connected, but they were arousing the imagination and provoking a whole generation of thinkers. As William James prophesied, the discussion of these ideas was to dominate the American intellectual scene for the next twenty-five years.

2. *Reflection and Valuation*

In 1904, because of increasing friction with the university administration concerning the Laboratory School, Dewey resigned from the University of Chicago. He started teaching the following year at Columbia University. During the previous decade, Dewey had gathered about him a group of sympathetic colleagues and students which James had dubbed the "Chicago School." Dewey now left this behind and took up residence in New York in a new intellectual and social climate. This philosopher from Vermont, mild in speech and manner but bold in philosophic speculation, was soon to exert a profound influence on his colleagues and students at Columbia and Teachers College and on a great part of the intellectual community of the United States as well.

The year 1904 was also the one in which Frederick J. E. Woodbridge founded the *Journal of Philosophy, Psychology, and Scientific Methods*. Dewey's arrival at Columbia and the appearance of this journal were a happy coincidence, for he shared the principles that led to its publication. It became an ideal place for critics of Dewey to raise their questions and objections, and for him to answer them and carefully explicate his views. Consistent with his belief that philosophy is reconstructive and is most fruitful when it deals with specific problems, Dewey publicly and forcefully disputed with his critics. This procedure also seemed to suit his philosophic temperament. He was much more comfortable dealing with an individual problem or contrasting his views with some other position than stating them in a general and systematic form. Though this type of philosophic encounter has the advantage of grounding the discussion in a specific context and illustrates the critical function of philosophy, it tends to obscure the affinities of his various ideas and the coherence of his position. Instead of following the devious ramifications of Dewey's investigations during the first quarter of the twentieth century, we will focus on his two central concerns: the analysis of reflective experience and valuation.

In *How We Think* (1910), written especially for educators and teachers, Dewey presents one of his most lucid statements of the structure of reflective experience.[13] While it is a simplified version of his view, we can use it as a skeletal framework, commenting on each of the steps in order to bring out the full meaning and significance of his instrumental logic. Five logical moments are discriminated within a reflective experience:

> (i) a felt difficulty; (ii) its location and definition; (iii) suggestion of possible solution; (iv) development by reasoning of the bearings of the suggestions; (v) further observation and experiment leading to its acceptance or rejection; that is, the conclusion of belief or disbelief.[14]

Reflection does not occur in a vacuum. It arises when there is a discrepancy or conflict, a felt difficulty. Reflection or inquiry arises out of, and because of, a disruption in the continuity of our nonreflective experiences. By "nonreflective" Dewey means the type of experience in which inquiring is not the dominant function. Suffering, enjoying a concert,

---

[13] He used a variety of terms to designate this experience, including "reflective experience," "reflection," and "knowing." Later he introduced the more technical term "inquiry" in the hope that it would avoid confusions that surround these other terms. For a technical analysis of the structure of inquiry, see "The Pattern of Inquiry" which is included in this collection.

[14] *How We Think* (New York: 1910), p. 72.

sculpturing involve cognitive awareness, but they are not primarily reflective experiences. Because philosophers have a special interest in knowledge, they have been tempted to think that all experience is a form of knowing. A repudiation of this claim is the pivotal point of Dewey's rejection of Hegel and his followers, as well as of his own early work. Dewey rebelled against the Hegelian conception of knowledge, thought, and reason in which all reality and experience are assimilated and consumed. Man is more than a knowing animal; his experience consists of doings and sufferings which are not simply knowing situations. Whereas for Hegel and the early Dewey all human experience is encompassed within reason and knowledge, now reason and knowledge are placed within the wider context of experience.

(i) *A felt difficulty.* The difficulty which is felt occurs because of a conflict within our experience. We will certainly be misled if we think that the difficulty is only something mental; the locus of the difficulty is in the situation. The felt difficulty exerts a regulative influence on the development of the situation. It forms the background of our thinking and guides us in seeking for possible solutions. In a later essay, Dewey subtly expresses these points when he says "the immediate existence of quality, and of dominant and pervasive quality, is the background, the point of departure, and the regulative principle of all thinking." (See "Qualitative Thought.")

There are two misconceptions about Dewey's theory of inquiry that we can here nip in the bud: the beliefs that men think only when they must, and that a practical difficulty is the only occasion for reflecting. If man were a passive creature prodded by his environment, then indeed he would think only when he was forced to think. But man is an active, exploring, and experimenting creature. Insofar as his explorations are deliberate and purposive, he will search for new problems to solve which are not simply grossly practical. When Dewey was challenged on this point, he made it clear that it is the mark of a scientific intelligence deliberately to search for important new problems.

(ii) Its location and definition. In a simple reflective situa- ——— ✳ ②
tion, the felt difficulty and our explicit understanding of the
problem may be merged, but in more complex situations a
great deal of ingenuity and experimentation may be essential in order to state the problem precisely. A careful formulation of the problem is essential if our inquiry is to be productive. The difference between the first two steps is one of degree
where the movement is from a difficulty directly grasped
toward the articulation and specification of the problem. And
as we come closer to solving the problem, its exact character
becomes sharper.

(iii) Suggestion of possible solution. Suggestion, hypothesis, ——— ✳ ③
or conjecture involves going beyond what is immediately
present to something absent. There is always an element of
adventure or risk in suggestion; there are no rigid rules for
coming up with illuminating and correct hypotheses. Making
relevant and fruitful suggestions is an art. Like all arts, a
certain amount of talent is necessary, though this art can be
cultivated through education.

There is, of course, an interplay between hypotheses and
data. The data which confront the inquirer may suggest some
hypothesis which will direct him to look more carefully at the
original data or to make some new observations which in turn *Data not*
may give rise to new hypotheses. There is no intrinsic mark *given —*
signifying that something is a datum. Data, properly speaking, *(taken) !*
are not given, they are *taken.* They are not independent
atomic facts; they are what are taken as primary for a specific
inquiry.

(iv) Development by reasoning of the bearings of the sug- ——— ✳ ④
gestions. This step involves reasoning or reflection when these
terms are used with a more restricted meaning. A hypothesis
may be rejected immediately upon examination of its logical
consequences, while at other times our reasoning about the
hypothesis may lead us to understand its relations with other
information and to devise a means for testing it. In this step,
we can see the importance of abstraction and formal systems
in inquiry. Formal systems can serve as powerful instruments

for constructing theories and deducing the logical consequences of hypotheses. In order to develop intellectual instruments for inquiry, we cannot limit ourselves to what now
appear to be "practical" tools. "The more theoretical, the
more abstract, an abstraction, or the farther away it is from
anything experienced in its concreteness, the better fitted it is
to deal with any one of the indefinite variety of things that
may later present themselves." [15]

(v) *Further observation and experiment leading to its acceptance or rejection.* The final stage of inquiry, which is the
one that Dewey emphasizes, is testing and confirming hypotheses. The relevant hypotheses which have not been rejected previously must now be tested. Sometimes simple observation is sufficient to settle the question, while at other
times it is necessary to construct elaborate experiments. The
critical examination of testing procedures and the study of the
rules of confirmation are means of perfecting this final stage.
Dewey's claim that the sharp dichotomy between theory and
practice, and knowledge and action, can no longer be maintained is based in part on the realization that critical common
sense and scientific knowledge are experimental, forms of
deliberate activity or practice.

These, then, are the five moments or stages of inquiry. The
discrimination of five moments does not mean that in a given
situation they are independent or occur in a fixed order.
Several of them may be fused into a single operation, and the
various stages can interact and influence each other. A problem does not even have to initiate an inquiry, for we may experiment and reflect for the purpose of discovering new problems.

What precisely is the significance of this analysis? Is it
intended to be an empirical report of how we think? If so,
what, if any, is it normative value? [16] Clearly, Dewey is not

---

[15] *Reconstruction in Philosophy* (New York: 1920), p. 150.

[16] For a further discussion of these and related points see my lecture
"Knowledge, Value, and Freedom" in *John Dewey and the Experimental
Spirit in Philosophy*

suggesting that this is the way in which we always think. Just the opposite. We are often muddled about a problem, or fail to think out the consequences or carefully test a proposed hypothesis. But the analysis is intended as a description of the structure of critical common sense and experimental science. By analyzing the methods which are effective in gaining reliable knowledge, we can derive rules for proceeding in other inquiries. Instrumental logic is normative: it establishes standards which guide inquiry, but these norms are *abducted* from the ways in which we do gain reliable knowledge. The standard objection that in order to evaluate the methods of knowing we must presuppose a norm of evaluation is a misleading half-truth. In our dealings with the world, we gradually learn the best means for gaining and warranting knowledge. Eventually rules are learned and explicated. They serve as leading principles for directing further inquiries and may be modified in the light of the consequences of these inquiries. There is a type of circularity, but it is not a vicious circularity. The process may be more aptly described as a spiral in which the regulative principles of inquiry are continually refined by further inquiry. There is no mystery here; this is the way in which science progresses.

This analysis of reflective experience also shows the significance of a community of inquirers. It is in and through such a community that regulative principles are developed and tested. Through the funded experience of such a community, rules are transmitted and become effective guides for future inquiry. It is more accurate to speak of types of inquiry, since Dewey, like Aristotle, realized that different subject matters require different rules of procedure, and the various types of inquiry will have differing degrees of precision. This point should be emphasized; it indicates that Dewey's empiricism as distinguished from other varieties is nonreductive. There are different qualities which cannot be reduced, in the sense of eliminated, to one basic type. Aesthetic and moral experiences, for example, have their own unique qualities which differentiate them from other modes of experience, and the procedures of inquiry can and ought to be adapted to the distinctive features of these varieties of experience without doing violence to the uniqueness of the subject matter.

The objection has been made that Dewey is interested primarily in how we gain knowledge rather than in the character of the knowledge gained. But Dewey's point is that the method by which knowledge is gained and justified is precisely what bestows cognitive status upon it. Knowledge is the end product of inquiries insofar as it is warranted by and through these inquiries. There is always an implicit reference to the future, for further inquiries may show that what has been taken as justified is no longer warranted. The consequence of this position is not philosophic skepticism which despairs at ever knowing anything, but the imperative that we must continually test our hypotheses and experiment with them in new contexts for the purpose of furthering our knowledge.

Dewey once said that all philosophy in the last analysis is philosophy of education, and we can see how this is relevant to his analysis of inquiry. The aim of education is to create habits of intelligence and this now has the more precise meaning of fostering the dispositions necessary for inquiry: sensitivity to the differences and demands of various situations, the ability to analyze carefully and to clarify problems, the imaginative capacity to envision new possibilities, rigor in reasoning, knowledge of how to test and evaluate hypotheses, and especially the courage to revise beliefs in the light of further experience. We also see more clearly why education is a social process; it is only in and through the community that the values and skills of inquiry become living norms.

Dewey's theory of valuation stems directly from this exposition of inquiry. His approach is existential insofar as he focuses on the concrete context in which valuation occurs. Men are constantly faced with situations in which there are practical conflicts and they are forced to make decisions about which course of action they ought to pursue. It is idle to speculate about whether men ought to be moral, for they do have values and are subject to obligations. In an actual moral situation, the primary question is What should I do? not What do I mean by "good" or "ought?" The task of a theory of valuation is to clarify the character of the type of situation in which valuation occurs and the nature of this process. This theory is normative in the same way that a general theory of inquiry is normative, for from a study of valuations we can derive standards and guides for the future. (The theory of valuation includes all values: practical, moral, and aesthetic. During this period, however, Dewey focused his attention on moral values. Later we shall extend our discussion to include aesthetic values.)

In order to understand the process of valuation Dewey distinguishes (two) basic meanings of "to value." We value something when we take an interest in it, enjoy it, prize it. "To value" in this sense signifies a direct or immediate experience. One *has* values insofar as he cherishes or esteems certain objects or experiences. The other meaning of "to value"—valuation—means to judge, to appraise, to evaluate. It is a deliberative process culminating in a value judgment. The difference between these two senses is illustrated in the following example. I may enjoy going to symphonic concerts; this is the type of experience that I prize or directly value. But when I am confronted with the question of whether I ought to go to a concert tonight, a judgment is called for. I must consider the specific situation, my finances, obligations, what will happen if I go or if I do not go, etc. In deliberating about these various factors, I must evaluate the alternative actions in order to decide what I ought to do.

What is the structure of this process of valuation? We have suggested that it is analogous to scientific judgment. It arises when there is a conflict within the course of experience, and we must attempt to define the exact character of the conflict, formulate possible actions, and appraise their consequences. There is even an analogue to the confirmation of a scientific hypothesis, for the actual consequences which follow from

Meanings of "to value"
① ②

initiating a course of activity can serve to test the correctness of the value judgment. And, as in science, the leading principles used in a specific valuation are derived from our past experience. But to say that valuation is analogous to making a scientific judgment is not to say that it is identical with it. Misunderstanding has resulted from a failure to realize that, while Dewey stressed the continuity of theoretical and practical inquiry, he was also sensitive to their differences.

If we fail to solve a theoretical problem we may move on to another one, while in a practical situation we are forced to make a decision. The urgency of a practical situation will also set limits on the extent to which we analyze the various factors involved. Further, a practical problem occurs when there is a conflict of our direct values, while this is not a necessary condition for an intellectual problem. The difference between a theoretical and a practical judgment is not an intrinsic difference in the process of deliberation, but is dependent on the context in which they occur. The total quality of a practical situation affects everything that enters into the situation.

"Sometimes every immediate good or intrinsic good goes back on us. . . . We are in the dark as to what we *should* regard with passionate esteem. . . . " We suspect that what we prized unquestioningly is "no longer worth our while, because of some growth on our part or some change in conditions." We may trust to luck for "something to turn up which will afford a new unquestioned object to cherish. . . . " But sometimes we deliberate and "search in order to form an estimate of what would be the good of the situation if we could attain it," though we cannot be sure that we will prize "the thing in question until it has been brought into existence. . . ." [17]

This description brings into focus the interplay of direct immediate values and valuation as a mediated reflective process. Valuation occurs when there is a conflict of our immediate values, of what we directly prize. Valuation is a reflective

[17] "The Objects of Valuation," *Journal of Philosophy,* XV (1918), 257.

process in which we decide "what we *should* regard with passionate esteem," what we ought to value. In making a value judgment, we *ascribe* value to something rather than describe our values. There is a sense in which every evaluation establishes a hierarchy of values for the specific situation. In this particular situation, we decide that x is more valuable than y. The fact that we institute a hierarchy of values in a specific evaluation has misled philosophers into thinking that values exist independently of any situation, and all we need to discover is the nature of this hierarchy to know what to do. This is only another instance of the fallacy of neglecting the context.

But then how do we determine what should be valued? We have said that careful understanding of the situation and knowledge of the consequences of alternative actions are essential. But they are necessary not sufficient conditions for evaluation. We must employ rules to determine what ought to be valued. These rules serve as the leading principles in judging what we ought to value and to do in a practical situation. Moral behavior, like scientific inquiry, is rule-regulated behavior. And as in science, rules are learned from, and modified by, experience.

Once again Dewey's analysis forces us to consider the role of education and the community. The rules which govern valuation are transmitted and funded in and through the community. They may in fact be accepted on blind faith, but we can and ought to inform them with critical reflection. Custom can thereby be brought into greater correspondence with the dictates of intelligence. If this is to be accomplished, it can only be through education in which values and rules are shared in social experience. Characteristic of Dewey's approach, the *theory* of valuation leads to a program of social *action* in which we constantly attempt to secure those values and rules which will encourage more intelligent evaluation. In answer to the classic question, Can virtue be taught? Dewey insists that it can, not by imposing a fixed code of values, or communicating a special type of knowledge, but by nurturing those personal and social dispositions required for making intelligent moral judgments.

Dewey's analysis of theoretical and practical inquiry was in the foreground of his philosophy during the first quarter of the twentieth century and persisted through his later writings. He frequently returned to these topics in order to bring out further subtleties. Throughout our discussion we have picked up fragments of his ideas about experience, and since our aim is to understand Dewey's theory of experience and nature it will be helpful now to put these pieces together.

A good starting place is Dewey's polemical essay "The Need for a Recovery of Philosophy" (1917), where he enumerates five contrasts between traditional accounts of experience and one that is "congenial to present conditions." [18] First of all, experience has been understood as primarily an affair of knowledge, but Dewey points out that experience includes far more than knowing situations. "Experience" designates the affairs of an organism interacting with its environment.

Secondly, while experience has come to mean something mental and subjective, "what experience suggests about itself is a genuinely objective world which enters into the actions and sufferings of men and undergoes modifications through their responses." Experience includes both the how of experiencing and what is experienced in a single unity. In itself, experience is neither subjective nor objective; these are distinctions instituted within it.

Thirdly, the past and the present are emphasized in traditional accounts of experience, although reference to the future is one of experience's salient traits. Theoretical and practical inquiry involve envisioning future possibilities. And we are dependent on future consequences in order to understand and evaluate present and past experiences.

Fourthly, traditional empiricisms have conceived of experience as consisting of discrete units, lacking genuine ex-

[18] This essay is included here. For a critical discussion of these five contrasts see Professor John E. Smith's lecture "John Dewey: Philosopher of Experience" in *John Dewey and the Experimental Spirit in Philosophy*.

istential connections. Contemporary philosophers including Bergson, James, and Whitehead have objected to this attempt to squeeze all connections and relations out of experience. In the same spirit and for similar reasons, Dewey argues that experience contains existential connections within itself; we are not under a delusion in supposing that experience is connected, nor do we impose these connections from some independent pure reason.

Fifthly, experience has been contrasted and separated from thought and reason. In Dewey's more liberal conception of experience, inquiry itself has been analyzed as a mode of experience. It might appear that this way of viewing experience entails giving up all distinction between sense experience and thought, where the former is a check and restriction on our thought. But the distinction is not given up; it is interpreted in a new way. *Within* experience, it is possible to isolate certain types of direct experience and observation for testing hypotheses. Through inquiry we come to know exactly what types of data are necessary and sufficient for grounding and testing our hypotheses.

These, then, are five major aspects of Dewey's reinterpretation of experience, the basis of his new empiricism. While his criticisms have the corrective value of ridding us of the dogmas which have been unquestioned in traditional empiricisms, the charge may be brought against Dewey that his view is so broad that its corrective value is nullified. "Experience" has been traditionally used as a contrast term, but it is difficult to know what would *not* be experience in Dewey's reinterpretation. What, for example, is the relation of experience to nature?

Dewey, who had escaped the pitfall of idealism in which everything becomes a form of knowledge, now appears to have fallen into another pitfall where everything becomes experience. There are serious problems here which Dewey was forced to investigate in his later writings. When he reached this more profound stage of development, too few seem to have been willing to follow him. Among those who remained faithful, it was the earlier Dewey alone which they stressed. The speculative, imaginative Dewey who grappled with the basic problems of philosophy, including the meaning of time, individuality, quality, nature, and freedom appears to have been generally neglected.

III. EXPERIENCE, NATURE, AND FREEDOM

In 1925, when Dewey had passed the age of sixty-five, he embarked on a new philosophic adventure with the publication of *Experience and Nature*. During the early part of the twentieth century, Dewey forged his philosophic position while parrying the thrusts of realists and idealists. Having survived these encounters, he now carried on his dialectic with the Greek philosophers. It is as if Dewey stepped back and took a long critical look at his philosophy to see how far he had come with his program of reconstruction.

Though at times sharply critical of Plato and Aristotle, Dewey felt a strong affinity with them. In 1930, just about the time that Whitehead wrote his famous passage about how the European philosophical tradition is a series of footnotes to Plato, Dewey wrote:

> Nothing could be more helpful to present philosophizing than a "Back to Plato" movement; but it would have to be back to the dramatic, restless Plato of the Dialogues, trying one mode of attack after another to see what it might yield, back to Plato whose highest flight of metaphysics always terminated with a social and practical turn. . . .
>
> ["From Absolutism to Experimentalism."]

As for Aristotle, Dewey favored his robust empiricism, his biological approach to problems of psychology, and his formulation of a logic of inquiry. Dewey conceived of his own instrumental logic as an attempt to achieve the same end, but because the nature of inquiry had radically changed since Aristotle's time as a result of the rise of modern science, so also the logic of inquiry had to change.

The Greek philosophers also had portrayed more authentically our direct experience, "the world in which we human beings act, suffer and enjoy." Experience consisted of the funded information and skills which had accumulated through a social past. Though this meaning of "experience" is reflected in our use of the term when we speak of an experienced artist or mechanic, it can be contrasted with modern accounts of experience as something so individual and subjective that it is forever cut off from a public objective world. (See "An Empirical Survey of Empiricisms.")

Dewey's affinity with the Greek philosophers goes deeper. He admired their enlightened naturalism, their appreciation of man as a genuine part of the natural world, where moral and political concerns are not an intrusion into nature but continuous with it, and their belief that theoretical knowledge is the source of intelligent moral activity. The history of modern philosophy, as Dewey viewed it, has been one of radical cleavages: metaphysical, epistemological, and ethical. So entrenched have these become in our thinking that philosophers have not been able to get man back into the natural and social world in which he finds himself. The prevailing dichotomies have affected every branch of philosophy, most seriously the domains of ethics and social philosophy. Dewey sought to overcome these cleavages, and to re-establish man's continuity with his social and natural environment. To accomplish this task there was no question of a simple return to the past, but rather a reconstruction was required of the fundamental categories of experience, nature, and freedom.

Experience, we have learned, is an interaction of organism-environment which has both spatial and temporal dimensions. Late in his career, Dewey characterized what he had previously called an organic interaction more precisely as a transaction.[19] And transaction is contrasted both with interaction and self-action. When an inherent capacity for activity is attributed to an entity by which it can act under its own

[19] Cf. "Interaction and Transaction" in *Knowing and the Known* (Boston: 1949), written with A. F. Bentley.

powers, we are using the concept of self-activity. For example, Plato argues that self-activity is the essence of the soul, and Aristotle tells us that those things which exist by nature have an innate impulse of self-motion. Self-action was a prominent concept in both ancient and medieval physics.

Self-motion

With the rise of modern science, a new concept of action became manifest and was in the foreground until the end of the nineteenth century. The classic example of the second concept of action—interaction—is Newton's mechanics. Newton suggested that in the beginning God formed matter in solid, massy, hard, impenetrable, movable particles and then set them in motion according to the laws of mechanics. From this point of view action takes place among entities which are themselves virtually unchangeable and immutable.

interaction

Transaction is a refinement of interaction. In a transaction, the components themselves are subject to change. Their character affects and is affected by the transaction. Properly speaking, they are not independent: they are phases in a unified transaction. Thus transaction is a more rigorous formulation of the category of the organic which is embedded in Dewey's earliest philosophic writings. Transaction is a generic trait of existence.

Transaction

N.B.

Quality too is a generic trait of existence. The investigation of quality is one of the most original features of Dewey's philosophy, yet until recently it has received scant attention. Looking back over his philosophy in 1939, Dewey defended his theory of experimental situations as "a *via media* between extreme atomistic pluralism and block universe monisms." [20] It is apparent that for Dewey the situation or context is the fundamental unit of significance. But to say that a situation is more than a composite of elements and less than the absolute is only to describe it negatively. What is it that gives a situation its unity and sets it off from other situations? Each situation has its unique pervasive quality which binds its

[20] "Experience, Knowledge, and Value: A Rejoinder," in *The Philosophy of John Dewey*, ed. Paul Arthur Schilpp (New York: 1939), p. 544.

Generic traits of existence: transaction, quality

constituents into a single whole. How does a quality pervade a situation? The following illustration gives us a clue:

> A painting is said to have quality, or a particular painting to have a Titian or Rembrandt quality. The word thus used most certainly does not refer to any particular line, color or part of the painting. It modifies all the constituents of the picture and all of their relations. It is not anything that can be expressed in words for it is something that must be *had*. Discourse may, however, point out the qualities, lines and relations by means of which pervasive and unifying quality is achieved.[21]

Something like this pervasive quality is present in every experience. Solving a difficult problem, making a moral decision, or recalling a memorable occasion, each has its own distinctive or aesthetic quality. These qualities are directly experienced. Of course, frequently we must know a good deal before we can grasp a specific quality. In the above example, we must know about different types of paintings before we can recognize that a painting has a "Rembrandt quality," though this prerequisite knowledge is not to be confused with experiencing the quality.

There is nothing mysterious about qualities which are directly experienced though not directly known; we can indicate to someone else a situation in which he can enjoy a similar quality. Just as discourse cannot adequately convey what it is like to see something which is red though we can indicate how one might go about seeing it, we can discursively indicate the necessary conditions for the experiencing of any quality. Qualities are felt, but it would be fallacious to conclude that they are merely feelings. This would be like concluding that chairs are "seeings" from the premise that they are seen. Agreeing with Peirce, who also thought of quality as a primary category, Dewey says that "anything that can be called feeling is objectively defined by reference to immediate quality." (See "Peirce's Theory of Quality.")

[21] *Logic: The Theory of Inquiry* (New York: 1938), p. 70.

The role of these pervasive qualities becomes clearer when we think of a situation in the process of development. In theoretical or practical inquiry the felt difficulty is in the background and, in part, guides our thinking. In artistic creation too, the artist starts with a vague undifferentiated quality. In the creative process, this quality is transformed through a medium into something definite, integrated, and concrete. "The underlying quality that defines the work, that circumscribes it externally and integrates it internally, controls the thinking of the artist; his logic is the logic of what I have called qualitative thinking." (See "Qualitative Thought.")

The qualitative dimension of experience helps to elucidate two other prominent features of Dewey's philosophy: the nature of consummatory experience and the continuity of experience and nature. Earlier we mentioned that when Dewey wrote about reflection and valuation, theoretical and practical inquiry, he stressed the conflicts within experience which we seek to overcome and resolve. Dewey was accused of glorifying the active restless life that is impatient with contemplation and aesthetic enjoyment. The role of consummatory experiences which Dewey stressed in his later writings balances his interpretation of experience. These are vital, integrated, coherent experiences. We can now add that they are pervaded by aesthetic quality, which unifies and intensifies them. Aesthetic quality can and ought to penetrate all our experiences. "The enemies of the aesthetic are neither the practical nor the intellectual." (See "Having an Experience.") They are the slack and the humdrum, coerced submission and rigid convention. Life, then, can consist of a rhythm of conflicts and consummations, each phase enriching the other.

Quality also helps us to understand the connection and the continuity of experience and nature. The qualities which we apprehend are the resultants, endings, or emergents of natural transactions. They are neither exclusively in the organism nor in its environment; they are as much a part of the experiencer as of the things experienced. In our awareness of qualities we have direct immediate contact with nature. In certain contexts, for the purpose of intellectual or practical control, we may refer the quality to the experiencer or to the object experienced. This is a subtle phenomenological point which has been obscured by the prevalence of the modern distinction between subject and object. Empirically we experience things as poignant, annoying, beautiful, harsh, fearful, etc. We do not experience these qualities as projections of a "subjective" mind on a colorless "objective" reality.

Scientific inquiry has taught us, however, that if we want to gain knowledge of nature, we must temporarily discount the unique and concrete qualitative appearance of things and seek for laws of change which are not immediately apparent. The uniqueness of directly experienced qualities is something we must transcend in order to further inquiry. If, for example, we are fascinated by the way in which the sunlight falls on a particular solution and brings out the richness of its color, we may enhance our aesthetic experience. But if we fail to get on with the experiment, we certainly will not learn anything about the chemical nature of the solution.

Scientific inquiry made a great advance when it was fully realized that to know nature we must turn our eyes from what is immediately most insistent in it. But the philosophy that grew up around modern science has led to intolerable paradoxes. Accepting the classic principle that the pre-eminently knowable is the pre-eminently real, it took scientific objects as reality par excellence, and devalued what is not instrumental for advancing scientific inquiry. Immediate qualities were relegated to a realm of appearance, illusion, and subjective consciousness, expelled from the determinate realm of objective reality. Consequently there is the paradox: What is most real for men in the sense of what they directly value and enjoy is condemned to unreality. Greek philosophy and science, on the other hand, appreciated the importance of immediate qualities and did not hesitate to countenance them as real and natural, though they made the mistake of thinking of qualities such as the dry and the wet as efficacious. It is possible, however, to reconcile the claims and insights of

good point N.B.

Greek and modern philosophy, and to resolve the bifurcation of nature.

Qualities which are directly experienced are not in competition with the refined objects of science for the title of "reality." The dispute arises only when we ignore the context of inquiry, and confuse what is stable and instrumental for inquiry with the exclusively real. Scientific inquiry ignores certain aspects of natural transactions not because they are unreal, but because they are not primarily important for the purposes of scientific inquiry. But there are other contexts, especially those of direct use and enjoyment in everyday life and distinctively aesthetic experience, where these qualities have the greatest significance. Pseudo arguments concerning the "reality" of immediate qualities and scientific objects result from a lack of sensitivity to the demands of different contexts. Artistic creation captures and intensifies the unique qualities of experience which are justifiably neglected in inquiry. (See "Time and Individuality" and "Qualitative Thought.")

We still have to answer questions which we have raised before. Is there anything which is outside of experience? And what is the relation of experience to nature? In *Experience and Nature,* Dewey squarely faced the task of showing that experience is not a self-enclosed whole that includes everything. It is grounded in, and limited by, other natural transactions. There are, for example, physical, psycho-physical, and human transactions. Though these are all natural, each type has its own qualities and behavior patterns which are continuous with, but distinguishable from other transactional plateaus. Human experience is natural in the sense that it manifests physical and psycho-physical qualities and behavior, and even what is novel in human experience has prototypes in less complex transactions. We can study human experience from a physical or biological perspective since it exhibits such traits. But there are features peculiar to human experience such as the use of spoken language and the nature of human societies. There is no need to presuppose a complete break with the rest of nature in order to explain these features, yet we must be sensitive to the uniqueness of human experience, just as we must be alert to the differences between organic and inorganic matter even though we do not postulate a break in nature.

Sensitivity to differences entails the use of categories which are appropriate for the emergent behavior. Consequently, Dewey argues that the social is a philosophic category because it is needed to account for distinctively human experience in which physical and psycho-physical phenomena are transformed. Dewey's naturalism achieves a delicate balance between continuity and uniqueness; he is not a materialist who falsely assumes that it is possible to explain away the uniqueness of more complex natural transactions by reducing them to physical behavior.

"Social" as a philosophic category

From this perspective, human experience consists of only one type of natural transaction and is included within, and conditioned by, the more extensive range of nature. But from another perspective, nature enters into experience. In our experience we encounter nature, not simply other experiences: we apprehend nature directly when we are aware of its qualities, and indirectly when through inquiry we gain knowledge of it. Experience then, is in nature, and nature is in experience, but we can understand this interpenetration when we carefully distinguish our perspective. (See "Nature in Experience.")

Experience and Nature

Although Dewey presupposed that man has freedom, only in his later years did he carefully explain and justify man's freedom. Since freedom is intimately bound up with individuality and time, we must first consider the meaning of these concepts.

—freedom —individuality —time

Everything that exists exhibits selective or preferential behavior. Whether an electron or a human being, it reacts positively or negatively in the presence of other things. These "preferences" express the constitution of the particular existences and are evidence of at least a rudimentary individuality in all things. But individuality is not only a matter of selective

Individuality

behavior; the individual is a history, an extensive event or course of events, each of which takes into itself something of the past and leads into the future. In other words, the unique ways of responding to presented conditions are, in part, the resultant of the ways in which an individual has responded to past occurrences. Man's individuality consists of his responses to opportunities, though these selective responses are conditioned by past experience. Historical development or temporal seriality which is not "simply external redistributions, rearrangements in space of what previously existed" but consists of "genuine qualitative changes" is the essence of individuality. (See "Time and Individuality," and also "Philosophies of Freedom.")

We must be careful here; terms like "development" and "individuality" are highly emotive and are too often used eulogistically, but Dewey is describing a trait which in itself is morally neutral. Individuality per se is neither good nor bad; the crucial issue is what we do with it. Our responses may become so routine and mechanical that in effect we lose our individuality. But individuality can be the source of the novel and fresh in experience.

Human freedom is grounded in this individuality. Unless we could respond uniquely to challenges, freedom would be impossible. This does not introduce an element of sheer chance which violates the laws of nature. In "Philosophies of Freedom," Dewey writes:

> In the description of causal sequences, we still have to start with and from existences, things that are individually and uniquely just what they are. The fact that we can state changes which occur by certain uniformities and regularities does not eliminate this original element of individuality, of preference and bias. On the contrary, the statement of laws presupposes just this capacity.

The issue of man's freedom is not whether or not his choices have causes, for Dewey insists that they do, but the type of cause which determines our choices. If we allow ourselves to be pushed and pulled, then for all practical purposes we have no freedom, but insofar as intelligent understanding, foresight, and deliberation enter into our choices, we *become* free.

Freedom then, is a possibility rooted in our capacity to respond uniquely to presented conditions. As a possibility, it must be concretely realized, and this can be done only through transaction with objective conditions. This point is reinforced by our purview of valuation and education, where we saw the significance of social conditions in fostering creative individuality. We cannot separate a metaphysical account of freedom from a concern with political and social freedom, for it is through political and social institutions that freedom is actualized by making our choices more enlightened. Once again, Dewey's dialectic moves from a metaphysical examination of the generic traits of existence to political and social issues.

In following Dewey's development from the speculations of a young Hegelian through the statement of the instrumental theory of inquiry and value, to a descriptive naturalistic metaphysics, we have sought to disclose the variety and comprehensiveness of his philosophy. Our exposition has been argumentative and interpretative, for a great injustice has been done to Dewey in the legend which has grown up around his name. There are signs, however, of a renewed interest in what Dewey sought to accomplish. For philosophers are once again becoming discontent with extreme specialization and a narrow view of philosophic analysis that avoids the more pressing and complex problems of men. There is a felt need for reunion in philosophy, for new perspective and vision that is informed by the lessons of careful analysis. In this search for new directions, there is much to be learned from John Dewey, who sought to unite speculative imagination with a sensitive concern for the variety of human experience and the specific "problems of men."

RICHARD J. BERNSTEIN

NOTE ON THE TEXT

All the articles are reprinted in their entirety. In the two instances where chapters have been taken from Dewey's books for the purpose of rounding out the discussion and supplementing the articles, the entire chapters have been reprinted. (Reference is to "The Pattern of Inquiry," from *Logic: The Theory of Inquiry;* and "Having an Experience," from *Art as Experience.*) The first footnote of each selection gives the place of original publication. Dewey's references and quotations have been checked, and all material supplied by the editor has been placed in square brackets. A few minor editorial corrections have been made in the selections for the sake of consistency.

R. J. B.

SELECTED BIBLIOGRAPHY[1]

Works by John Dewey

The School and Society, Chicago, 1900; and *The Child and The Curriculum,* Chicago, 1902. (Reprinted together by Phoenix Books.)

The Influence of Darwin on Philosophy, New York, 1910.

Essays in Experimental Logic, Chicago, 1916. (Reprinted by Dover Publications.)

Democracy and Education, New York, 1916.

Reconstruction in Philosophy, New York, 1920. (Reprinted, with a new introduction, by the Beacon Press.)

Human Nature and Conduct, New York, 1922. (Reprinted, with a new introduction, by the Modern Library.)

Experience and Nature, Chicago, 1925. (Revised edition reprinted by Dover Publications.)

The Public and Its Problems, New York, 1927.

The Quest for Certainty, New York, 1929.

Philosophy and Civilization, New York, 1931.

Art as Experience, New York, 1934. (Reprinted by Capricorn.)

A Common Faith, New Haven, 1934.

Logic: The Theory of Inquiry, New York, 1938.

Intelligence in the Modern World, ed. Joseph Ratner, New York, 1939.

Freedom and Culture, New York, 1939.

Theory of Valuation, Chicago, 1939.

Knowing and the Known, with A. F. Bentley, Boston, 1949.

[1] For a detailed bibliography of Dewey's works, see *The Philosophy of John Dewey,* ed. by Paul Arthur Schilpp, second edition, New York, 1951.

Collateral Reading

Geiger, George R., *John Dewey in Perspective,* New York, 1958.

Hendel, Charles W. (ed.), *John Dewey and The Experimental Spirit in Philosophy,* New York, 1959.

Hook, Sidney, *John Dewey: An Intellectual Portrait,* New York, 1939.

Schilpp, Paul Arthur (ed.), *The Philosophy of John Dewey,* New York, 1939. (Second edition 1951.)

JOHN DEWEY

On Experience, Nature,
and Freedom

FROM ABSOLUTISM TO EXPERIMENTALISM [1]

In this intimate autobiographical account, written in 1930, Dewey describes the men and ideas which influenced his intellectual development. He conveys a vivid sense of the atmosphere and transition of American intellectual life from the end of the nineteenth century, when it was strongly under European influence, to the twentieth century, when it set out in new and independent directions. The story of Dewey's discovery of Hegel, the personal and philosophic reasons for the strong attraction to his speculative philosophy, and the subsequent drifting away from Hegel is told with directness and frankness. Though Dewey explicitly broke with Hegel and his followers early in his philosophic career, there is a strong mark of Hegel throughout Dewey's writings. Dewey attempted to "naturalize" Hegel, to extract the insights from his speculative philosophy and incorporate them into a position more congenial to, and in closer co-operation with, the experimental sciences. Dewey concludes with a sketch of four motifs which recur, are developed and interwoven throughout the selections presented here. They are (1) a basic concern with the "practice and theory of education (2) an attempt to formulate a "method of effective inquiry" which would bridge the gap between science and morals (3) a biological orientation in understanding experience as a life activity (4) and "the importance of distinctive social categories" in philosophy. Dewey's remarks about Plato have a special relevance to his own philosophy, for in Dewey as in Plato, the "highest flight of metaphysics always terminated with a social and practical turn."

I N THE LATE 'seventies, when I was an undergraduate, "electives" were still unknown in the smaller New England colleges. But in the one I attended, the University of Vermont, the tradition of a "senior-year course" still subsisted. This course was regarded as a kind of intellectual coping to

[1] *Contemporary American Philosophy,* ed. George P. Adams and Wm. Pepperell Montague (New York: 1930), II, 13-27.

the structure erected in earlier years, or, at least, as an inser-
tion of the key-stone of the arch. It included courses in political economy, international law, history of civilization
(Guizot),[2] psychology, ethics, philosophy of religion (Butler's
Analogy), logic, etc., not history of philosophy, save incidentally. The enumeration of these titles may not serve the
purpose for which it was made; but the idea was that after
three years of somewhat specialized study in languages and
sciences, the last year was reserved for an introduction into
serious intellectual topics of wide and deep significance—an
introduction into the world of ideas. I doubt if in many cases
it served its alleged end; however, it fell in with my own in-
clinations, and I have always been grateful for that year of my
schooling. There was, however, one course in the previous year
that had excited a taste that in retrospect may be called philosophical. That was a rather short course, without laboratory
work, in Physiology, a book of Huxley's being the text.[3] It is
difficult to speak with exactitude about what happened to me
intellectually so many years ago, but I have an impression that
there was derived from that study a sense of interdependence
and interrelated unity that gave form to intellectual stirrings
that had been previously inchoate, and created a kind of type
or model of a view of things to which material in any field
ought to conform. Subconsciously, at least, I was led to desire
a world and a life that would have the same properties as had
the human organism in the picture of it derived from study of
Huxley's treatment. At all events, I got great stimulation from
the study, more than from anything I had had contact with
before; and as no desire was awakened in me to continue that
particular branch of learning, I date from this time the
awakening of a distinctive philosophic interest.

The University of Vermont rather prided itself upon its

2 [F. P. G. Guizot, *The History of Civilization from the Fall of the
Roman Empire to the French Revolution,* trans. by William Hazlitt
(London: 1846).]

3 [Thomas H. Huxley, *Lessons in Elementary Physiology* (London:
1866).]

tradition in philosophy. One of its earlier teachers, Dr. Marsh, *Marsh* was almost the first person in the United States to venture upon the speculative and dubiously orthodox seas of German thinking—that of Kant, Schelling, and Hegel. The venture, to be sure, was made largely by way of Coleridge; Marsh edited an American edition of Coleridge's *Aids to Reflection*. Even this degree of speculative generalization, in its somewhat obvious tendency to rationalize the body of Christian theological doctrines, created a flutter in ecclesiastical dovecots. In particular, a controversy was carried on between the Germanizing rationalizers and the orthodox representatives of the Scottish school of thought through the representatives of the latter at Princeton. I imagine—although it is a very long time since I have had any contact with this material—that the controversy still provides data for a section, if not a chapter, in the history of thought in this country.

Although the University retained pride in its pioneer work, and its atmosphere was for those days theologically "liberal"— of the Congregational type—the teaching of philosophy had become more restrained in tone, more influenced by the still dominant Scotch school. Its professor, Mr. H. A. P. Torrey, *Torrey* was a man of genuinely sensitive and cultivated mind, with marked esthetic interest and taste, which, in a more congenial atmosphere than that of northern New England in those days, would have achieved something significant. He was, however, constitutionally timid, and never really let his mind go. I recall that, in a conversation I had with him a few years after graduation, he said: "Undoubtedly pantheism is the most satisfactory form of metaphysics intellectually, but it goes counter to religious faith." I fancy that remark told of an inner conflict that prevented his native capacity from coming to full fruition. His interest in philosophy, however, was genuine, not perfunctory; he was an excellent teacher, and I owe to him a double debt, that of turning my thoughts definitely to the study of philosophy as a life pursuit, and of a generous gift of time to me during a year devoted privately under his direction to a reading of classics in the history of

Dewey is concerned with the stifling of philosophical speculation by religious dogma

philosophy and learning to read philosophic German. In our walks and talks during this year, after three years on my part of high-school teaching, he let his mind go much more freely than in the classroom, and revealed potentialities that might have placed him among the leaders in the development of a freer American philosophy—but the time for the latter had not yet come.

Teachers of philosophy were at that time, almost to a man, clergymen; the supposed requirements of religion, or theology, dominated the teaching of philosophy in most colleges. Just how and why Scotch philosophy lent itself so well to the exigencies of religion I cannot say; probably the causes were more extrinsic than intrinsic; but at all events there was a firm alliance established between religion and the cause of "intuition." It is probably impossible to recover at this date the almost sacrosanct air that enveloped the idea of intuitions; but somehow the cause of all holy and valuable things was supposed to stand or fall with the validity of intuitionalism; the only vital issue was that between intuitionalism and a sensational empiricism that explained away the reality of all higher objects. The story of this almost forgotten debate, once so urgent, is probably a factor in developing in me a certain skepticism about the depth and range of purely contemporary issues; it is likely that many of those which seem highly important today will also in a generation have receded to the status of the local and provincial. It also aided in generating a sense of the value of the history of philosophy; some of the claims made for this as a sole avenue of approach to the study of philosophic problems seem to me misdirected and injurious. But its value in giving perspective and a sense of proportion in relation to immediate contemporary issues can hardly be overestimated.

I do not mention this theological and intuitional phase because it had any lasting influence upon my own development, except negatively. I learned the terminology of an intuitional philosophy, but it did not go deep, and in no way did it satisfy what I was dimly reaching for. I was brought up in a conventionally evangelical atmosphere of the more "liberal" sort; and the struggles that later arose between acceptance of that faith and the discarding of traditional and institutional creeds came from personal experiences and not from the effects of philosophical teaching. It was not, in other words, in this respect that philosophy either appealed to me or influenced me—though I am not sure that Butler's *Analogy*, with its cold logic and acute analysis, was not, in a reversed way, a factor in developing "skepticism."

During the year of private study, of which mention has been made, I decided to make philosophy my life study, and accordingly went to Johns Hopkins the next year (1884) to enter upon that new thing, "graduate work." It was something of a risk; the work offered there was almost the only indication that there were likely to be any self-supporting jobs in the field of philosophy for others than clergymen. Aside from the effect of my study with Professor Torrey, another influence moved me to undertake the risk. During the years after graduation I had kept up philosophical readings and I had even written a few articles which I sent to Dr. W. T. Harris, the well-known Hegelian, and the editor of the *Journal of Speculative Philosophy*, the only philosophic journal in the country at that time, as he and his group formed almost the only group of laymen devoted to philosophy for nontheological reasons. In sending an article I asked Dr. Harris for advice as to the possibility of my successfully prosecuting philosophic studies. His reply was so encouraging that it was a distinct factor in deciding me to try philosophy as a professional career.

The articles sent were, as I recall them, highly schematic and formal; they were couched in the language of intuitionalism; [4] of Hegel I was then ignorant. My deeper interests had not as yet been met, and in the absence of subject matter that would correspond to them, the only topics at my command were such as were capable of a merely formal treatment. I imagine that my development has been controlled largely by

[4] ["The Metaphysical Assumptions of Materialism" and "The Pantheism of Spinoza," *Journal of Speculative Philosophy*, Vol. XVI (1882).]

a struggle between a native inclination toward the schematic and formally logical, and those incidents of personal experience that compelled me to take account of actual material. Probably there is in the consciously articulated ideas of every thinker an overweighting of just those things that are contrary to his natural tendencies, an emphasis upon those things that are contrary to his intrinsic bent, and which, therefore, he has to struggle to bring to expression, while the native bent, on the other hand, can take care of itself. Anyway, a case might be made out for the proposition that the emphasis upon the concrete, empirical, and "practical" in my later writings is partly due to considerations of this nature. It was a reaction against what was more natural, and it served as a protest and protection against something in myself which, in the pressure of the weight of actual experiences, I knew to be a weakness. It is, I suppose, becoming a commonplace that when anyone is unduly concerned with controversy, the remarks that seem to be directed against others are really concerned with a struggle that is going on inside himself. The marks, the stigmata, of the struggle to weld together the characteristics of a formal, theoretic interest and the material of a maturing experience of contacts with realities also showed themselves, naturally, in style of writing and manner of presentation. During the time when the schematic interest predominated, writing was comparatively easy; there were even compliments upon the clearness of my style. Since then thinking and writing have been hard work. It is easy to give way to the dialectic development of a theme; the pressure of concrete experiences was, however, sufficiently heavy, so that a sense of intellectual honesty prevented a surrender to that course. But, on the other hand, the formal interest persisted, so that there was an inner demand for an intellectual technique that would be consistent and yet capable of flexible adaptation to the concrete diversity of experienced things. It is hardly necessary to say that I have not been among those to whom the union of abilities to satisfy these two opposed requirements, the formal and the material, came easily. For that very reason I have been acutely aware, too much so, doubtless, of a tendency of other thinkers and writers to achieve a specious lucidity and simplicity by the mere process of ignoring considerations which a greater respect for concrete materials of experience would have forced upon them.

It is a commonplace of educational history that the opening of Johns Hopkins University marked a new epoch in higher education in the United States. We are probably not in a condition as yet to estimate the extent to which its foundation and the development of graduate schools in other universities, following its example, mark a turn in our American culture. The 'eighties and 'nineties seem to mark the definitive close of our pioneer period, and the turn from the Civil-War era into the new industrialized and commercial age. In philosophy, at least, the influence of Johns Hopkins was not due to the size of the provision that was made. There was a half-year of lecturing and seminar work given by Professor George Sylvester Morris, of the University of Michigan; belief in the "demonstrated" (a favorite word of his) truth of the substance of German idealism, and of belief in its competency to give direction to a life of aspiring thought, emotion, and action. I have never known a more single-hearted and whole-souled man—a man of a single piece all the way through; while I long since deviated from his philosophic faith, I should be happy to believe that the influence of the spirit of his teaching has been an enduring influence.

While it was impossible that a young and impressionable student, unacquainted with any system of thought that satisfied his head and heart, should not have been deeply affected, to the point of at least a temporary conversion, by the enthusiastic and scholarly devotion of Mr. Morris, this effect was far from being the only source of my own "Hegelianism." The 'eighties and 'nineties were a time of new ferment in English thought; the reaction against atomic individualism and sensationalistic empiricism was in full swing. It was the time of Thomas Hill Green, of the two Cairds, of Wallace, of the appearance of the *Essays in Philosophical Criticism,* co-operatively produced by a younger group under the leadership of the late Lord Haldane.[5] This movement was at the time the vital and constructive one in philosophy. Naturally its influence fell in with and reinforced that of Professor Morris. There was but one marked difference, and that, I think, was in favor of Mr. Morris. He came to Kant through Hegel instead of to Hegel by way of Kant, so that his attitude toward Kant was the critical one expressed by Hegel himself. Moreover, he retained something of his early Scotch philosophical training in a common-sense belief in the existence of the external world. He used to make merry over those who thought the *existence* of this world and of matter were things to be proved by philosophy. To him the only philosophical question was as to the *meaning* of this existence; his idealism was wholly of the objective type. Like his contemporary, Professor John Watson, of Kingston, he combined a logical and idealistic metaphysics with a realistic epistemology. Through his teacher at Berlin, Trendelenburg, he had acquired a great reverence for Aristotle, and he had no difficulty in uniting Aristotelianism with Hegelianism.

There were, however, also "subjective" reasons for the appeal that Hegel's thought made to me; it supplied a demand for unification that was doubtless an intense emotional craving, and yet was a hunger that only an intellectualized subject matter could satisfy. It is more than difficult, it is impossible, to recover that early mood. But the sense of divisions and separations that were, I suppose, borne in upon me as a consequence of a heritage of New England culture, divisions by way of isolation of self from the world, of soul from body, of nature from God, brought a painful oppression—or, rather, they were an inward laceration. My earlier philosophic study had been an intellectual gymnastic. Hegel's synthesis of subject and object, matter and spirit, the divine and the human, was, however, no mere intellectual formula; it operated as an immense release, a liberation. Hegel's treatment of human culture, of institutions and the arts, involved the same dissolu-

[5] [London: 1883.]

tion of hard-and-fast dividing walls, and had a special attraction for me.

As I have already intimated, while the conflict of traditional religious beliefs with opinions that I could myself honestly entertain was the source of a trying personal crisis, it did not at any time constitute a leading philosophical problem. This might look as if the two things were kept apart; in reality it was due to a feeling that any genuinely sound religious experience could and should adapt itself to whatever beliefs one found oneself intellectually entitled to hold—a half unconscious sense at first, but one which ensuing years have deepened into a fundamental conviction. In consequence, while I have, I hope, a due degree of personal sympathy with individuals who are undergoing the throes of a personal change of attitude, I have not been able to attach much importance to religion as a philosophic problem; for the effect of that attachment seems to be in the end a subornation of candid philosophic thinking to the alleged but factitious needs of some special set of convictions. I have enough faith in the depth of the religious tendencies of men to believe that they will adapt themselves to any required intellectual change, and that it is futile (and likely to be dishonest) to forecast prematurely just what forms the religious interest will take as a final consequence of the great intellectual transformation that is going on. As I have been frequently criticized for undue reticence about the problems of religion, I insert this explanation: it seems to me that the great solicitude of many persons, professing belief in the universality of the need for religion, about the present and future of religion proves that in fact they are moved more by partisan interest in a particular religion than by interest in religious experience.

The chief reason, however, for inserting these remarks at this point is to bring out a contrast effect. Social interests and problems from an early period had to me the intellectual appeal and provided the intellectual sustenance that many seem to have found primarily in religious questions. In undergraduate days I had run across, in the college library,

Harriet Martineau's exposition of Comte.[6] I cannot remember that his law of "the three stages" affected me particularly; but his idea of the disorganized character of Western modern culture, due to a disintegrative "individualism," and his idea of a synthesis of science that should be a regulative method of an organized social life, impressed me deeply. I found, as I thought, the same criticisms combined with a deeper and more far-reaching integration in Hegel. I did not, in those days when I read Francis Bacon, detect the origin of the Comtean idea in him, and I had not made acquaintance with Condorcet, the connecting link.

I drifted away from Hegelianism in the next fifteen years; the word "drifting" expresses the slow and, for a long time, imperceptible character of the movement, though it does not convey the impression that there was an adequate cause for the change. Nevertheless I should never think of ignoring, much less denying, what an astute critic occasionally refers to as a novel discovery—that acquaintance with Hegel has left a permanent deposit in my thinking. The form, the schematism, of his system now seems to me artificial to the last degree. But in the content of his ideas there is often an extraordinary depth; in many of his analyses, taken out of their mechanical dialectical setting, an extraordinary acuteness. Were it possible for me to be a devotee of any system, I still should believe that there is greater richness and greater variety of insight in Hegel than in any other single systematic philosopher— though when I say this I exclude Plato, who still provides my favorite philosophic reading. For I am unable to find in him that all-comprehensive and overriding system which later interpretation has, as it seems to me, conferred upon him as a dubious boon. The ancient skeptics overworked another aspect of Plato's thought when they treated him as their spiritual father, but they were nearer the truth, I think, than those who force him into the frame of a rigidly systematized doctrine. Although I have not the aversion to system as such

[6] [*The Positive Philosophy of Auguste Comte,* Freely Translated and Condensed by Harriet Martineau (London: 1853).]

that is sometimes attributed to me, I am dubious of my own ability to reach inclusive systematic unity, and in consequence, perhaps, of that fact also dubious about my contemporaries. Nothing could be more helpful to present philosophizing than a "Back to Plato" movement; but it would have to be back to the dramatic, restless, co-operatively inquiring Plato of the Dialogues, trying one mode of attack after another to see what it might yield; back to the Plato whose highest flight of metaphysics always terminated with a social and practical turn, and not to the artificial Plato constructed by unimaginative commentators who treat him as the original university professor.

The rest of the story of my intellectual development I am unable to record without more faking than I care to indulge in. What I have so far related is so far removed in time that I can talk about myself as another person; and much has faded, so that a few points stand out without my having to force them into the foreground. The philosopher, if I may apply that word to myself, that I became as I moved away from German idealism, is too much the self that I still am and is still too much in process of change to lend itself to record. I envy, up to a certain point, those who can write their intellectual biography in a unified pattern, woven out of a few distinctly discernible strands of interest and influence. By contrast, I seem to be unstable, chameleon-like, yielding one after another to many diverse and even incompatible influences; struggling to assimilate something from each and yet striving to carry it forward in a way that is logically consistent with what has been learned from its predecessors. Upon the whole, the forces that have influenced me have come from persons and from situations more than from books—not that I have not, I hope, learned a great deal from philosophical writings, but that what I have learned from them has been technical in comparison with what I have been forced to think upon and about because of some experience in which I found myself entangled. It is for this reason that I cannot say with candor that I envy completely, or envy beyond a certain point, those to whom I have referred. I like to think, though it may be a defence reaction, that with all the inconveniences of the road I have been forced to travel, it has the compensatory advantage of not inducing an immunity of thought to experiences—which perhaps, after all, should not be treated even by a philosopher as the germ of a disease to which he needs to develop resistance.

While I cannot write an account of intellectual development without giving it the semblance of a continuity that it does not in fact own, there are four special points that seem to stand out. One is the importance that the practice and theory of education have had for me: especially the education of the young, for I have never been able to feel much optimism regarding the possibilities of "higher" education when it is built upon warped and weak foundations. This interest fused with and brought together what might otherwise have been separate interests—that in psychology and that in social institutions and social life. I can recall but one critic who has suggested that my thinking has been too much permeated by interest in education. Although a book called *Democracy and Education* was for many years that in which my philosophy, such as it is, was most fully expounded, I do not know that philosophic critics, as distinct from teachers, have ever had recourse to it. I have wondered whether such facts signified that philosophers in general, although they are themselves usually teachers, have not taken education with sufficient seriousness for it to occur to them that any rational person could actually think it possible that philosophizing should focus about education as the supreme human interest in which, moreover, other problems, cosmological, moral, logical, come to a head. At all events, this handle is offered to any subsequent critic who may wish to lay hold of it.

A second point is that as my study and thinking progressed, I became more and more troubled by the intellectual scandal that seemed to me involved in the current (and traditional) dualism in logical standpoint and method between something called "science" on the one hand and something called "morals" on the other. I have long felt that the construction of a logic, that is, a method of effective inquiry, which would apply without abrupt breach of continuity to the fields designated by both of these words, is at once our needed theoretical solvent and the supply of our greatest practical want. This belief has had much more to do with the development of what I termed, for lack of a better word, "instrumentalism," than have most of the reasons that have been assigned.

The third point forms the great exception to what was said about no very fundamental vital influence issuing from books; it concerns the influence of William James. As far as I can discover, one specifiable philosophic factor which entered into my thinking so as to give it a new direction and quality, it is this one. To say that it proceeded from his *Psychology* rather than from the essays collected in the volume called *Will to Believe,* his *Pluralistic Universe,* or *Pragmatism,* is to say something that needs explanation. For there are, I think, two unreconciled strains in the *Psychology.* One is found in the adoption of the subjective tenor of prior psychological tradition; even when the special tenets of that tradition are radically criticized, an underlying subjectivism is retained, at least in vocabulary—and the difficulty in finding a vocabulary which will intelligibly convey a genuinely new idea is perhaps the obstacle that most retards the easy progress of philosophy. I may cite as an illustration the substitution of the "stream of consciousness" for discrete elementary states: the advance made was enormous. Nevertheless the point of view remained that of a realm of consciousness set off by itself. The other strain is objective, having its roots in a return to the earlier biological conception of the *psyche,* but a return possessed of a new force and value due to the immense progress made by biology since the time of Aristotle. I doubt if we have as yet begun to realize all that is due to William James for the introduction and use of this idea; as I have already intimated, I do not think that he fully and consistently realized it himself. Anyway, it worked its way more and more into all my ideas and acted as a ferment to transform old beliefs.

If this biological conception and mode of approach had been prematurely hardened by James, its effect might have been merely to substitute one schematism for another. But it is not tautology to say that James's sense of life was itself vital. He had a profound sense, in origin artistic and moral, perhaps, rather than "scientific," of the difference between the categories of the living and of the mechanical; some time, I think, someone may write an essay that will show how the most distinctive factors in his general philosophic view, pluralism, novelty, freedom, individuality, are all connected with his feeling for the qualities and traits of that which lives. Many philosophers have had much to say about the idea of organism; but they have taken it structurally and hence statically. It was reserved for James to think of life in terms of life in action. This point, and that about the objective biological factor in James's conception of thought (discrimination, abstraction, conception, generalization), is fundamental when the role of psychology in philosophy comes under consideration. It is true that the effect of its introduction into philosophy has often, usually, been to dilute and distort the latter. But that is because the psychology was bad psychology.

I do not mean that I think that in the end the connection of psychology with philosophy is, in the abstract, closer than is that of other branches of science. Logically it stands on the same plane with them. But historically and at the present juncture the revolution introduced by James had, and still has, a peculiar significance. On the negative side it is important, for it is indispensable as a purge of the heavy charge of bad psychology that is so embedded in the philosophical tradition that is not generally recognized to be psychology at all. As an example, I would say that the problem of "sense data," which occupies such a great bulk in recent British thinking, has to my mind no significance other than as a survival of an old and outworn psychological doctrine—although those who deal with the problem are for the most part among those who stoutly assert the complete irrelevance of psychology to philosophy. On the positive side we have the obverse of this situation. The newer objective psychology supplies the easiest way, pedagogically if not in the abstract, by which to reach a fruitful conception of thought and its work, and thus to better our logical theories—provided thought and logic have anything to do with one another. And in the present state of men's minds the linking of philosophy to the significant issues of actual experience is facilitated by constant interaction with the methods and conclusions of psychology. The more abstract sciences, mathematics and physics, for example, have left their impress deep upon traditional philosophy. The former, in connection with an exaggerated anxiety about formal certainty, has more than once operated to divorce philosophic thinking from connection with questions that have a source in existence. The remoteness of psychology from such abstractions, its nearness to what is distinctively human, gives it an emphatic claim for a sympathetic hearing at the present time.

In connection with an increasing recognition of this human aspect, there developed the influence which forms the fourth heading of this recital. The objective biological approach of the Jamesian psychology led straight to the perception of the importance of distinctive social categories, especially communication and participation. It is my conviction that a great deal of our philosophizing needs to be done over again from this point of view, and that there will ultimately result an integrated synthesis in a philosophy congruous with modern science and related to actual needs in education, morals, and religion. One has to take a broad survey in detachment from immediate prepossessions to realize the extent to which the characteristic traits of the science of today are connected with the development of social subjects—anthropology, history, politics, economics, language and literature, social and abnormal psychology, and so on. The movement is both so new, in an intellectual sense, and we are so much of it and it so much of us, that it escapes definite notice. Technically the influence of mathematics upon philosophy is more obvious; the great change that has taken place in recent years in the ruling ideas and methods of the physical sciences attracts attention much more easily than does the growth of the social subjects, just because it is farther away from impact upon us. Intellectual prophecy is dangerous; but if I read the cultural signs of the times aright, the next synthetic movement in philosophy will emerge when the significance of the social sciences and arts has become an object of reflective attention in the same way that mathematical and physical sciences have been made the objects of thought in the past, and when their full import is grasped. If I read these signs wrongly, nevertheless the statement may stand as a token of a factor significant in my own intellectual development.

In any case, I think it shows a deplorable deadness of imagination to suppose that philosophy will indefinitely revolve within the scope of the problems and systems that two thousand years of European history have bequeathed to us. Seen in the long perspective of the future, the whole of western European history is a provincial episode. I do not expect to see in my day a genuine, as distinct from a forced and artificial, integration of thought. But a mind that is not too egotistically impatient can have faith that this unification will issue in its season. Meantime a chief task of those who call themselves philosophers is to help get rid of the useless lumber that blocks our highways of thought, and strive to make straight and open the paths that lead to the future. Forty years spent in wandering in a wilderness like that of the present is not a sad fate—unless one attempts to make himself believe that the wilderness is after all itself the promised land.

THE NEED FOR A RECOVERY
OF PHILOSOPHY[1]

This passionate and highly polemical essay was written as
the lead article in a collection of "essays in the pragmatic
attitude." It appeared at a time when the First World War
was having a disturbing effect on men's intellectual convictions and when it had become popular for opposing
schools of realists and idealists to issue credos in the form
of collections of essays. Dewey strikes out against the double-
headed monster of "the idea of invidiously real reality" and
"the spectator theory of knowledge," which he claims is
responsible for the artificiality of "current philosophizing."
In the course of his fervent plea for "faith in the power of
intelligence to imagine a future which is the projection of
the desirable in the present, and to invent the instrumentalities of its realization," Dewey outlines five contrasts between
the traditional notion of experience and one more congenial to contemporary times. Experience had been regarded as a knowledge-affair, but it encompasses all modes
of interaction of the human organism with its environment; experience had been conceived of as primarily subjective and private, but subject-object is a functional
distinction instituted within experience; traditional empiricisms, Dewey claims, had been concerned with the
present and the past in experience, but experience "is characterized by projection" into the future; experience had
been understood as consisting of discrete disconnected particulars, but it contains within itself genuine connections;
and finally, experience had been divorced from, and contrasted with, reason, but experience is "full of inference"
and can become funded with intelligence. While these five
points are developed in this essay, it is easier to see what
Dewey opposes rather than what he precisely means. In
his later writings Dewey attempted to explicate more subtly

[1] *Creative Intelligence: Essays in the Pragmatic Attitude* (New York:
1917), pp. 3-69.

the meaning of experience and to deal with some of the difficult issues which he raises here. (See "An Empirical Survey of Empiricisms" and "Nature in Experience.")

INTELLECTUAL advance occurs in two ways. At times increase of knowledge is organized about old conceptions, while these are expanded, elaborated and refined, but not seriously revised, much less abandoned. At other times, the increase of knowledge demands qualitative rather than quantitative change; alteration, not addition. Men's minds grow cold to their former intellectual concerns; ideas that were burning fade; interests that were urgent seem remote. Men face in another direction; their older perplexities are unreal; considerations passed over as negligible loom up. Former problems may not have been solved, but they no longer press for solution.

Philosophy is no exception to the rule. But it is unusually conservative—not, necessarily, in proffering solutions, but in clinging to problems. It has been so allied with theology and theological morals as representative of men's chief interests, that radical alteration has been shocking. Men's activities took a decidedly new turn, for example, in the seventeenth century, and it seemed as if philosophy, under the lead of thinkers like Bacon and Descartes, was to execute an about-face. But, in spite of the ferment, it turned out that many of the older problems were but translated from Latin into the vernacular or into the new terminology furnished by science.

The association of philosophy with academic teaching has reinforced this intrinsic conservatism. Scholastic philosophy persisted in universities after men's thoughts outside of the walls of colleges had moved in other directions. In the last hundred years intellectual advances of science and politics have in like fashion been crystallized into material of instruction and now resist further change. I would not say that the spirit of teaching is hostile to that of liberal inquiry, but a philosophy which exists largely as something to be taught rather than wholly as something to be reflected upon is conducive to discussion of views held by others rather than to immediate response. Philosophy when taught inevitably magnifies the history of past thought, and leads professional philosophers to approach their subject matter through its formulation in received systems. It tends, also, to emphasize points upon which men have divided into schools, for these lend themselves to retrospective definition and elaboration. Consequently, philosophical discussion is likely to be a dressing out of antithetical traditions, where criticism of one view is thought to afford proof of the truth of its opposite (as if formulation of views guaranteed logical exclusives). Direct preoccupation with contemporary difficulties is left to literature and politics.

If changing conduct and expanding knowledge ever required a willingness to surrender not merely old solutions but old problems it is now. I do not mean that we can turn abruptly away from all traditional issues. This is impossible; it would be the undoing of the one who attempted it. Irrespective of the professionalizing of philosophy, the ideas philosophers discuss are still those in which Western civilization has been bred. They are in the backs of the heads of educated people. But what serious-minded men not engaged in the professional business of philosophy most want to know is what modifications and abandonments of intellectual inheritance are required by the newer industrial, political, and scientific movements. They want to know what these newer movements mean when translated into general ideas. Unless professional philosophy can mobilize itself sufficiently to assist in this clarification and redirection of men's thoughts, it is likely to get more and more sidetracked from the main currents of contemporary life.

This essay may, then, be looked upon as an attempt to forward the emancipation of philosophy from too intimate and exclusive attachment to traditional problems. It is not in intent a criticism of various solutions that have been offered, but raises a question *as to the genuineness under the present conditions of science and social life, of the problems.*

The limited object of my discussion will, doubtless, give an exaggerated impression of my conviction as to the artificiality of much recent philosophizing. Not that I have wilfully exaggerated in what I have said, but that the limitations of my purpose have led me not to say many things pertinent to a broader purpose. A discussion less restricted would strive to enforce the genuineness, in their own context, of questions now discussed mainly because they have been discussed rather than because contemporary conditions of life suggest them. It would also be a grateful task to dwell upon the precious contributions made by philosophic systems which as a whole are impossible. In the course of the development of unreal premises and the discussion of artificial problems, points of view have emerged which are indispensable possessions of culture. The horizon has been widened; ideas of great fecundity struck out; imagination quickened; a sense of the meaning of things created. It may even be asked whether these accompaniments of classic systems have not often been treated as a kind of guarantee of the systems themselves. But while it is a sign of an illiberal mind to throw away the fertile and ample ideas of a Spinoza, a Kant, or a Hegel, because their setting is not logically adequate, it is surely a sign of an undisciplined one to treat their contributions to culture as confirmations of premises with which they have no necessary connection.

Cf.
"Philoso-
phy + Civilization"

Distinction between traditional notion of experience and & his own¹ notion of experience

A criticism of current philosophizing from the standpoint of the traditional quality of its problems must begin somewhere, and the choice of a beginning is arbitrary. It has appeared to me that the notion of experience implied in the questions most actively discussed gives a natural point of departure. For, if I mistake not, it is just the inherited view of experience common to the empirical school and its opponents which keeps alive many discussions even of matters that on their face are quite remote from it, while it is also this view which is most untenable in the light of existing science and social practice. Accordingly I set out with a brief statement of some of the chief contrasts between the orthodox description of experience and that congenial to present conditions.

(i) In the orthodox view, experience is regarded primarily as a knowledge-affair. But to eyes not looking through ancient spectacles, it assuredly appears as an affair of the intercourse of a living being with its physical and social environment. (ii) According to tradition experience is (at least primarily) a psychical thing, infected throughout by "subjectivity." What experience suggests about itself is a genuinely objective world which enters into the actions and sufferings of men and undergoes modifications through their responses. (iii) So far as anything beyond a bare present is recognized by the established doctrine, the past exclusively counts. Registration of what has taken place, reference to precedent, is believed to be the essence of experience. Empiricism is conceived of as tied up to what has been, or is, "given." But experience in its vital form is experimental, an effort to change the given; it is characterized by projection, by reaching forward into the unknown; connection with a future is its salient trait. (iv) The empirical tradition is committed to particularism. Connections and continuities are supposed to be foreign to experience, to be by-products of dubious validity. An experience that is an undergoing of an environment and a striving for its control in new directions is pregnant with connections. (v) In the traditional notion experience and thought are antithetical terms. Inference, so far as it is other than a revival of what has been given in the past, goes beyond experience; hence it is either invalid, or else a measure of desperation by which, using experience as a springboard, we jump out to a world of stable things and other selves. But experience, taken free of the restrictions imposed by the older concept, is full of inference. There is, apparently, no conscious experience without inference; reflection is native and constant.

These contrasts, with a consideration of the effect of substituting the account of experience relevant to modern life for the inherited account, afford the subject matter of the following discussion.

Suppose we take seriously the contribution made to our idea of experience by biology—not that recent biological science discovered the facts, but that it has so emphasized them that there is no longer an excuse for ignoring them or treating them as negligible. Any account of experience must now fit into the consideration that experiencing means living; and that living goes on in and because of an environing medium, not in a vacuum. Where there is experience, there is a living being. Where there is life, there is a double connection maintained with the environment. In part, environmental energies constitute organic functions; they enter into them. Life is not possible without such direct support by the environment. But while all organic changes depend upon the natural energies of the environment for their origination and occurrence, the natural energies sometimes carry the organic functions prosperously forward, and sometimes act counter to their continuance. Growth and decay, health and disease, are alike continuous with activities of the natural surroundings. The difference lies in the bearing of what happens upon future life activity. From the standpoint of this future reference environmental incidents fall into groups: those favorable-to-life activities, and those hostile.

The successful activities of the organism, those within which environmental assistance is incorporated, react upon the environment to bring about modifications favorable to their own future. The human being has upon his hands the problem of responding to what is going on around him so that these changes will take one turn rather than another, namely, that required by its own further functioning. While backed in part by the environment, its life is anything but a peaceful exhalation of environment. It is obliged to struggle—that is to say, to employ the direct support given by the environment in order indirectly to effect changes that would not otherwise occur. In this sense, life goes on by means of controlling the environment. Its activities must change the changes going on around it; they must neutralize hostile occurrences; they must transform neutral events into co-operative factors or into an efflorescence of new features.

Dialectic developments of the notion of self-preservation, of the *conatus essendi,* often ignore all the important facts of the actual process. They argue as if self-control, self-development, went on directly as a sort of unrolling push from within. But life endures only in virtue of the support of the environment. And since the environment is only incompletely enlisted in our behalf, self-preservation—or self-realization or whatever—is always indirect—always an affair of the way in which our present activities affect the direction taken by independent changes in the surroundings. Hindrances must be turned into means.

We are also given to playing loose with the conception of adjustment, as if that meant something fixed—a kind of accommodation once for all (ideally at least) of the organism *to* an environment. But as life requires the fitness of the environment to the organic functions, adjustment to the environment means not passive acceptance of the latter, but acting so that the environing changes take a certain turn. The 'higher' the type of life, the more adjustment takes the form of an adjusting of the factors of the environment to one another in the interest of life; the less the significance of living, the more it becomes an adjustment to a given environment till at the lower end of the scale the differences between living and the nonliving disappear.

These statements are of an external kind. They are about the conditions of experience, rather than about experiencing itself. But assuredly experience as it concretely takes place bears out the statements. Experience is primarily a process of undergoing: a process of standing something; of suffering and passion, of affection, in the literal sense of these words. The organism has to endure, to undergo, the consequences of its own actions. Experience is no slipping along in a path fixed by inner consciousness. Private consciousness is an incidental outcome of experience of a vital objective sort; it is not its source. Undergoing, however, is never mere passivity. The most patient patient is more than a receptor. He is also an agent—a reactor, one trying experiments, one concerned with undergoing in a way which may influence what is still to happen. Sheer endurance, side-stepping evasions, are, after all, ways of treating the environment with a view to what such treatment will accomplish. Even if we shut ourselves up in the most clam-like fashion, we are doing something; our passivity is an active attitude, not an extinction of response. Just as there is no assertive action, no aggressive attack upon things as they are, which is all action, so there is no undergoing which is not on our part also a going on and a going through.

Experience, in other words, is a matter of *simultaneous* doings and sufferings. Our undergoings are experiments in varying the course of events; our active tryings are trials and tests of ourselves. This duplicity of experience shows itself in our happiness and misery, our successes and failures. Triumphs are dangerous when dwelt upon or lived off from; successes use themselves up. Any achieved equilibrium of adjustment with the environment is precarious because we cannot evenly keep pace with changes in the environment. These are so opposed in direction that we must choose. We must take the risk of casting in our lot with one movement or the other. Nothing can eliminate all risk, all adventure; the one thing doomed to failure is to try to keep even with the whole environment at once—that is to say, to maintain the happy moment when all things go our way.

The obstacles which confront us are stimuli to variation, to novel response, and hence are occasions of progress. If a favor done us by the environment conceals a threat, so its disfavor is a potential means of hitherto unexperienced modes of success. To treat misery as anything but misery, as for example a blessing in disguise or a necessary factor in good, is disingenuous apologetics. But to say that the progress of the race has been stimulated by ills undergone, and that men have been moved by what they suffer to search out new and better courses of action is to speak veraciously.

The preoccupation of experience with things which are coming (are now coming, not just to come) is obvious to any one whose interest in experience is empirical. Since we live forward; since we live in a world where changes are going on whose issue means our weal or woe; since every act of ours modifies these changes and hence is fraught with promise, or charged with hostile energies—what should experience be but a future implicated in a present! Adjustment is no timeless state; it is a continuing process. To say that a change takes time may be to say something about the event which is external and uninstructive. But adjustment of organism to environment takes time in the pregnant sense; every step in the process is conditioned by reference to further changes which it effects. What is going on in the environment is the concern of the organism; not what is already "there" in accomplished and finished form. In so far as the issue of what is going on may be affected by intervention of the organism, the moving event is a challenge which stretches the agent-patient to meet what is coming. Experiencing exhibits things in their unterminated aspect moving toward determinate conclusions. The finished and done with is of import as affecting the future, not on its own account: in short, because it is not, really, done with.

Anticipation is therefore more primary than recollection; projection than summoning of the past; the prospective than the retrospective. Given a world like that in which we live, a world in which environing changes are partly favorable and partly callously indifferent, and experience is bound to be prospective in import; for any control attainable by the living creature depends upon what is done to alter the state of things. Success and failure are the primary "categories" of life; achieving of good and averting of ill are its supreme interests; hope and anxiety (which are not self-enclosed states of feeling, but active attitudes of welcome and wariness) are dominant qualities of experience. Imaginative forecast of the future is this forerunning quality of behavior rendered available for guidance in the present. Day-dreaming and castle-building and esthetic realization of what is not practically achieved are offshoots of this practical trait, or else practical intelligence is a chastened fantasy. It makes little difference. Imaginative recovery of the bygone is indispensable to successful invasion of the future, but its status is that of an instrument. To ignore its import is the sign of an undisciplined agent; but to isolate the past, dwelling upon it for its own sake and giving it the eulogistic name of knowledge, is to substitute the reminiscence of old age for effective intelligence. The movement of the agent-patient to meet the future is partial and passionate; yet detached and impartial study of the past is the only alternative to luck in assuring success to passion.

Centrality of Relations and Connections to Experience

II

This description of experience would be but a rhapsodic celebration of the commonplace were it not in marked contrast to orthodox philosophical accounts. The contrast indicates that traditional accounts have not been empirical, but have been deductions, from unnamed premises, of what experience *must* be. Historic empiricism has been empirical in a technical and controversial sense. It has said, Lord, Lord, Experience, Experience; but in practice it has served ideas *forced into* experience, not *gathered from* it.

The confusion and artificiality thereby introduced into philosophical thought is nowhere more evident than in the empirical treatment of relations or dynamic continuities. The experience of a living being struggling to hold its own and make its way in an environment, physical and social, partly facilitating and partly obstructing its actions, is of necessity a matter of ties and connections, of bearings and uses. The very point of experience, so to say, is that it doesn't occur in a vacuum; its agent-patient instead of being insulated and disconnected is bound up with the movement of things by most intimate and pervasive bonds. Only because the organism is in and of the world, and its activities correlated with those of other things in multiple ways, is it susceptible to undergoing things and capable of trying to reduce objects to means of securing its good fortune. That these connections are of diverse kinds is irresistibly proved by the fluctuations which occur in its career. Help and hindrance, stimulation and inhibition, success and failure mean specifically different modes of correlation. Although the actions of things in the world are taking place in one continuous stretch of existence, there are all kinds of specific affinities, repulsions, and relative indifferencies.

Dynamic connections are qualitatively diverse, just as are the centers of action. *In this sense*, pluralism, not monism, is an established empirical fact. The attempt to establish monism from consideration of the very nature of a relation is a mere piece of dialectics. Equally dialectical is the effort to establish by a consideration of the nature of relations an ontological Pluralism of Ultimates: *simple and independent beings.* To attempt to get results from a consideration of the "external" nature of relations is of a piece with the attempt to deduce results from their "internal" character. Some things are relatively insulated from the influence of other things; some things are easily invaded by others; some things are fiercely attracted to conjoin their activities with those of others. Experience exhibits every kind of connection[2] from the most intimate to mere external juxtaposition.

Empirically, then, active bonds of continuities of all kinds, together with static discontinuities, characterize existence. To deny this qualitative heterogeneity is to reduce the struggles and difficulties of life, its comedies and tragedies, to illusion: to the nonbeing of the Greeks or to its modern counterpart, the "subjective." Experience is an affair of facilitations and

2 The word relation suffers from ambiguity. I am speaking here of *connection,* dynamic and functional interaction. "Relation" is a term used also to express logical reference. I suspect that much of the controversy about internal and external relations is due to this ambiguity. One passes at will from existential connections of things to logical relationship of terms. Such an identification of existences with *terms* is congenial to idealism, but is paradoxical in a professed realism.

checks, of being sustained and disrupted, being let alone, being helped and troubled, of good fortune and defeat in all the countless qualitative modes which these words pallidly suggest. The existence of genuine connections of all manner of heterogeneity cannot be doubted. Such words as conjoining, disjoining, resisting, modifying, saltatory, and ambulatory (to use James's picturesque term) only hint at their actual heterogeneity.

Among the revisions and surrenders of historic problems demanded by this feature of empirical situations, those centering in the rationalistic-empirical controversy may be selected for attention. The implications of this controversy are twofold: First, that connections are as homogeneous in fact as in name; and, secondly, if genuine, are all due to thought, or, if empirical, are arbitrary by-products of past particulars. The stubborn particularism of orthodox empiricism is its outstanding trait; consequently the opposed rationalism found no justification of bearings, continuities, and ties save to refer them in gross to the work of a hyper-empirical Reason.

Of course, not all empiricism prior to Hume and Kant was sensationalistic, pulverizing "experience" into isolated sensory qualities or simple ideas. It did not all follow Locke's lead in regarding the entire content of generalization as the "workmanship of the understanding." On the Continent, prior to Kant, philosophers were content to draw a line between empirical generalizations regarding matters of fact and necessary universals applying to truths of reason. But logical atomism was implicit even in this theory. Statements referring to empirical fact were mere quantitative summaries of particular instances. In the sensationalism which sprang from Hume (and which was left unquestioned by Kant as far as any strictly empirical element was concerned) the implicit particularism was made explicit. But the doctrine that sensations and ideas are so many separate existences was not derived from observation nor from experiment. It was a logical deduction from a prior unexamined concept of the nature of experience. From the same concept it followed that the appearance of stable objects and of general principles of connection was but an appearance.[3]

Kantianism, then, naturally invoked universal bonds to restore objectivity. But, in so doing, it accepted the particularism of experience and proceeded to supplement it from nonempirical sources. A sensory manifold being all which is really empirical in experience, a reason which transcends experience must provide synthesis. The net outcome might have suggested a correct account of experience. For we have only to forget the apparatus by which the net outcome is arrived at, to have before us the experience of the plain man—a diversity of ceaseless changes connected in all kinds of ways, static and dynamic. This conclusion would deal a deathblow to both empiricism and rationalism. For, making clear the nonempirical character of the alleged manifold of unconnected particulars, it would render unnecessary the appeal to functions of the understanding in order to connect them. With the downfall of the traditional notion of experience, the appeal to reason to supplement its defects becomes superfluous.

The tradition was, however, too strongly entrenched; especially as it furnished the subject matter of an alleged science of states of mind which were directly known in their very presence. The historic outcome was a new crop or artificial puzzles about relations; it fastened upon philosophy for a long time the quarrel about the *a priori* and the *a posteriori* as its chief issue. The controversy is today quiescent. Yet it is not at all uncommon to find thinkers modern in tone and intent who regard any philosophy of experience as necessarily committed to denial of the existence of genuinely general propositions, and who take empiricism to be inherently averse to the recognition of the importance of an organizing and constructive intelligence.

[3] There is some gain in substituting a doctrine of flux and interpenetration of psychical states, *à la* Bergson, for that of rigid discontinuity. But the substitution leaves untouched the fundamental misstatement of experience, the conception of experience as directly and primarily "inner" and psychical.

The quiescence alluded to is in part due, I think, to sheer weariness. But it is also due to a change of standpoint introduced by biological conceptions; and particularly the discovery of biological continuity from the lower organisms to man. For a short period, Spencerians might connect the doctrine of evolution with the old problem, and use the long temporal accumulation of "experiences" to generate something which, for human experience, is *a priori*. But the tendency of the biological way of thinking is neither to confirm or negate the Spencerian doctrine, but to shift the issue. In the orthodox position *a posteriori* and *a priori* were affairs of knowledge. But it soon becomes obvious that while there is assuredly something *a priori*—that is to say, native, unlearned, original— in human experience, that something is *not* knowledge, but is activities made possible by means of established connections of neurones. This empirical fact does not solve the orthodox problem; it dissolves it. It shows that the problem was misconceived, and solution sought by both parties in the wrong direction.

Organic instincts and organic retention, or habit-forming, are undeniable factors in actual experience. They are factors which effect organization and secure continuity. They are among the specific facts which a description of experience cognizant of the correlation of organic action with the action of other natural objects will include. But while fortunately the contribution of biological science to a truly empirical description of experiencing has outlawed the discussion of the *a priori* and *a posteriori,* the transforming effect of the same contributions upon other issues has gone unnoticed, save as pragmatism has made an effort to bring them to recognition.

Problem of the place of — Thought or intelligence in experience (*reason*)

III

The point seriously at issue in the notion of experience common to both sides in the older controversy thus turns out to be the place of thought or intelligence in experience. Does reason) have a distinctive office? Is there a characteristic order of relations contributed by it?

Experience, to return to our positive conception, is primarily what is undergone in connection with activities whose import lies in their objective consequences—their bearing upon future experiences. Organic functions deal with things as things in course, in operation, in a state of affairs not yet given or completed. What is done with, what is just "there," is of concern only in the potentialities which it may indicate. As ended, as wholly given, it is of no account. But as a sign of what may come, it becomes an indispensable factor in behavior dealing with changes, the outcome of which is not yet determined.

The only power the organism possesses to control its own future depends upon the way its present responses modify changes which are taking place in its medium. A living being may be comparatively impotent, or comparatively free. It is all a matter of the way in which its present reactions to things influence the future reactions of things upon it. Without regard to its wish or intent every act it performs makes some difference in the environment. The change may be trivial as respects its own career and fortune. But it may also be of incalculable importance; it may import harm, destruction, or it may procure well-being.

Is it possible for a living being to increase its control of welfare and success? Can it manage, in any degree, to assure its future? Or does the amount of security depend wholly upon the accidents of the situation? Can it learn? Can it gain ability to assure its future in the present? These questions center attention upon the significance of reflective intelligence in the process of experience. The extent of an agent's capacity for inference, its power to use a given fact as a sign of something not yet given, measures the extent of its ability systematically to enlarge its control of the future.

A being which can use given and finished facts as signs of things to come; which can take given things as evidences of absent things, can, in that degree, forecast the future; it can form reasonable expectations. It is capable of achieving ideas; it is possessed of intelligence. For use of the given or finished to anticipate the consequence of processes going on is precisely what is meant by "ideas," by "intelligence."

As we have already noted, the environment is rarely all of a kind in its bearing upon organic welfare; its most whole-hearted support of life activities is precarious and temporary. Some environmental changes are auspicious; others are menacing. The secret of success—that is, of the greatest attainable success—is for the organic response to cast in its lot with present auspicious changes to strengthen them and thus to avert the consequences flowing from occurrences of ill-omen. Any reaction is a venture; it involves risk. We always build better or worse than we can foretell. But the organism's fateful intervention in the course of events is blind, its choice is random, except as it can employ what happens to it as a basis of inferring what is likely to happen later. In the degree in which it can read future results in present on-goings, its responsive choice, its partiality to this condition or that, become intelligent. Its bias grows reasonable. It can deliberately, intentionally, participate in the direction of the course of affairs. Its foresight of different futures which result according as this or that present factor predominates in the shaping of affairs permits it to partake intelligently instead of blindly and fatally in the consequences its reactions give rise to. Participate it must, and to its own weal or woe. Inference, the use of what happens, to anticipate what will—or at least may—happen, makes the difference between directed and undirected participation. And this capacity for inferring is precisely the same as that use of natural occurrences for the discovery and determination of consequences—the formation of new dynamic connections—which constitutes knowledge.

The fact that thought is an intrinsic feature of experience is fatal to the traditional empiricism which makes it an artificial by-product. But for that same reason it is fatal to the historic rationalisms whose justification was the secondary and retrospective position assigned to thought by empirical philosophy. According to the particularism of the latter, thought was inevitably only a bunching together of hard-and-fast separate items; thinking was but the gathering together and tying of items already completely given, or else an equally artificial untying—a mechanical adding and subtracting of the given. It was but a cumulative registration, a consolidated merger; generality was a matter of bulk, not of quality. Thinking was therefore treated as lacking constructive power; even its organizing capacity was but simulated, being in truth but arbitrary pigeon-holing. Genuine projection of the novel, deliberate variation and invention, are idle fictions in such a version of experience. If there ever was creation, it all took place at a remote period. Since then the world has only recited lessons.

The value of inventive construction is too precious to be *Rationalism* disposed of in this cavalier way. Its unceremonious denial afforded an opportunity to assert that in addition to experience the subject has a ready-made faculty of thought or reason which transcends experience. Rationalism thus accepted the account of experience given by traditional empiricism, and introduced reason as extra-empirical. There are still thinkers who regard any empiricism as necessarily committed to a belief in a cut-and-dried reliance upon disconnected precedents, and who hold that all systematic organization of past experiences for new and constructive purposes is alien to strict empiricism.

Rationalism never explained, however, how a reason extraneous to experience could enter into helpful relation with concrete experiences. By definition, reason and experience were antithetical, so that the concern of reason was not the fruitful expansion and guidance of the course of experience, but a realm of considerations too sublime to touch, or be touched by, experience. Discreet rationalists confined themselves to theology and allied branches of abstruse science, and to mathematics. Rationalism would have been a doctrine reserved for academic specialists and abstract formalists had it not assumed the task of providing an apologetics for traditional morals and theology, thereby getting into touch with actual human beliefs and concerns. It is notorious that historic empiricism was strong in criticism and in demolition of outworn beliefs, but weak for purposes of constructive social direction. But we frequently overlook the fact that whenever rationalism cut free from conservative apologetics, it was also simply an instrumentality for pointing out inconsistencies and absurdities in existing beliefs—a sphere in which it was immensely useful, as the Enlightenment shows. Leibniz and Voltaire were contemporary rationalists in more senses than one.[4]

Reflection

The recognition that reflection is a genuine factor within experience and an indispensable factor in that control of the world which secures a prosperous and significant expansion of experience undermines historic rationalism as assuredly as it abolishes the foundations of historic empiricism. The bearing of a correct idea of the place and office of reflection upon modern idealisms is less obvious, but no less certain.

One of the curiosities of orthodox empiricism is that its outstanding speculative problem is the existence of an "external world." For in accordance with the notion that experience is attached to a private subject as its exclusive possession, a world like the one in which we appear to live must be "external" to experience instead of being its subject matter. I call it a curiosity, for if anything seems adequately grounded empirically it is the existence of a world which resists the characteristic functions of the subject of experience; which goes its way, in some respects, independently of these functions, and which frustrates our hopes and intentions. Ignorance which is fatal; disappointment; the need of adjusting means and ends to the course of nature, would seem to be

[4] Mathematical science in its formal aspects, or as a branch of formal logic, has been the empirical stronghold of rationalism. But an empirical empiricism, in contrast with orthodox deductive empiricism, has no difficulty in establishing its jurisdiction as to deductive functions.

facts sufficiently characterizing empirical situations as to render the existence of an external world indubitable.

That the description of experience was arrived at by forcing actual empirical facts into conformity with dialectic developments from a concept of a knower outside of the real world of nature is testified to by the historic alliance of empiricism and idealism.[5] According to the most logically consistent editions of orthodox empiricism, all that can be experienced is the fleeting, the momentary, mental state. That alone is absolutely and indubitably present; therefore, it alone is cognitively certain. It alone is *knowledge.* The existence of the past (and of the future), of a decently stable world and of other selves—indeed, of one's own self—falls outside this datum of experience. These can be arrived at only by inference which is "ejective"—a name given to an alleged type of inference that jumps from experience, as from a springboard, to something beyond experience.

I should not anticipate difficulty in showing that this doctrine is, dialectically, a mass of inconsistencies. Avowedly it is a doctrine of desperation, and as such it is cited here to show the desperate straits to which ignoring empirical facts has reduced a doctrine of experience. More positively instructive are the objective idealisms which have been the offspring of the marriage between the "reason" of historic rationalism and the alleged immediate psychical stuff of historic empiricism. These idealisms have recognized the genuineness of connections and the impotency of "feeling." They have then identified connections with logical or rational connections, and thus treated "the real World" as a synthesis of sentient consciousness by means of a rational self-consciousness introducing objectivity: stability and universality of reference.

---

[5] It is a shame to devote the word idealism, with its latent moral, practical connotations, to a doctrine whose tenets are the denial of the existence of a physical world, and the psychical character of all objects— at least as far as they are knowable. But I am following usage, not attempting to make it.

Here again, for present purposes, criticism is unnecessary. It suffices to point out that the value of this theory is bound up with the genuineness of the problem of which it purports to be a solution. If the basic concept is a fiction, there is no call for the solution. The more important point is to perceive how far the "thought" which figures in objective idealism comes from meeting the empirical demands made upon actual thought. Idealism is much less formal than historic rationalism. It treats thought, or reason, as constitutive of experience by means of uniting and constructive functions, not as just concerned with a realm of eternal truths apart from experience. On such a view thought certainly loses its abstractness and remoteness. But, unfortunately, in thus gaining the whole world it loses its own self. A world already, in its intrinsic structure, dominated by thought is not a world in which, save by contradiction of premises, thinking has anything to do.

That the doctrine logically results in making change unreal and error unaccountable are consequences of importance in the technique of professional philosophy; in the denial of empirical fact which they imply they seem to many a *reductio ad absurdum* of the premises from which they proceed. But, after all, such consequences are of only professional import. What is serious, even sinister, is the implied sophistication regarding the place and office of reflection in the scheme of things. A doctrine which exalts thought in name while ignoring its efficacy in fact (that is, its use in bettering life) is a doctrine which cannot be entertained and taught without serious peril. Those who are not concerned with professional philosophy but who are solicitous for intelligence as a factor in the amelioration of actual conditions can but look askance at any doctrine which holds that the entire scheme of things is already, if we but acquire the knack of looking at it aright, fixedly and completely rational. It is a striking manifestation of the extent in which philosophies have been compensatory in quality.[6] But the matter cannot be passed over as if it were

[6] See Dr. Kallen's essay . . . . ["Value and Existence in Philosophy, Art and Religion" in *Creative Intelligence*.]

simply a question of not grudging a certain amount of consolation to one amid the irretrievable evils of life. For as to these evils no one knows how many are retrievable; and a philosophy which proclaims the ability of a dialectic theory of knowledge to reveal the world as already and eternally a self-luminous rational whole, contaminates the scope and use of thought at its very spring. To substitute the otiose insight gained by manipulation of a formula for the slow co-operative work of a humanity guided by reflective intelligence is more than a technical blunder of speculative philosophers.

A practical crisis may throw the relationship of ideas to life into an exaggerated Brocken-like spectral relief, where exaggeration renders perceptible features not ordinarily noted. The use of force to secure narrow because exclusive aims is no novelty in human affairs. The deploying of all the intelligence at command in order to increase the effectiveness of the force used is not so common, yet presents nothing intrinsically remarkable. The identification of force—military, economic, and administrative—with moral necessity and moral culture is, however, a phenomenon not likely to exhibit itself on a wide scale except where intelligence has already been suborned by an idealism which identifies "the actual with the rational," and thus finds the measure of reason in the brute event determined by superior force. If we are to have a philosophy which will intervene between attachment to rule of thumb muddling and devotion to a systematized subordination of intelligence to pre-existent ends, it can be found only in a philosophy which finds the ultimate measure of intelligence in consideration of a desirable future and in search for the means of bringing it progressively into existence. When professed idealism turns out to be a narrow pragmatism—narrow because taking for granted the finality of ends determined by historic conditions—the time has arrived for a pragmatism which shall be empirically idealistic, proclaiming the essential connection of intelligence with the unachieved future—with possibilities involving a transfiguration.

Self at the basis of the non-empirical conception of experience IV

Why has the description of experience been so remote from the facts of empirical situations? To answer this question throws light upon the submergence of recent philosophizing in epistemology—that is, in discussions of the nature, possibility, and limits of knowledge in general, and in the attempt to reach conclusions regarding the ultimate nature of reality from the answers given to such questions.

The reply to the query regarding the currency of a non-empirical doctrine of experience (even among professed empiricists) is that the traditional account is derived from a conception once universally entertained regarding the subject or bearer or center of experience. The description of experience has been forced into conformity with this prior conception; it has been primarily a deduction from it, actual empirical facts being poured into the moulds of the deductions. The characteristic feature of this prior notion is the assumption that experience centers in, or gathers about, or proceeds from a center or subject which is outside the course of natural existence, and set over against it—it being of no importance, for present purposes, whether this antithetical subject is termed soul, or spirit, or mind, or ego, or consciousness, or just knower or knowing subject.

N. B.

There are plausible grounds for thinking that the currency of the idea in question lies in the form which men's religious preoccupations took for many centuries. These were deliberately and systematically other-worldly. They centered about a Fall which was not an event in nature, but an aboriginal catastrophe that corrupted Nature; about a redemption made possible by supernatural means; about a life in another world —essentially, not merely spatially, Other. The supreme drama of destiny took place in a soul or spirit which, under the circumstances, could not be conceived other than as nonnatural—extranatural, if not, strictly speaking, supernatural. When Descartes and others broke away from medieval in-

Descartes

terests, they retained as commonplaces its intellectual apparatus: Such as, knowledge is exercised by a power that is extranatural and set over against the world to be known. Even if they had wished to make a complete break, they had nothing to put as knower in the place of the soul. It may be doubted whether there was any available empirical substitute until science worked out the fact that physical changes are functional correlations of energies, and that man is continuous with other forms of life, and until social life had developed an intellectually free and responsible individual as its agent.

But my main point is not dependent upon any particular theory as to the historic origin of the notion about the bearer of experience. The point is there on its own account. The essential thing is that the bearer was conceived as outside of the world; so that experience consisted in the bearer's being affected through a type of operations not found anywhere in the world, while knowledge consists in surveying the world, looking at it, getting the view of a spectator.

N. B.

The theological problem of attaining knowledge of God as ultimate reality was transformed in effect into the philosophical problem of the possibility of attaining knowledge of reality. For how is one to get beyond the limits of the subject and subjective occurrences? Familiarity breeds credulity oftener than contempt. How can a problem be artificial when men have been busy discussing it almost for three hundred years? But if the assumption that experience is something set over against the world is contrary to fact, then the problem of how self or mind or subjective experience or consciousness can reach knowledge of an external world is assuredly a meaningless problem. Whatever questions there may be about knowledge, they will not be the kind of problems which have formed epistemology.

The problem of knowledge as conceived in the industry of epistemology is the problem of knowledge *in general*—of the possibility, extent, and validity of knowledge in general. What does this "in general" mean? In ordinary life there are problems a-plenty of knowledge in particular; every conclusion we try to reach, theoretical or practical, affords such a problem. But there is no problem of knowledge in general. I do not mean, of course, that general statements cannot be made about knowledge, or that the problem of attaining these general statements is not a genuine one. On the contrary, specific instances of success and failure in inquiry exist, and are of such a character that one can discover the conditions conducing to success and failure. Statement of these conditions constitutes logic, and is capable of being an important aid in proper guidance of further attempts at knowing. But this logical problem of knowledge is at the opposite pole from the epistemological. Specific problems are about right conclusions to be reached—which means, in effect, right ways of going about the business of inquiry. They imply a difference between knowledge and error consequent upon right and wrong methods of inquiry and testing; not a difference between experience and the world. The problem of knowledge *überhaupt* exists because it is assumed that there is a knower in general, who is outside of the world to be known, and who is defined in terms antithetical to the traits of the world. With analogous assumptions, we could invent and discuss a problem of digestion in general. All that would be required would be to conceive the stomach and food material as inhabiting different worlds. Such an assumption would leave on our hands the question of the possibility, extent, nature, and genuineness of any transaction between stomach and food.

But because the stomach and food inhabit a continuous stretch of existence, because digestion is but a correlation of diverse activities in one world, the problems of digestion are specific and plural: What are the particular correlations which constitute it? How does it proceed in different situations? What is favorable and what unfavorable to its best performance?—and so on. Can one deny that if we were to take our clue from the present empirical situation, including the scientific notion of evolution (biological continuity) and the existing arts of control of nature, subject and object would be treated as occupying the same natural world as unhesitatingly as we assume the natural conjunction of an animal and its food? Would it not follow that knowledge is one way in which natural energies co-operate? Would there be any problem save discovery of the peculiar structure of this co-operation, the conditions under which it occurs to best effect, and the consequences which issue from its occurrence?

It is a commonplace that the chief divisions of modern philosophy, idealism in its different kinds, realisms of various brands, so-called common-sense dualism, agnosticism, relativism, phenomenalism, have grown up around the epistemological problem of the general relation of subject and object. Problems not openly epistemological, such as whether the relation of changes in consciousness to physical changes is one of interaction, parallelism, or automatism have the same origin. What becomes of philosophy, consisting largely as it does of different answers to these questions, in case the assumptions which generate the questions have no empirical standing? Is it not time that philosophers turned from the attempt to determine the comparative merits of various replies to the questions to a consideration of the claims of the questions?

When dominating religious ideas were built up about the idea that the self is a stranger and pilgrim in this world; when morals, falling in line, found true good only in inner states of a self inaccessible to anything but its own private introspection; when political theory assumed the finality of disconnected and mutually exclusive personalities, the notion that the bearer of experience is antithetical to the world instead of being in and of it was congenial. It at least had the warrant of other beliefs and aspirations. But the doctrine of biological continuity or organic evolution has destroyed the scientific basis of the conception. Morally, men are now concerned with the amelioration of the conditions of the common lot in this world. Social sciences recognize that associated life is not a matter of physical juxtaposition, but of genuine intercourse—of community of experience in a non-metaphorical sense of

Trouble with the problem

community. Why should we longer try to patch up and refine and stretch the old solutions till they seem to cover the change of thought and practice? Why not recognize that the trouble is with the problem?

A belief in organic evolution which does not extend unreservedly to the way in which the subject of experience is thought of, and which does not strive to bring the entire theory of experience and knowing into line with biological and social facts, is hardly more than Pickwickian. There are many, for example, who hold that dreams, hallucinations, and errors cannot be accounted for at all except on the theory that a self (or "consciousness") exercises a modifying influence upon the "real object." The logical assumption is that consciousness is outside of the real object; that it is something different in kind, and therefore has the power of changing "reality" into appearance, of introducing "relativities" into things as they are in themselves—in short, of infecting real things with subjectivity. Such writers seem unaware of the fact that this assumption makes consciousness supernatural in the literal sense of the word; and that, to say the least, the conception can be accepted by one who accepts the doctrine of biological continuity only after every other way of dealing with the facts has been exhausted.

Realists, of course (at least some of the Neorealists), deny any such miraculous intervention of consciousness. But they [7] admit the reality of the problem; denying only this particular solution, they try to find some other way out, which will still preserve intact the notion of knowledge as a relationship of a general sort between subject and object.

Now dreams and hallucinations, errors, pleasures, and pains, possibly "secondary" qualities, do not occur save where there are organic centers of experience. They cluster about a subject. But to treat them as things which inhere exclusively

[7] The "they" means the "some" of the prior sentence—those whose realism is epistemological, instead of being a plea for taking the facts of experience as we find them without refraction through epistemological apparatus.

in the subject; or as posing the problem of a distortion of *the* real object by a knower set over against the world, or as presenting facts to be explained primarily as cases of contemplative knowledge, is to testify that one has still to learn the lesson of evolution in its application to the affairs in hand.

If biological development be accepted, the subject of experience is at least an animal, continuous with other organic forms in a process of more complex organization. An animal in turn is at least continuous with chemico-physical processes which, in living things, are so organized as really to constitute the activitives of life with all their defining traits. And experience is not identical with brain action; it is the entire organic agent-patient in all its interaction with the environment, natural and social. The brain is primarily an organ of a certain kind of behavior, not of knowing the world. And to repeat what has already been said, experiencing *is* just certain modes of interaction, of correlation, of natural objects among which the organism happens, so to say, to be one. It follows with equal force that experience means primarily not knowledge, but ways of doing and suffering. Knowing must be described by discovering what particular mode—qualitatively unique—of doing and suffering it is. As it is, we find experience assimilated to a nonempirical concept of knowledge, derived from an antecedent notion of a spectator outside of the world.[8]

What is knowing?

In short, the epistemological fashion of conceiving dreams, errors, "relativities," etc., depends upon the isolation of mind

[8] It is interesting to note that some of the realists who have assimilated the cognitive relation to other existential relations in the world (instead of treating it as an unique or epistemological relation) have been forced in support of their conception of knowledge as a "presentative" or spectatorial affair to extend the defining features of the latter to all relations among things, and hence to make all the "real" things in the world pure "simples," wholly independent of one another. So conceived the doctrine of external relations appears to be rather the doctrine of complete externality of *things*. Aside from this point, the doctrine is interesting for its dialectical ingenuity and for the elegant development of assumed premises, rather than convincing on account of empirical evidence supporting it.

from intimate participation with other changes in the same continuous nexus. Thus it is like contending that when a bottle bursts, the bottle is, in some self-contained miraculous way, exclusively responsible. Since it is the nature of a bottle to be whole so as to retain fluids, bursting is an abnormal event—comparable to a hallucination. Hence it cannot belong to the "real" bottle; the "subjectivity" of glass is the cause. It is obvious that since the breaking of glass is a case of specific correlation of natural energies, its accidental and abnormal character has to do with *consequences,* not with causation. Accident is interference with the consequences for which the bottle is intended. The bursting considered apart from its bearing on these consequences is on a plane with any other occurrence in the wide world. But from the standpoint of a desired future, bursting is an anomaly, an interruption of the course of events.

The analogy with the occurrence of dreams, hallucinations, etc., seems to me exact. Dreams are not something outside of the regular course of events; they are in and of it. They are not cognitive distortions of real things; they are *more* real things. There is nothing abnormal in their existence, any more than there is in the bursting of a bottle.[9] But they may be abnormal, from the standpoint of their influence, of their operation as stimuli in calling out responses to modify the future. Dreams have often been taken as prognostics of what is to happen; they have modified conduct. A hallucination may lead a man to consult a doctor; such a consequence is right and proper. But the consultation indicates that the subject regarded it as an indication of consequences which he feared: as a symptom of a disturbed life. Or the hallucination may lead him to anticipate consequences which in fact flow only from the possession of great wealth. Then the hallucination is a disturbance of the normal course of events; the occurrence is wrongly *used* with reference to eventualities.

[9] In other words, there is a general "problem of error" only because there is a general problem of evil, concerning which see Dr. Kallen's essay . . . . [*Loc. cit.*]

To regard reference to use and to desired and intended consequences as involving a "subjective" factor is to miss the point, for this has regard to the future. The uses to which a bottle are put are not mental; they do not consist of physical states; they are further correlations of natural existences. Consequences in use are genuine natural events; but they do not occur without the intervention of behavior involving anticipation of a future. The case is not otherwise with a hallucination. The differences it makes are in any case differences in the course of the one continuous world. The important point is whether they are good or bad differences. To use the hallucination as a sign of organic lesions that menace health means the beneficial result of seeing a physician; to respond to it as a sign of consequences such as actually follow only from being persecuted is to fall into error—to be abnormal. The persecutors are "unreal"; that is, there are no things which act as persecutors act; but the hallucination exists. Given its conditions it is as natural as any other event, and poses only the same kind of problem as is put by the occurrence of, say, a thunderstorm. The "unreality" of persecution is not, however, a subjective matter; it means that conditions do not exist for producing the *future* consequences which are now anticipated and reacted to. Ability to anticipate future consequences and to respond to them as stimuli to present behavior may well *define* what is meant by a mind or by "consciousness." [10] But this is only a way of saying just what kind of a real or natural existence the subject is; it is not to fall back on a preconception about an unnatural subject in order to characterize the occurrence of error.

Although the discussion may be already labored, let us take another example—the occurrence of disease. By definition it is pathological, abnormal. At one time in human history this abnormality was taken to be something dwelling in the intrinsic nature of the event—in its existence irrespective of future consequences. Disease was literally extranatural and

[10] Compare the paper by Professor Bode. ["Consciousness and Psychology" in *Creative Intelligence*.]

to be referred to demons or to magic. No one today questions its naturalness—its place in the order of natural events. Yet it is abnormal—for it operates to effect results different from those which follow from health. The difference is a genuine empirical difference, not a mere mental distinction. From the standpoint of bearing on a subsequent course of events disease is unnatural, in spite of the naturalness of its occurrence and origin.

The habit of ignoring reference to the future is responsible for the assumption that to admit human participation in any form is to admit the "subjective" in a sense which alters the objective into the phenomenal. There have been those who, like Spinoza, regarded health and disease, good and ill, as equally real and equally unreal. However, only a few consistent materialists have included truth along with error as merely phenomenal and subjective. But if one does not regard movement toward possible consequences as genuine, wholesale denial of existential validity to all these distinctions is the only logical course. To select truth as objective and error as "subjective" is, on this basis, an unjustifiably partial procedure. Take everything as fixedly given, and both truth and error are arbitrary insertions into fact. Admit the genuineness of changes going on, and capacity for its direction through organic action based on foresight, and both truth and falsity are alike existential. It is human to regard the course of events which is in line with our own efforts as the *regular* course of events, and interruptions as abnormal, but this partiality of human desire is itself a part of what actually takes place.

It is now proposed to take a particular case of the alleged epistemological predicament for discussion, since the entire ground cannot be covered. I think, however, the instance chosen is typical, so that the conclusion reached may be generalized.

The instance is that of so-called relativity in perception. There are almost endless instances; the stick bent in water; the whistle changing pitch with change of distance from the ear; objects doubled when the eye is pushed; the destroyed star still visible, etc., etc. For our consideration we may take the case of a spherical object that presents itself to one observer as a flat circle, to another as a somewhat distorted elliptical surface. This situation gives empirical proof, so it is argued, of the difference between a real object and mere appearance. Since there is but one object, the existence of two *subjects* is the sole differentiating factor. Hence the two appearances of the one real object [are] proof of the intervening distorting action of the subject. And many of the Neorealists who deny the difference in question, admit the case to be one of knowledge and accordingly to constitute an epistemological problem. They have in consequence developed wonderfully elaborate schemes of sundry kinds to maintain "epistemological monism" intact.

Let us try to keep close to empirical facts. In the first place the two unlike appearances of the one sphere are physically necessary because of the laws of reaction of light. If the one sphere did *not* assume these two appearances under given conditions, we should be confronted with a hopelessly irreconcilable discrepancy in the behavior of natural energy. That the result is natural is evidenced by the fact that two cameras— or other arrangements of apparatus for reflecting light—yield precisely the same results. Photographs are as genuinely physical existence as the original sphere; and they exhibit the two geometrical forms.

The statement of these facts makes no impression upon the confirmed epistemologist; he merely retorts that as long as it is admitted that the organism is the cause of a sphere being seen, from different points, as a circular and as an elliptical surface, the essence of his contention—the modification of the real object by the subject—is admitted. To the question why the same logic does not apply to photographic records he makes, as far as I know, no reply at all.

The source of the difficulty is not hard to see. The objection assumes that the alleged modifications of *the* real object are cases of *knowing* and hence attributable to the influence of a *knower*. Statements which set forth the doctrine will always be found to refer to the organic factor, to the eye, as an observer or a percipient. Even when reference is made to a lens or a mirror, language is sometimes used which suggests that the writer's naïveté is sufficiently gross to treat these physical factors as if they were engaged in perceiving the sphere. But as it is evident that the lens operates as a physical factor in correlation with other physical factors—notably light—so it ought to be evident that the intervention of the optical apparatus of the eye is a purely noncognitive matter. The relation in question is not one between a sphere and a would-be knower of it, unfortunately condemned by the nature of the knowing apparatus to alter the thing he would know; it is an affair of the dynamic interaction of two physical agents in producing a third thing, an effect—an affair of precisely the same kind as in any physical conjoint action, say the operation of hydrogen and oxygen in producing water. To regard the eye as primarily a knower, an observer, of things, is as crass as to assign that function to a camera. But unless the eye (or optical apparatus, or brain, or organism) be so regarded, there is absolutely no problem of observation or of knowledge in the case of the occurrence of elliptical and circular surfaces. Knowledge does not enter into the affair at all till *after* these forms of refracted light have been produced. About them there is nothing unreal. Light is really, physically, existentially, refracted into these forms. If the same spherical form upon refracting light to physical objects in two quite different positions produced the same geometric forms, there would, indeed, be something to marvel at—as there would be if wax produced the same results in contact simultaneously with a cold body and with a warm one. Why talk about *the real* object in relation to *a knower* when what is given is one real thing in dynamic connection with another real thing?

The way of dealing with the case will probably meet with a retort; at least, it has done so before. It has been said that the account given above and the account of traditional subjectivism differ only verbally. The essential thing in both, so it is said, is the admission that an activity of a self or subject or organism makes a difference in the real object. Whether the subject makes this difference in the very process of knowing or makes it prior to the act of knowing is a minor matter; what is important is that the known thing has, by the time it is known, been "subjectified."

The objection gives a convenient occasion for summarizing the main points of the argument. On the one hand, the retort of the objector depends upon talking about *the* real object. Employ the term *a* real object," and the change produced by the activity characteristic of the optical apparatus is of just the same kind as that of the camera lens or that of any other physical agency. Every event in the world marks a difference made to one existence in active conjunction with some other existence. And, as for the alleged subjectivity, if subjective is used merely as an adjective to designate the specific activity of a particular existence, comparable, say, to the term feral, applied to tiger, or metallic, applied to iron, then of course reference to subjective is legitimate. But it is also tautological. It is like saying that flesh eaters are carnivorous. But the term "subjective" is so consecrated to other uses, usually implying invidious contrast with objectivity (while subjective in the sense just suggested means specific mode *of* objectivity), that it is difficult to maintain this innocent sense. Its use in any disparaging way in the situation before us—any sense implicating contrast with a real object—assumes that the organism *ought* not to make any difference when it operates in conjunction with other things. Thus we run to earth that assumption that the subject is heterogeneous from every other natural existence; it is to be the one otiose, inoperative thing in a moving world—our old assumption of the self as outside of things.[11]

[11] As the attempt to retain the epistemological problem and yet to reject idealistic and relativistic solutions has forced some Neorealists into the doctrine of isolated and independent simples, so it has also led to a doctrine of Eleatic pluralism. In order to maintain the doctrine [that] the subject makes no difference to anything else, it is held that *no* ultimate real

What and where is knowledge in the case we have been considering? Not, as we have already seen, in the production of forms of light having a circular and elliptical surface. These forms are natural happenings. They may enter into knowledge or they may not, according to circumstances. Countless such refractive changes take place without being noted.[12] When they become subject matter for knowledge, the inquiry they set on foot may take on an indefinite variety of forms. One may be interested in ascertaining more about the structural peculiarities of the forms themselves; one may be interested in the mechanism of their production; one may find problems in projective geometry, or in drawing and painting—all depending upon the specific matter-of-fact context. The forms may be *objectives* of knowledge—of reflective examination—or they may be means of knowing something else. It may happen—under some circumstances it does happen—that the objective of inquiry is the nature of the geometric form which, when refracting light, gives rise to these other forms. In this case the sphere is the thing known, and in this case, the forms of light are signs or evidence of the conclusion to be drawn. There is no more reason for supposing that they *are* (mis)-knowledges of the sphere—that the sphere is necessarily and from the start what one is trying to know—than for supposing that the position of the mercury in the thermometer tube is a cognitive distortion of atmospheric pressure. In each case (that of the mercury and that of, say, a circular surface) the primary datum is a physical happening. In each case it may be used, upon occasion, as a sign or evidence of the nature of the causes which brought it about. Given the position in

---

makes any difference to anything else—all this rather than surrender once for all the genuineness of the problem and to follow the lead of empirical subject matter.

12 There is almost no end to the various dialectic developments of the epistemological situation. When it is held that all the relations of the type in question are cognitive, and yet it is recognized (as it must be) that many such "transformations" go unremarked, the theory is supplemented by introducing "unconscious" psychical modifications.

question, the circular form would be an intrinsically *unreliable* evidence of the nature and position of the spherical body only in case it, as the direct datum of perception, were *not* what it is—a circular form.

I confess that all this seems so obvious that the reader is entitled to inquire into the motive for reciting such plain facts. Were it not for the persistence of the epistemological problem it would be an affront to the reader's intelligence to dwell upon them. But as long as such facts as we have been discussing furnish the subject matter with which philosophizing is peculiarly concerned, these commonplaces must be urged and reiterated. They bear out two contentions which are important at the juncture, although they will lose special significance as soon as these are habitually recognized: Negatively, a prior and nonempirical notion of the self is the source of the prevailing belief that experience as such is primarily cognitional—a knowledge affair; positively, *knowledge is always a matter of the use that is made of experienced natural events,* a use in which given things are treated as indications of what will be experienced under different conditions.

Negatively

Positively

Let us make one effort more to clear up these points. Suppose it is a question of knowledge of water. The thing to be known does not present itself primarily as a matter of knowledge-and-ignorance at all. It occurs as a stimulus to action and as the source of certain undergoings. It is something to react to—to drink, to wash with, to put out fire with, and also something that reacts unexpectedly to our reactions, that makes us undergo disease, suffocation, drowning. In this two-fold way, water or anything else enters into experience. Such presence in experience has of itself nothing to do with knowledge or consciousness; nothing that is in the sense of depending upon them, though it has everything to do with knowledge and consciousness in the sense that the latter depends upon prior experience of this noncognitive sort. Man's experience is what it is because his response to things (even successful response) and the reactions of things to his life, are so radically different from knowledge. The difficulties and tragedies

Experience radically different from knowledge

of life, the stimuli to acquiring knowledge, lie in the radical disparity of presence-in-experience and presence-in-knowing. Yet the immense importance of knowledge experience, the fact that turning presence-in-experience over into presence-in-a-knowledge-experience is the sole mode of control of nature, has systematically hypnotized European philosophy since the time of Socrates into thinking that all experiencing is a mode of knowing, if not good knowledge, then a low-grade or confused or implicit knowledge.

When water is an adequate stimulus to action or when its reactions oppress and overwhelm us, it remains outside the scope of knowledge. When, however, the bare presence of the thing (say, as optical stimulus) ceases to operate directly as stimulus to response and begins to operate in connection with a forecast of the consequences it will effect when responded to, it begins to acquire meaning—to be known, to be an object. It is noted as something which is wet, fluid, satisfies thirst, allays uneasiness, etc. The conception that we begin with a known visual quality which is thereafter enlarged by adding on qualities apprehended by the other senses does not rest upon experience; it rests upon making experience conform to the notion that every experience *must* be a cognitive noting. As long as the visual stimulus operates as a stimulus on its own account, there is no apprehension, no noting, of color or light at all. To much the greater portion of sensory stimuli we react in precisely this wholly noncognitive way. In the attitude of suspended response in which consequences are anticipated, the direct stimulus becomes a sign or index of something else—and thus matter of noting or apprehension or acquaintance, or whatever term may be employed. This difference (together, of course, with the consequences which go with it) is the difference which the natural event of knowing makes to the natural event of direct organic stimulation. It is no change of a reality into an unreality, of an object into something subjective; it is no secret, illicit, or epistemological transformation; it is a genuine acquisition of new and distinctive features through entering into relations with things with which it was not formerly connected—namely, possible and future things.

But, replies some one so obsessed with the epistemological point of view that he assumes that the prior account is a rival epistemology in disguise, all this involves no change in Reality, no difference made to Reality. Water was all the time all the things it is ever found out to be. Its real nature has not been altered by knowing it; any such alteration means a misknowing.

In reply let it be said—once more and finally—there is no assertion or implication about *the* real object or *the* real world or *the* reality. Such an assumption goes with that epistemological universe of discourse which has to be abandoned in an empirical universe of discourse. The change is of *a* real object. An incident of the world operating as a physiologically direct stimulus is assuredly a reality. Responded to, it produces specific consequences in virtue of the response. Water is not drunk unless somebody drinks it; it does not quench thirst unless a thirsty person drinks it—and so on. Consequences occur whether one is aware of them or not; they are integral facts in experience. But let one of these consequences be anticipated and let it, as anticipated, become an indispensable element in the stimulus, and then there is a known object. It is not that knowing *produces* a change, but that it *is* a change of the specific kind described. A serial process, the successive portions of which are as such incapable of simultaneous occurrence, is telescoped and condensed into an object, a unified interreference of contemporaneous properties, most of which express potentialities rather than completed data.

Because of this change, an *object* possesses truth or error (which the physical occurrence as such never has); it is classifiable as fact or fantasy; it is of a sort or kind, expresses an essence or nature, possesses implications, etc., etc. That is to say, it is marked by specifiable *logical* traits not found in physical occurrences as such. Because objective idealisms have seized upon these traits as constituting the very essence of Reality is no reason for proclaiming that they are ready-made

argument against knowledge as presentational

features of physical happenings, and hence for maintaining that knowing is nothing but an appearance of things on a stage for which "consciousness" supplies the footlights. For only the epistemological predicament leads to "presentations" being regarded as cognitions of things which were previously unpresented. In any empirical situation of everyday life or of science, knowledge signifies something stated or inferred of another thing. Visible water is not a more or less erroneous presentation of H_2O, but H_2O is a knowledge about the thing we see, drink, wash with, sail on, and use for power.

A further point and the present phase of discussion terminates. Treating knowledge as a presentative relation between the knower and object makes it necessary to regard the mechanism of *presentation* as constituting the act of knowing. Since things may be presented in sense-perception, in recollection, in imagination and in conception, and since the mechanism in every one of these four styles of presentation is sensory-cerebral the problem of knowing becomes a mind-body problem.[13] The psychological, or physiological, mechanism of presentation involved in seeing a chair, remembering what I ate yesterday for luncheon, imagining the moon the size of a cart wheel, conceiving a mathematical continuum is identified with the operation of knowing. The evil consequences are two fold. The problem of the relation of mind and body has become a part of the problem of the possibility of knowledge in general, to the further complication of a matter already hopelessly constrained. Meantime the actual process of knowing, namely, operations of controlled observation, inference, reasoning, and testing, the only process with *intellectual* import, is dismissed as irrelevant to the theory of knowing. The methods of knowing practiced in daily life and science are excluded from consideration in the philosophical theory of

[13] Conception-presentation has, of course, been made by many in the history of speculation an exception to this statement; "pure" memory is also made an exception by Bergson. To take cognizance of this matter would, of course, accentuate, not relieve, the difficulty remarked upon in the text.

So → Logic: Theory of Inquiry
(not a purely formal logic)

knowing. Hence the constructions of the latter become more and more elaborately artificial because there is no definite check upon them. It would be easy to quote from epistemological writers statements to the effect that these processes (which supply the only empirically verifiable facts of knowing) are *merely* inductive in character, or even that they are of purely psychological significance. It would be difficult to find a more complete inversion of the facts than in the latter statement, since presentation constitutes in fact the psychological affair. A confusion of logic with physiological [psychology] has bred hybrid epistemology, with the amazing result that the technique of effective inquiry is rendered irrelevant to the theory of knowing, and those physical events involved in the occurrence of data for knowing are treated as if they constituted the act of knowing.

V

What are the bearings of our discussion upon the conception of the present scope and office of philosophy? What do our conclusions indicate and demand with reference to philosophy itself? For the philosophy which reaches such conclusions regarding knowledge and mind must apply them, sincerely and wholeheartedly, to its idea of its own nature. For philosophy claims to be one form or mode of knowing. If, then, the conclusion is reached that knowing is a way of employing empirical occurrences with respect to increasing power to direct the consequences which flow from things, the application of the conclusion must be made to philosophy itself. It, too, becomes not a contemplative survey of existence nor an analysis of what is past and done with, but an outlook upon future possibilities with reference to attaining the better and averting the worse. Philosophy must take, with good grace, its own medicine.

It is easier to state the negative results of the changed idea of philosophy than the positive ones. The point that occurs to mind most readily is that philosophy will have to surrender all pretension to be peculiarly concerned with ultimate reality, or with reality as a complete (i.e., completed) whole: with *the* real object. The surrender is not easy of achievement. The philosophic tradition that comes to us from classic Greek thought and that was reinforced by Christian philosophy in the Middle Ages discriminates philosophical knowing from other modes of knowing by means of an alleged peculiarly intimate concern with supreme, ultimate, true reality. To deny this trait to philosophy seems to many to be the suicide of philosophy; to be a systematic adoption of skepticism or agnostic positivism.

The pervasiveness of the tradition is shown in the fact that so vitally a contemporary thinker as Bergson, who finds a philosophic revolution involved in abandonment of the traditional identification of the truly real with the fixed (an identification inherited from Greek thought), does not find it in his heart to abandon the counterpart identification of philosophy with search for the truly Real; and hence he finds it necessary to substitute an ultimate and absolute flux for an ultimate and absolute permanence. Thus his great empirical services in calling attention to the fundamental importance of considerations of time for problems of life and mind get compromised with a mystic, nonempirical "Intuition"; and we find him preoccupied with solving, by means of his new idea of ultimate reality, the traditional problems of realities-in-themselves and phenomena, matter and mind, free will and determinism, God and the world. Is not that another evidence of the influence of the classic idea about philosophy?

Even the new realists are not content to take their realism as a plea for approaching subject matter directly instead of through the intervention of epistemological apparatus; they find it necessary first to determine the status of *the* real object. Thus they too become entangled in the problem of the possibility of error, dreams, hallucinations, etc., in short, the problem of evil. For I take it that an uncorrupted realism would accept such things as real events, and find in them no other problems than those attending the consideration of any real occurrence—namely, problems of structure, origin, and operation.

It is often said that pragmatism, unless it is content to be a contribution to mere methodology, must develop a theory of Reality. But the chief characteristic trait of the pragmatic notion of reality is precisely that no theory of Reality in general, *überhaupt,* is possible or needed. It occupies the position of an emancipated empiricism or a thoroughgoing naïve realism. It finds that "reality" is a *denotative* term, a word used to designate indifferently everything that happens. Lies, dreams, insanities, deceptions, myths, theories are all of them just the events which they specifically are. Pragmatism is content to take its stand with science; for science finds all such events to be subject matter of description and inquiry—just like stars and fossils, mosquitoes and malaria, circulation and vision. It also takes its stand with daily life, which finds that such things really have to be reckoned with as they occur interwoven in the texture of events.

The only way in which the term reality can ever become more than a blanket denotative term is through recourse to specific events in all their diversity and thatness. Speaking summarily, I find that the retention by philosophy of the notion of a Reality feudally superior to the events of everyday occurrence is the chief source of the increasing isolation of philosophy from common sense and science. For the latter do not operate in any such region. As with them of old, philosophy in dealing with real difficulties finds itself still hampered by reference to realities more real, more ultimate, than those which directly happen.

I have said that identifying the cause of philosophy with the notion of superior reality is the cause of an *increasing* isolation from science and practical life. The phrase reminds us that there was a time when the enterprise of science and the moral interests of men both moved in a universe invidiously distinguished from that of ordinary occurrence. While all that happens is equally real—since it really happens—happenings are not of equal worth. Their respective consequences, their import, varies tremendously. Counterfeit money, although real (or rather *because* real) is really different from valid circulatory medium, just as disease is really different from health; different in specific structure and so different in consequences. In occidental thought, the Greeks were the first to draw the distinction between the genuine and the spurious in a generalized fashion and to formulate and enforce its tremendous significance for the conduct of life. But since they had at command no technique of experimental analysis and no adequate technique of mathematical analysis, they were compelled to treat the difference of the true and the false, the dependable and the deceptive, as signifying two kinds of existence, the truly real and the apparently real.

Two points can hardly be asserted with too much emphasis. The Greeks were wholly right in the feeling that questions of good and ill, as far as they fall within human control, are bound up with discrimination of the genuine from the spurious, of "being" from what only pretends to be. But because they lacked adequate instrumentalities for coping with this difference in specific situations, they were forced to treat the difference as a wholesale and rigid one. Science was concerned with vision of ultimate and true reality; opinion was concerned with getting along with apparent realities. Each had its appropriate region permanently marked off. Matters of opinion could never become matters of science; their intrinsic nature forbade. When the practice of science went on under such conditions, science and philosophy were one and the same thing. Both had to do with ultimate reality in its rigid and insuperable difference from ordinary occurrences.

We have only to refer to the way in which medieval life wrought the philosophy of an ultimate and supreme reality into the context of practical life to realize that for centuries political and moral interests were bound up with the distinction between the absolutely real and the relatively real. The difference was no matter of a remote technical philosophy, but one which controlled life from the cradle to the grave, from the grave to the endless life after death. By means of a vast institution, which in effect was state as well as church, the claims of ultimate reality were enforced; means of access to it were provided. Acknowledgment of The Reality brought security in this world and salvation in the next. It is not necessary to report the story of the change which has since taken place. It is enough for our purposes to note that none of the modern philosophies of a superior reality, or *the* real object, idealistic or realistic, holds that its insight makes a difference like that between sin and holiness, eternal condemnation and eternal bliss. While in its own context the philosophy of ultimate reality entered into the vital concerns of men, it now tends to be an ingenious dialectic exercised in professorial corners by a few who have retained ancient premises while rejecting their application to the conduct of life.

The increased isolation from science of any philosophy identified with the problem of *the* real is equally marked. For the growth of science has consisted precisely in the invention of an equipment, a technique of appliances and procedures, which, accepting all occurrences as homogeneously real, proceeds to distinguish the authenticated from the spurious, the true from the false, by specific modes of treatment in specific situations. The procedures of the trained engineer, of the competent physician, of the laboratory expert, have turned out to be the only ways of discriminating the counterfeit from the valid. And they have revealed that the difference is not one of antecedent fixity of existence, but one of mode of treatment and of the consequences thereon attendant. After mankind has learned to put its trust in specific procedures in order to make its discriminations between the false and the true, philosophy arrogates to itself the enforcement of the distinction at its own cost.

More than once, this essay has intimated that the counterpart of the idea of invidiously real reality is the spectator notion of knowledge. If the knower, however defined, is set over against the world to be known, knowing consists in possessing a transcript, more or less accurate but otiose, of real things. Whether this transcript is presentative in character (as realists say) or whether it is by means of states of consciousness which represent things (as subjectivists say), is a matter of great importance in its own context. But, in another regard, this difference is negligible in comparison with the point in which both agree. Knowing is viewing from outside. But if it be true that the self or subject of experience is part and parcel of the course of events, it follows that the self *becomes* a knower. It becomes a mind in virtue of a distinctive way of partaking in the course of events. The significant distinction is no longer between the knower *and* the world; it is between different ways of being in and of the movement of things; between a brute physical way and a purposive, intelligent way.

There is no call to repeat in detail the statements which have been advanced. Their net purport is that the directive presence of future possibilities in dealing with existent conditions is what is meant by knowing; that the self becomes a knower or mind when anticipation of future consequences operates as its stimulus. What we are now concerned with is the effect of this conception upon the nature of philosophic knowing.

As far as I can judge, popular response to pragmatic philosophy was moved by two quite different considerations. By some it was thought to provide a new species of sanctions, a new mode of apologetics, for certain religious ideas whose standing had been threatened. By others, it was welcomed because it was taken as a sign that philosophy was about to surrender its otiose and speculative remoteness; that philosophers were beginning to recognize that philosophy is of account only if, like everyday knowing and like science, it affords guidance to action and thereby makes a difference in the event. It was welcomed as a sign that philosophers were willing to have the worth of their philosophizing measured by responsible tests.

I have not seen this point of view emphasized, or hardly recognized, by professional critics. The difference of attitude can probably be easily explained. The epistemological universe of discourse is so highly technical that only those who have been trained in the history of thought think in terms of it. It did not occur accordingly, to nontechnical readers to interpret the doctrine that the meaning and validity of thought are fixed by differences made in consequences and in satisfactoriness, to mean consequences in personal feelings. Those who were professionally trained, however, took the statement to mean that consciousness or mind in the mere act of looking at things modifies them. It understood the doctrine of test of validity by consequences to mean that apprehensions and conceptions are true if the modifications affected by them were of an emotionally desirable tone.

Prior discussion should have made it reasonably clear that the source of this misunderstanding lies in the neglect of temporal considerations. The change made in things by the self in knowing is not immediate and, so to say, cross-sectional. It is longitudinal—in the redirection given to changes already going on. Its analogue is found in the changes which take place in the development of, say, iron ore into a watch spring, not in those of the miracle of transubstantiation. For the static, cross-sectional, nontemporal relation of subject and object, the pragmatic hypothesis substitutes apprehension of a thing in terms of the results in other things which it is tending to effect. For the unique epistemological relation, it substitutes a practical relation of a familiar type—responsive behavior which changes in time the subject matter to which it applies. The unique thing about the responsible behavior which constitutes knowing is the specific difference which marks it off from other modes of response, namely, the part played in it by anticipation and prediction. Knowing is the act, stimulated by this foresight, of securing and averting consequences. The success of the achievement measures the standing of the foresight by which response is directed. The popular impression that pragmatic philosophy means that philosophy shall develop ideas relevant to the actual crises of life, ideas influential in dealing with them and tested by the assistance they afford, is correct.

Reference to practical response suggests, however, another

misapprehension. Many critics have jumped at the obvious
association of the word pragmatic with practical. They have
assumed that the intent is to limit all knowledge, philosophic
included, to promoting "action," understanding by action
either just any bodily movement, or those bodily movements
which conduce to the preservation and grosser well-being of
the body. James's statement that general conceptions must
"cash in" has been taken (especially by European critics) to
mean that the end and measure of intelligence lies in the
narrow and coarse utilities which it produces. Even an acute
American thinker, after first criticizing pragmatism as a kind
of idealistic epistemology, goes on to treat it as a doctrine
which regards intelligence as a lubricating oil facilitating the
workings of the body.

One source of the misunderstanding is suggested by the fact
that "cashing in" to James meant that a general idea must
always be capable of verification in specific existential cases.
The notion of "cashing in" says nothing about the breadth or
depth of the specific consequences. As an empirical doctrine,
it could not say anything about them in general; the specific
cases must speak for themselves. If one conception is verified
in terms of eating beefsteak, and another in terms of a favorable credit balance in the bank, that is not because of anything in the theory, but because of the specific nature of the
conceptions in question, and because there exist particular
events like hunger and trade. If there are also existences in
which the most liberal esthetic ideas and the most generous
moral conceptions can be verified by specific embodiment,
assuredly so much the better. The fact that a strictly empirical
philosophy was taken by so many critics to imply an *a priori*
dogma about the kind of consequences capable of existence is
evidence, I think, of the inability of many philosophers to
think in concretely empirical terms. Since the critics were
themselves accustomed to get results by manipulating the concepts of "consequences" and of "practice," they assumed that
even a would-be empiricist must be doing the same sort of
thing. It will, I suppose, remain for a long time incredible to

some that a philosopher should really intend to go to specific experiences to determine of what scope and depth practice admits, and what sort of consequences the world permits to come into being. Concepts are so clear; it takes so little time to develop their implications; experiences are so confused, and it requires so much time and energy to lay hold of them. And yet these same critics charge pragmatism with adopting subjective and emotional standards!

As a matter of fact, the pragmatic theory of intelligence means that the function of mind is to project new and more complex ends—to free experience from routine and from caprice. Not the use of thought to accomplish purposes already given either in the mechanism of the body or in that of the existent state of society, but the use of intelligence to liberate and liberalize action, is the pragmatic lesson. Action restricted to given and fixed ends may attain great technical efficiency; but efficiency is the only quality to which it can lay claim. Such action is mechanical (or becomes so), no matter what the scope of the preformed end, be it the Will of God or *Kultur*. But the doctrine that intelligence develops within the sphere of action for the sake of possibilities not yet given is the opposite of a doctrine of mechanical efficiency. Intelligence *as* intelligence is inherently forward-looking; only by ignoring its primary function does it become a mere means for an end already given. The latter *is* servile, even when the end is labeled moral, religious, or esthetic. But action directed to ends to which the agent has not previously been attached inevitably carries with it a quickened and enlarged spirit. A pragmatic intelligence is a creative intelligence, not a routine mechanic.

All this may read like a defense of pragmatism by one concerned to make out for it the best case possible. Such is not, however, the intention. The purpose is to indicate the extent to which intelligence frees action from a mechanically instrumental character. Intelligence is, indeed, instrumental *through* action to the determination of the qualities of future experience. But the very fact that the concern of intelligence is with

ends not simply given

Critical view of "ends"

the future, with the as-yet-unrealized (and with the given and the established only as conditions of the realization of possibilities), makes the action in which it takes effect generous and liberal; free of spirit. Just that action which extends and approves intelligence has an intrinsic value of its own in being instrumental—the intrinsic value of being informed with intelligence in behalf of the enrichment of life. By the same stroke, intelligence becomes truly liberal: knowing is a human undertaking, not an esthetic appreciation carried on by a refined class or a capitalistic possession of a few learned specialists, whether men of science or of philosophy.

More emphasis has been put upon what philosophy is not than upon what it may become. But it is not necessary, it is not even desirable, to set forth philosophy as a scheduled program. There are human difficulties of an urgent, deep-seated kind which may be clarified by trained reflection, and whose solution may be forwarded by the careful development of hypotheses. When it is understood that philosophic thinking is caught up in the actual course of events, having the office of guiding them toward a prosperous issue, problems will abundantly present themselves. Philosophy will not solve these problems; philosophy is vision, imagination, reflection—and these functions, apart from action, modify nothing and hence resolve nothing. But in a complicated and perverse world, action which is not informed with vision, imagination, and reflection, is more likely to increase confusion and conflict than to straighten things out. It is not easy for generous and sustained reflection to become a guiding and illuminating method in action. Until it frees itself from identification with problems which are supposed to depend upon Reality as such, or its distinction from a world of Appearance, or its relation to a Knower as such, the hands of philosophy are tied. Having no chance to link its fortunes with a responsible career by suggesting things to be tried, it cannot identify itself with questions which actually arise in the vicissitudes of life. Philosophy recovers itself when it ceases to be a device for dealing with the problems of philosophers and becomes a method, cultivated by philosophers, for dealing with the problems of men.

Emphasis must vary with the stress and special impact of the troubles which perplex men. Each age knows its own ills, and seeks its own remedies. One does not have to forecast a particular program to note that the central need of any program at the present day is an adequate conception of the nature of intelligence and its place in action. Philosophy cannot disavow responsibility for many misconceptions of the nature of intelligence which now hamper its efficacious operation. It has at least a negative task imposed upon it. It must take away the burdens which it has laid upon the intelligence of the common man in struggling with his difficulties. It must deny and eject that intelligence which is naught but a distant eye, registering in a remote and alien medium the spectacle of nature and life. To enforce the fact that the emergence of imagination and thought is relative to the connection of the sufferings of men with their doings is of itself to illuminate those sufferings and to instruct those doings. To catch mind in its connection with the entrance of the novel into the course of the world is to be on the road to see that intelligence is itself the most promising of all novelties, the revelation of the meaning of that transformation of past into future which is the reality of every present. To reveal intelligence as the organ for the guidance of this transformation, the sole director of its quality, is to make a declaration of present untold significance for action. To elaborate these convictions of the connection of intelligence with what men undergo because of their doings and with the emergence and direction of the creative, the novel, in the world is of itself a program which will keep philosophers busy until something more worth while is forced upon them. For the elaboration has to be made through application to all the disciplines which have an intimate connection with human conduct: to logic, ethics, esthetics, economics, and the procedure of the sciences formal and natural.

I also believe that there is a genuine sense in which the

enforcement of the pivotal position of intelligence in the world and thereby in control of human fortunes (so far as they are manageable) is the peculiar problem in the problems of life which come home most closely to ourselves—to ourselves living not merely in the early twentieth century but in the United States. It is easy to be foolish about the connection of thought with national life. But I do not see how any one can question the distinctively national color of English, or French, or German philosophies. And if of late the history of thought has come under the domination of the German dogma of an inner evolution of ideas, it requires but a little inquiry to convince oneself that that dogma itself testifies to a particularly nationalistic need and origin. I believe that philosophy in America will be lost between chewing a historic cud long since reduced to woody fiber, or an apologetics for lost causes (lost to natural science), or a scholastic, schematic formalism, unless it can somehow bring to consciousness America's own needs and its own implicit principle of successful action.

This need and principle, I am convinced, is the necessity of a deliberate control of policies by the method of intelligence, an intelligence which is not the faculty of intellect honored in textbooks and neglected elsewhere, but which is the sum-total of impulses, habits, emotions, records, and discoveries which forecast what is desirable and undesirable in future possibilities, and which contrive ingeniously in behalf of imagined good. Our life has no background of sanctified categories upon which we may fall back; we rely upon precedent as authority only to our own undoing—for with us there is such a continuously novel situation that final reliance upon precedent entails some class interest guiding us by the nose whither it will. British empiricism, with its appeal to what has been in the past, is, after all, only a kind of *a priorism*. For it lays down a fixed rule for future intelligence to follow; and only the immersion of philosophy in technical learning prevents our seeing that this is the essence of *a priorism*.

We pride ourselves upon being realistic, desiring a hard-headed cognizance of facts, and devoted to mastering the means of life. We pride ourselves upon a practical idealism, a lively and easily moved faith in possibilities as yet unrealized, in willingness to make sacrifice for their realization. Idealism easily becomes a sanction of waste and [carelessness [14]], and realism a sanction of legal formalism in behalf of things as they are—the rights of the possessor. We thus tend to combine a loose and ineffective optimism with assent to the doctrine of take who take can: a deification of power. All peoples at all times have been narrowly realistic in practice and have then employed idealization to cover up in sentiment and theory their brutalities. But never, perhaps, has the tendency been so dangerous and so tempting as with ourselves. Faith in the power of intelligence to imagine a future which is the projection of the desirable in the present, and to invent the instrumentalities of its realization, is our salvation. And it is a faith which must be nurtured and made articulate: surely a sufficiently large task for our philosophy.   *Task of philosophy*

14 [The original text has "carefulness," which is obviously a typographical error—Ed.]

AN EMPIRICAL SURVEY OF EMPIRICISMS[1]

Dewey maintained that philosophy must be understood in the context of its cultural setting, for philosophy both reflects and shapes the character of a culture. (See "Context and Thought.") This general thesis is illustrated here with a survey of three concepts of experience: the Greek view as exemplified by Plato and Aristotle, the modern view stemming from Locke, and a new concept of experience which is still in the "process of development." Dewey's reconstructive approach to the history of philosophy is clearly illustrated, for he attempts to use the insights and relevance of older views for understanding present conditions. The new concept of experience that Dewey advocates has been influenced by two basic themes: the character of the experimental sciences with their emphasis on future consequences and use of hypotheses to direct new observations; and the breakdown of a subjective introspectionist psychology which is being replaced by an objective biological orientation to psychological problems. While new cultural pressures and scientific conditions have demanded a reconstruction of "experience," the emerging view is also continuous with other views. It incorporates the Greek idea that experience consists of the accumulated information and skills of a social past, transmitted and refined through the medium of custom and habit, as well as the Lockian idea that experience is coercive and is the final test and "safeguard against the vagaries of fancy and accidents of conventional belief."

THERE ARE three historic conceptions of experience. The first is that formulated in classic antiquity, which persisted well into the seventeenth century and, as far as time is concerned, is the most important and influential. The second is that characteristic of two centuries, the eighteenth

1 *Studies in the History of Ideas,* edited by the Department of Philosophy of Columbia University (New York: 1935), III, 3-32.

and the nineteenth. Although it is more recent, it is what now generally comes to mind when the term empiricism is used. 3)The third is the latest movement, still in process of development. In discussing them it will be well to forget about empiricists and to consider the various concepts of experience. For if we start with the "ism," there is danger of becoming involved, as most discussions of "isms" do, in a somewhat sterile dialectic; while the conceptions of experience behind the different forms of empiricism and the various controversies concerning them are at least attempts to interpret a definite subject matter.

The clue to the Greek conception of the nature and limitations of experience may be derived most easily and directly from a present use of the word "empirical," as in the saying that medicine for a long time was on a purely empirical basis and that for the most part the practitioners of medicine were empiricists. It is well illustrated in the story that James tells in his Psychology of the brakeman in the old-fashioned railway car. The car filled with smoke from the stove while the train was at the station, and when the passengers complained, the brakeman replied, "Well, it will stop just as soon as the train starts." The man asked why, and the brakeman said, "It always does." [2] That is a good illustration of the meaning of experience and the empirical as conceived from the Greek point of view. The great mass of weather prophecies, the bulk of information upon which the arts and crafts depend, medicine to some extent, blacksmithing, carpentering, shoemaking, etc., are examples of empirical knowledge. Putting it negatively, while "experience" supplied fairly dependable information, dependable for purposes of practical utility or of action, it did not involve or depend upon any insight into the cause or reason of the occurrence. That is essentially what we have to do with when we give, in general outline, a Greek philosopher's account of experience. It denotes the accumulated information of the past, not merely the individual's own

[2] [See William James, *The Principles of Psychology* (New York: 1890), II, 342.]

past but the social past, transmitted through language and even more through apprenticeship in the various crafts, so far as this information was condensed in matter-of-fact generalizations about how to do certain things like building a house, making a statue, leading an army, or knowing what to expect under given circumstances.

With Plato, experience begins to get the depreciatory meaning which has clung to it all through the classic strain in philosophy. The reason for the derogatory view is, I think, fairly obvious. This kind of knowledge does stand in unfavorable contrast with knowledge that depends on insight as to why things happen, or on understanding the reason and the cause of things, for, on the whole, in earlier thought the terms "reason for a thing" and "cause of a thing" are largely synonymous. If you knew *why* a thing happened, then you understood it, you grasped the reason for its occurrence. Consequently, experience and empirical knowledge were set in very definite contrast with science, since science meant, of course, understanding or rational comprehension. This difference was illustrated for Plato in the contrast between the knowledge a geometer built up in a systematic, rational way and the kind of generalizations a carpenter might use. Experience had all the limitations which custom has. Indeed, the whole concept of experience was closely connected with the idea of habit and custom, if not identical with it. It was a collective memory or funded deposit of the past, just like the brakeman's "The smoke will stop because it always has done so." The recurrent events of the past leave behind them a certain definite expectation that things will continue in that way. Consequently, experience cannot give rise to knowledge in the honorific sense of science, but only to opinion, and, although opinions may sometimes be correct, that occurs, so to speak, by accident, because there is no knowledge of why they are true.

In Aristotle we have a more systematic account of the nature of experience and the reason for giving it a low status in philosophy. It is well to recognize that for him experience is not sensation nor perception, but rather the funded, practical, organized information about things that has come by the accumulation of past experience and the sifting out of the successful elements in the past experience from the unsuccessful ones.

Aristotle has the idea—of course the idea came to him ultimately from Plato—of a stepladder in knowledge, a series of grades: first is sensation, then comes perception involving organization of sense qualities. Now to Aristotle there are forms rather than mere stuff or material, since we grasp characters, characteristics, features. To know a chair is to know a certain structure that defines a whole class of objects; to perceive a thing as a chair is to grasp an element which therefore is, as far as it goes, general. Next in order comes the imagination. It preserves the formal element, the structural element, at the expense of matter. Our imagination, that is, our reproductive imagination or memory, while it does not grasp the form in its purity, lays hold of it with less immersion in sense or matter than is the case in direct sense perception. Now, by a kind of subconscious psychical mechanism which, like all of Aristotle's psychology, has its biological side, the images are preserved and more or less integrated with one another, the images that are similar, reinforcing one another. Thus we get an idea, a nonscientific idea but none the less an idea, of a *kind* of things, an empirical classification or generalization, and that is experience.

First sensation, then perception, then the reproductive memory or reproductive imagination, and then the consolidation or organization of these images in experience. And with this generalized idea there is also a general tendency to action in a certain direction toward a certain end form, in other words, a habit. As in the case of Plato, it is assumed that through language, through education, the cumulative process goes on in the arts and crafts not simply through the individual's lifetime but also through successive generations.

Thus experience comes to consist of standardized ways of action and a standardized body of beliefs, expectations, materials, and techniques.

Experience thus in both Plato and Aristotle, more on the whole in Aristotle than in Plato, serves the useful purpose of giving us the consolidated net results of past experience in the form that makes them available for further action. But there is also the same contrast, as in the case of Plato, between experience and science, understanding, or comprehension, which depend on reason. In fact, this contrast defines reason: whatever gives us forms entirely pure from matter is reason, the *intellectus purus* of scholastic and early modern philosophy. The chief way in which Aristotle modifies the Platonic concept of experience is in formulating this graded emerging of rational understanding out of experience.

There are certain things, according to Aristotle, concerning which empirical knowledge is the only kind possible. Where there is no necessity and universality in the objects and occurrences themselves, and where the element of contingency enters in, empirical knowledge is the only kind we can arrive at, though it is not the demonstrative knowledge which constitutes science. Thus social, political, and moral matters are the kind of material in which universality and necessity do not exist; and, as Aristotle was wont to say, it is the mark of an educated person not to expect more exactness in the ideas about a subject matter than the subject matter itself permits of.

I might note in passing, though it is perhaps not strictly related to my subject, that this is one great difference between Plato and Aristotle, more important to my mind than many of the differences that have been emphasized. Plato was quite aware that political and social matters were not regulated by reason and did not have a rational and necessary form, but a large part of the problem for him was to consider under what conditions morals and politics might really become a science and lawmaking in the community be rationally regulated. Thus his *Republic* is an attempt at least to sketch ideally the conditions under which politics and morals might become truly rational. Aristotle had no such ambition. He was perfectly willing, I won't say to throw morals and politics to the dogs, but he was willing to leave them to probability and opinion, to a certain amount of guesswork, especially to the intuition of the shrewd expert. Rational or scientific control is reserved for purely theoretical and intellectual matters. Thus Aristotle made a sharper distinction between matters of practice—even moral and political practice—and theory than Plato had done.

This is, I think, why Aristotle is conventionally treated as more empirical than Plato. Aristotle held that, historically and psychologically, reason can function only as the outcome of a series of graded steps up from sensation. For him there was no original, separate, and independent rational intuition. The latter had to pass through the stage of experience so that even a scientist, dealing with demonstrable and rational matters, would, as a matter of his own development and education, need the preparation of an empirical stage. This dependence of rational insight upon experience is not in any way logical or epistemological. It is a biological and, one might say, a biographical and a pedagogical matter. There is no logical connection between arriving at a certain height and climbing a ladder, yet things are so constituted that under certain conditions we cannot get to a particular place unless we climb a ladder.

I wish to emphasize a point which is now rarely mentioned but is necessary to an understanding of Plato and Aristotle, namely, that the Greeks did not separate the cognitive or intellectual from the active in the way in which the separation has become current in modern thought largely through the influence of Immanuel Kant, who was not satisfied until he had separated, if he possibly could, everything that belonged together. I do not mean that the Greeks attempted to derive one from the other, but that they always saw them in pairs, so that different stages of activity corresponded directly and intimately to different stages of intellectual cognitive grasp.

It is rather elementary in Platonic and Aristotelian psychology that the connection of sense with appetite is much closer than it is with knowledge. If we begin with taste and smell, the connection with the appetite of hunger is obvious; but even in sight and hearing, the higher senses, the senses as such are essentially organs of biological activity connected with the appetite. You may remember the incident in Plato where he describes from a moral point of view the appetite of a man whose sense of decency was restraining him from viewing a corpse, but who finally opened his eyes wide and said, "There, take your fill." In other words, there was a hunger expressed through the eyes that had to be satisfied, just as there is in taste and smell. The imagination as memory corresponded to a *particular* line of action associated with the reproductive image of some form of experience. Custom and habit were the practical or active correspondents or correlates of empirical knowledge. And then, finally, the beholding with esthetic satisfaction of perfect forms, ideas or ideals, being pure intuition with Plato, or self-inclosed rational activity in the case of Aristotle, corresponded to the essentially divine activity, *theoria,* of pure reason.

The reason I am calling attention to this now is that, especially through the influence of Aristotle, experience is commonly limited to that form of activity ordinarily called "practice." We say, "That is practical," "That is a practical man," and we mean the kind of activity that is adapted to securing certain rather limited utilities—utilities rather than higher values. The supreme activity is that of the pure intellect, and therefore it must be distinguished from every kind of practical doing and making. Subsequent philosophy inherited this depreciation of "experience" as being connected with lower and practical activity in contrast with the superior worth of purely rational activity.

Experience was thus identified with action concerned with material and limited utilities, as well as set in antithesis to science. Because of its limitation to "practice" in its restricted utilitarian sense, experience cannot rise above mundane things. The artisan, the typical exemplar of experience, is *practical activity* dependent upon his tools and his materials; his activity is therefore never wholly independent, free, liberal. But theorectical activity is carried on by reason within reason and thus *theoretical activity* is independent of all extraneous aids. Even moral and political activity is practical, and, since it requires the co-operation of others, is not self-contained as is pure thinking.

Here then are three great limitations of experience as it *3 limitations of experience as conceived by classical philosophy* was conceived by classical philosophy. (1) There is the contrast of empirical knowledge (strictly speaking, of belief and opinion rather than knowledge) with science. (2) There is the restricted and dependent nature of practice in contrast with the free character of rational thought. (3) And there is the metaphysical basis for these two defects of experience: the fact that sense and bodily action are confined to the realm of phenomena while reason in its inherent nature is akin to ultimate reality. The threefold contrast thus implies a metaphysical depreciation of experience, an epistemological one, and, coloring both of the others and giving them their human value, a moral one: the difference in worth between (1) activity that is limited to the body and to physical things, originating in need and serving temporal utilities, and (2) that which soars to ideal and eternal values.

Even when the concept of experience was greatly transformed in later thought, the stock criticism against the knowledge that is based on experience remained. No amount of experience can establish a universal and necessary truth. It cannot get beyond the general, *i.e.*, the usual and customary. Since reality was conceived to be immutable and eternal, manifested in essences that make things to be necessarily what they are, empirical "knowledge" is limited to the changing and the contingent. Mathematics, for example, which is the only truly scientific element in the physical sciences themselves, is beyond its capacity. While Aristotle was content with the conclusions of experience in social morals and politics, since he regarded them as falling within the realm of the probable, with the advent of Christianity there was a demand for basing morals on absolute truth. So in this sphere also empiricism became suspect, because it could not provide universal and necessary truth.

In many respects, the account of experience given by Plato and Aristotle was, on its positive side, itself an honest empirical report. For the kind of experience which the ancient world had, and the medieval, too, until the rise of the new experimental science, was of the kind described. There was no technique by which a rational control of empirical observation and expectation could be brought about. There was no way, so far as I can see, of anticipating the fact that such a technique would ever come into existence. There was no way of seeing how rational thought could gain a leverage within experience, so that experience could be fruitful of new truths and capable of testing the beliefs to which it gave rise. The gap between experience and a rational ideal seemed fixed and impassable. Experience might grow quantitatively but it could not alter its quality.

In short, the account given of experience was a correct statement of the conditions of contemporary culture. The mistake involved in the philosophy of the period was in its assumption that the implications of a particular state of culture were eternal—a mistake that philosophers as well as others readily fall into. If the experience of the time had been the measure of all possible, all future, experience, I do not see how this conception of the nature of experience could be attacked. But the significant point to be borne in mind (one that philosophers of the present period have little excuse for ignoring) is that subsequent developments show that experience is capable of incorporating rational control within itself.

In speaking of the second typical concept of experience, I shall make a long and abrupt jump and come to the ideas enunciated by John Locke, passing by, for lack of time, the important anticipations of thinkers prior to his date. I cannot, however, refrain from noting a radical shift in evaluation which marked Roger as well as Francis Bacon. Classical philosophy, as we have seen, identified experience with the beliefs and skills that were due to custom and consolidated memory, and regarded it as in consequence inevitably enslaved to the past. Thinkers began to put the shoe on the other foot. What had passed for rational truths seemed to them infected with stale repetition and blind acceptance of authority. In contrast "experience" suggested something fresh and personal, while "reason" signified dogmas and doctrines that owed their power to convention and tradition. It is interesting to note that this shift was accompanied by another, equally radical. Classical thought had glorified the universal and regarded the individual as valid only in the degree in which it was an organ of the universal. There was a growing tendency in the centuries preceding Locke to regard what had been considered as universal and objective as a kind of dead weight and imposed upon men from without, and to regard the individual as the seat of freedom and the source of all advance, intellectual and political. This double reversal of valuation is perhaps more significant as an indication of the change taking place in culture than any one of the elements in the technical concept of experience.

John Locke was carrying further this new spirit when he defined experience as consisting essentially of observation, a view which implies that it is a direct, first-hand, personal contact with nature. Now observation proceeds through the senses. If, then, observation is made the test of the origin of valid knowledge, only "ideas" coming through the senses are to be trusted in physical matters. His faith in observation is the source of his hostility to innate ideas. His polemic against them, if carefully read, will show that his objection is not technical. Innate ideas, according to his reading of the times, had become the great bulwark of unfounded tradition and arbitrarily exercised authority. By definition they are not open to criticism and test. Say that a particular "principle" is innate and you have automatically exempted it from critical examination.

Locke held that a large part of so-called innate ideas, especially in the realm of morals were in fact picked up from grandparents and nursemaids in early childhood, so early, indeed, that not being able to remember their origin we suppose they have always been in the mind, implanted in its very constitution. Locke's objection to what we now call the a priori was an objection against the imposed and the secondhand, and its motive is repeated in what he says about an undue dependence on uncritical reading of books. Its spirit is that of Montaigne and other "moderns." Like many things in all philosophers, his emphasis on observation and sensation can be understood only when we recall against what it was directed among the tendencies contemporary with him. His emphasis is a part of that spirit we call the Enlightenment—a movement which, manifested first in theological and then in political circles, is known as "rationalism"—so great are the turns that changes in culture bring about in terms.

Experience

What characterizes sensation and observation, and hence experience, is, in Locke's thought, their coerciveness. They are forced upon us whether we like them or not; if we open our eyes and ears we cannot help receiving certain "simple ideas." This coercion of will and of opinion is the essential guarantee of their validity—at least the only guarantee our constitution permits. Compulsion is the safeguard against vagaries of fancy and accidents of conventional belief. In contrast with this inescapable force, the ideas which we construct and label "rational" are our own constructions and hence suspect, unless we can check them by "experience"—that is, observation. For the latter, according to Locke, is something which nature, rather than mind, does. Hence his emphasis upon the blank tablet and passivity in reception of impressions.

Locke adhered to the classical tradition in holding that experience cannot supply universal knowledge, and drew the conclusion that there is no exact science of natural phenomena, but only probability sufficient for the conduct of life. The candle of understanding set up in us shines brightly enough to guide us on our path. On the other hand, he held that morals and mathematics may be true sciences, since, while the ideas with which they set out are derived from observation, *relations* between them are under our control, being made by mind, and hence do not have to agree with any external "archetype." They are their own models and originals and hence may be regulative of experience, being themselves patterns instead of having to conform to some other pattern. In other words, Locke himself was not the thoroughgoing empiricist of the sensationalist type he is sometimes represented to be. He recognized *relations* as essential to truly scientific knowledge and regarded them as the "workmanship of the understanding," although the elements that are related come from observation.

The next stage in the development of Locke's point of view was to reduce relations, as well as elements, to sensational form. Pleasures and pains were treated as kinds of sensation; and, according to the eighteenth-century French followers of Locke, attention, desire, and volition can all be derived from suitable associations of sensation. To Locke himself association had been a force by which objective or "natural" connections among things were supplanted by unnatural associations—such as jingles that sometimes haunt the mind and refuse to be expelled. To those who wrought his ideas out into a comprehensive logical system, association was the sole possible tie holding together sensations as elements of experience.

The system thus developed was adopted wholeheartedly in Great Britain by James Mill and his disciples. The system developed was so inclusive and so warmly espoused that its vogue has led many who ought to know better to regard associational sensationalism as the sole owner of the right to the name of a philosophy of experience. Some of them, while rejecting the philosophy, seem to go to the length of regarding it as an adequate account of experience as such. Indeed, Kant himself accepted it as an adequate description of what is empirical *in* experience, holding that for that very reason it had to be supplemented by *a priori* factors if experience was to be coherent and cognitive.

This sensational philosophy, in its general outline, passed over into psychology and for a time had the prestige of being truly "scientific." It was, as Mr. Santayana has called it, a malicious psychology in its impact upon a mass of common-sense beliefs. But, taking the philosophy in its relation to the culture of its own day, it is necessary to see what its malice was directed against, for in its own intention it was not aimed at science nor at common sense, but against various influential forms of superstitious dogmatism and arbitrary political authority. As far as science was concerned, it was taken for granted that science, freed from the oppression of these forces, would flourish and become the ruling principle of life. In this sense, this group of empiricists were indeed "rationalists" and of a radical character.

Their philosophy was intended to be, and was used as, an instrument of criticism for dissolving institutions then dominant, ecclesiastical and political. It used Locke's criterion to demand that all institutions produce the credentials of originating in experience by means of the action of nature upon us, forgetful that, according to the *conclusions* of their philosophy, "nature" had no longer any standing in court. Looking back, however, it is clear that this inconsistency in uniting nature with experience as the sole guarantee of validity rendered sensational empiricism a much more powerful tool of criticism and disintegration than would have been the skepticism which was its logical conclusion. Its power as a weapon was increased by the fact that it combined the force belonging to the idea of a natural order with that of fresh, unhampered personal experience.

On the positive side this empirical philosophy was used to magnify the importance, or according to Helvetius the omnipotence, of education. In connection with the coercive quality of observation, Locke had insisted on the passiveness, the receptiveness, of the mind. The world cannot stamp itself accurately on the mind if it does not have a blank on which to work. The French thinkers, starting from this idea of a passive, empty mind, virtually said (at least a few extremists did) that you can build up any type of mind or character you wish by controlling the impressions, sensations, observations, of that mind, especially by controlling associations that are formed with pleasure and pain. The worst thing about bad institutions and all laws is that they corrupt minds. They associate happiness and success with the wrong kind of thing. A proper political and social order would associate sensations of pleasure with things that are socially useful, and of personal pain with things that are socially detrimental. It would *Education* be the business of education to further this action—an idea that was taken over not merely with regard to education but *Bentham* with regard to legislation and judicial procedures by Jeremy Bentham.

On the positive side, empiricism was thus an ideal, whether realized or not, associated with the eighteenth-century concept of progress and the opening up of vistas of the infinite perfectibility of humanity, when once the corruption that comes from bad institutions, political and ecclesiastical, had been done away with and education and rationality given a chance.

While then it had a definite intellectual basis in Locke, the typical empiricism of the eighteenth and the early nineteenth century is explicable as a social doctrine and a doctrine in which emphasis fell upon its use as a weapon. Therefore, because that phase is emphasized in all histories, I pass over *Hume* the skeptical direction which Hume gave the earlier empirical doctrine, showing that, with the dialectic development of Locke's simple ideas, the result was complete skepticism as to the existence of an external world and a self. The truly empirical contribution of Hume lay in his revival of the concepts of habit and of custom and their importance. Of course the biology and the physiology of the time did not enable him to explain the importance of habit. It remained for him a simple and mysterious tie, but he did introduce, even if through the back door, a principle of connection and of organization which undid the consequences of Locke's "simple ideas." But in any case the important thing, to my mind, in this empirical movement was its critical, negative side. Its power as a dissolvent of tradition and doctrine was much greater than any impetus it could give to construction. When the general cultural situation became such that a positive, constructive direction and impetus were required, there was the cultural opportunity for a new type of philosophy.

Thus we have the reaction of German philosophy of the nineteenth century, beginning with Kant and going through the whole romantic and neoromantic period of German philosophy, later taken up in the England of the 1880's and '90's and becoming in the universities, the former centers of empirical or modified empirical philosophy, the dominant mode of thought. There was wanted some guarantee against the destructive, dissolvent tendency of empiricism carried to extremes. And the French Revolution served as a convenient symbol of what that philosophy would come to if it were allowed to go on unchecked.

I mention this rationalistic, spiritualistic reaction because it influenced so strongly some of the members of the empirical school, especially John Stuart Mill. Of course he was brought up in the strictest sect of empiricists by his father, James Mill, but through personal experiences, through social problems of the time, through the direct influence especially of Coleridge and Wordsworth, he felt the defects of historical empiricism and the need of something that would give a more stable, constructive ground for belief and conduct. He tried various devices to get it without giving up essentially his empiricism. Perhaps his most characteristic device was the invention of indissoluble associations. What troubled him first was that if associations can build up a positive action, that also can be destroyed and the person left without any guide. And so he discovered, I think more likely he invented, a mechanism for creating association that could not be broken and that was so solid as to serve all the practical purposes of necessary and universal principles.

More important, however, in John Stuart Mill than his psychological experimentations, which were, logically, vagaries, was his interest in logic, in transferring the center of attention regarding experience from its psychological formulation to certain problems of scientific method. It is an easily ascertainable fact that Mill's interest in logic was primarily due to his interest in social, economic, and political questions. His real problem was how the method used in the natural sciences could be employed in thinking about political and economic affairs so that they would be taken out of the field of mere opinion and prejudice.

His logic itself, almost anybody would admit, is an incoherent mixture of certain psychological premises derived from sensational association and a genuine interest in scientific method and scientific procedure on its own account. Indirectly rather than directly, I think it is fair to say (though I do not think the statement can be proved) that this change had a rather definite effect as an antecedent of and a stimulus to the development of the third concept of experience, which brings us down into recent times and into the present. It is a fact, or seems to be a fact, that the natural sciences, at least if for the sake of simplicity we leave mathematics out of account, depend upon experience. At the same time, it is unanswerable that if experience were what a sensational-associationist said it was, it could not possibly produce science. Therefore there is a mistake somewhere. Either natural sciences do not have the intimate dependence on experience that the enthusiasts on this subject think they have, or experience is a different sort of thing from what it had been analyzed as being either by the classic conception or by the eighteenth-century conception.

Moreover, there is a feature obviously present in the natural sciences which sensationalism does not explain or make possible, and this is experimentation. For all experiment involves regulated activity, directed by ideas, by thought. And in the present state of, say, physics, highly elaborate, intricate schemes of thought are here involved, beyond the reach of sense or of any form of observation. Therefore it would seem that those ideas which function as theories and hypotheses in scientific experimentation and organization are not copies of sensations nor suggested by past experience, by past observation, but that they have a free, imaginative quality that no direct sensation or observation can have.

Now, following this line of thought, one would deduce at least one phase of the philosophy of William James, namely, that validity is not a matter of origin nor of antecedents, but of consequents. This statement, associated with the philosophy of all pragmatism, is often treated as if it were directed merely against previous rationalisms. Its more direct objective of attack is previous empiricism. Mill, for example, following the empirical tradition, had said very definitely that all proof or demonstration of validity is a matter of the antecedents out of which an idea is constructed. And the whole point of James's philosophy, which comes out better in some chapters of his *Psychology,* I think, especially in the last chapter of the second volume, than in his lectures on *Pragmatism,* is that the value of ideas is independent of their origin, that it is a matter of their outcome as they are used in directing new observation and new experiment. Therefore there is at least one factor in generating a new concept of experience and a new type of empiricism which cannot be understood when it is classified in terms of either of the two earlier historical systems. That is one difficulty with the history of philosophy. The tendency is to discourage originality, not directly, but by cultivating the temper of mind that believes every idea must be interpreted or understood in terms of some pre-existing system. It is obvious that if it is a good idea, I mean a really significant idea, it may involve a departure from any previously formulated system, and the criterion judging it must be worked out both by its critics and by those who have attained that idea.

The prevalence of experimental habits, looking ahead, looking forward, and using ideas, made one fundamental transformation in the concept of experience now in the process of developing. Another factor was the breakdown of the old introvert psychology and the development of a psychology having an objective basis, essentially a biological basis. It is impossible to get the same concept of sensation, to take one case, if sensations are approached from the biological and physiological side as was given by the old analytic psychology. In many respects we are getting much nearer Aristotle's psychology on this particular point in the approach to the problem. From the physiological standpoint it is quite obvious that sensations are part of the mechanisms of behavior and have a direct connection with the motor apparatus, and that they are stimuli to the outgoing patterns and remain their stimuli except when trained connections come into play, and that in that case, they become conscious sensations or sensory qualities. In other words, they have to do with the determination of new modes of behavior, thus setting up internal relations through the tracks that will lead to a mode of action that had not existed before.

This third view of experience in the history of thought is still more or less inchoate, because it is still in process of development, but I have tried to call attention to two trends, or two motifs, that are influential in developing this newer type of interpretation of experience and therefore a new type of empiricism: namely, the practice of science, especially with reference to the use of ideas, hypotheses, and experimentation, in the process of verification or validation through results; and secondly, the radically different psychological approach that comes from looking at things objectively, from the standpoint of biology rather than of introspective analysis.

CONTEXT AND THOUGHT [1]

Dewey looked upon modern philosophies as moving between two extremes: atomistic monadisms which claim that
reality and knowledge are constructed out of discrete and
independent elements, and monisms which claim that
everything is so interrelated that reality and knowledge are
ultimately a single whole. He argued against both extremes,
pointing out that they are based on the same fallacy, neglect
of context—"the greatest single disaster which philosophic
thinking can incur." Dewey's contextual approach is intended to avoid the disaster of this Scylla and Charybdis.
Within a context there is a spatial and temporal background which affects all thinking, and a selective interest
or bias which conditions the subject matter of thinking.
(In "Qualitative Thought" there is a further discussion of
how the background of a context qualifies the material in
the foreground, and in "Time and Individuality" and
"Philosophies of Freedom" there is an explication of the
meaning and significance of selective interest.) Once the
nature of a context has been clarified, Dewey concludes by
considering the context and function of philosophy. The
ultimate context of philosophy is a living culture, and it is
the task of philosophy to criticize, clarify, test the internal
coherence, and make explicit the consequences of the beliefs, customs, and social institutions of a culture.

I N A SUPPLEMENTARY essay in Ogden and Richards' *Meaning of Meaning,* Mr. Malinowski gives a striking example
of the need for understanding context in connection with
the use of language. The literal translation into English of
an utterance of New Guinea natives runs as follows: "We
run frontwards ourselves; we paddle in place; we turn, we see

1 *University of California Publications in Philosophy* (Berkeley: 1931),
XII, 203-24.

companion ours; he runs rearward behind their sea-arm Bilolu." [2] As he says, the speech sounds like a meaningless jumble. If one is to understand it one must be informed about the situation in which the words were spoken and have them placed in their own context of culture. As a matter of fact, the utterance refers to a victory in an overseas trading expedition of the natives, in which several canoes have taken part in a competitive spirit. "This feature of rivalry (he adds) also explains the emotional nature of the utterance; it is not a mere statement of fact, but a boast, a piece of self-glorification, extremely characteristic of the Trobrianders' culture in general and of their ceremonial barter in particular." [3]

After going into some detail of explanation, he remarks that in trying to give an adequate analysis of meaning "we are faced by a long and not altogether simple process of describing wide fields of custom, of social psychology, of tribal organization, which correspond to one term or another. Linguistic analysis inevitably leads us into the study of all the subjects covered by ethnographic field-work." [4] Furthermore, as he points out, knowledge of ethnography will not remove all difficulties; even those of exclusively linguistic problems can, some of them, be solved only on the basis of psychological analysis. He sums up by saying that "in the reality of a spoken

[2] [Dewey's quotations from Malinowski's supplementary essay, "The Problem of Meaning in Primitive Languages," vary slightly from the original text. I have therefore included Malinowski's exact statements. All references are to the eighth edition of *The Meaning of Meaning* (New York: 1956). "We run front-wood ourselves; we paddle in place; we turn we see companion ours; he runs rear-wood behind their sea-arm Pilolu." (Pp. 300-1.)]

[3] ["This . . . feature explains also the emotional nature of the utterance: it is not a mere statement of fact, but a boast, a piece of self-glorification, extremely characteristic of the Trobrianders' culture in general and of their ceremonial barter in particular." P. 301.]

[4] [". . . we are faced by a long and not altogether simple process of describing wide fields of custom, of social psychology and of tribal organization which correspond to one term or another. We see that linguistic analysis inevitably leads us into the study of all the subjects covered by Ethnographic field-work." Pp. 301-2.]

living language, the utterance has no meaning except in the context of a situation." [5]

We should all, I suppose, admit this contention in the case of the speech of an alien and remote savage tribe. But it would be a great mistake to imagine that the principle is limited in application to such peoples. There is indeed a great contrast with our own modes of utterance. But the contrast is significant because it throws into relief familiar traits which very familiarity tends to conceal from us. We grasp the meaning of what is said in our own language not because appreciation of context is unnecessary but because context is so unescapably present. It is taken for granted; it is a matter of course, and accordingly is not explicitly specified. Habits of speech, including syntax and vocabulary, and modes of interpretation have been formed in the face of inclusive and defining situations of context. The latter are accordingly implicit in most of what is said and heard. We are not explicitly aware of the role of context just because our every utterance is so saturated with it that it forms the significance of what we say and hear.

The illustrative episode with which I began refers to language. But in it there is contained in germ all that I have to say for the indispensability of context for thinking, and therefore for a theory of logic and ultimately of philosophy itself. What is true of the meaning of words and sentences is true of all meaning. Such a statement need not, however, involve us in controversy about the relation of thought to language. If language is identified with speech, there is undoubtedly thought without speech. But if "language" is used to signify all kinds of signs and symbols, then assuredly there is no thought without language; while signs and symbols depend for their meaning upon the contextual situation in which they appear and are used.

For the meaning of symbols is not inherent but derived. This appears from the fact that they *are* symbols. It is true

[5] [". . . in the reality of a spoken living tongue, the utterance has no meaning except in the *context of situation*." P. 307.]

that when we talk and write the meaning of a particular verbal symbol is given us by the context of other symbols in which it occurs. It is also true that there are systems of symbols, notably in mathematics, where the system determines the meaning of any particular symbol. We cannot however infer from these facts that symbols are capable of supplying the ultimate context which provides meaning and understanding. Continued and systematic discourse enables us to determine the meaning of special symbols within the discourse only because it enables us to build up a nonverbal and nonsymbolic context to which the whole refers. The mathematician does not stop to think of the ulterior context of existences, which gives his system of symbols import; long familiarity and a long tradition behind it have made the connection highly indirect and tenuous. He would not only have difficulty in making the connection, but he would perhaps be irritated, as at a useless interruption and distraction, at any suggestion that he attempt to make the connection. But expertness in treating symbols as if they were things does not alter their symbolic character. Multiplication of symbols and increase in their intricacy facilitates manipulation. But reference of one symbol to another cannot destroy their character as symbols.

Now thought lives, moves, and has its being in and through symbols, and, therefore, depends for meaning upon context as do the symbols. We think *about* things, but not *by* things. Or rather when we do think by and with things, we are not experiencing the things in their own full nature and content. Sounds, for example, and marks in printed books are themselves existential things. But they operate in thought only as they stand for something else; if we become absorbed in them as things, they lose their value for thinking. If a man thinks, as he may do, by means of blocks and stones, he is not, as far as he is thinking, engaged in complete and intimate realization of them in their own intrinsic qualities. If he does become concerned with them in this fashion, he indulges in something that is either more or less than thought; more, if it is an esthetic absorption, less if it relapse into dumb stupor.

The concern of thinking is with things as they carry the mind beyond themselves; they are vehicles not terminal stations.

These remarks have themselves an implicit context. Negatively, this context is the habit of philosophers of neglecting the indispensability of context, both in particular and in general. I should venture to assert that the most pervasive fallacy of philosophic thinking goes back to neglect of context. In the face to face communications of everyday life, context may be safely ignored. For, as we have already noted, it is irrevocably there. It is taken for granted, not denied, when it is passed over without notice. It gives point to everything said. A man engaged in a business transaction does not, for example, need to remind himself specifically of that fact—unless he is falling asleep. Context is incorporated in what is said and forms the arbiter of the value of every utterance. The same ideas and words apart from context would be the extravagancies of a madman. But in philosophizing there is rarely an immediately urgent context which controls the course of thought. Neglect of specific acknowledgment of it is, then, too readily converted into a virtual denial.

Let us consider an instance or two of virtual denial of context in philosophy and its effect. Some philosophers have attacked the validity of analysis. They have held that while it is important in "science," that fact is itself evidence of the partial nature of science, of its abstraction from the "whole" with which philosophy is concerned. Other thinkers reach much the same conclusion when they assert that all valid analysis is attended by a synthetic act of thought which deliberately restores what is left out of account in the act of analysis. Now I do not see how a superadded act of synthesis can be other than arbitrary. But I can see how analysis falsifies when its results are interpreted as complete in themselves apart from any context. And it seems to me that the fault found with analysis would be more correctly as well as more simply directed against the ignoring of context. When a physician sets out to diagnose a disease he analyzes what is before him by the best technique at command. He does not at the end require another and further act of synthesis. The situation from the first has been one of disease and that situation provides the connection between the particular details analytically detected. One always identifies by discovering differences that are characteristic. This is true whether the identification be that of a criminal, of a plant or an animal, a metal, a disease, or a law. So far there is no defect in analysis and no demand for an added act of synthesis. But if the physician were to so forget the presence of a human being as a patient, if he were virtually to deny that context, he certainly would have a meaningless heap of atomic particulars on hand, and might be led to appeal to some transcendental synthesis to bring them to significant unity.

And so in philosophy. The trouble is not with analysis, but with the philosopher who ignores the context in which and for the sake of which the analysis occurs. In this sense, a characteristic defect of philosophy *is* connected with analysis. There are a multitude of ways of committing the analytic fallacy. It is found whenever the distinctions or elements that are discriminated are treated as if they were final and self-sufficient. The result is invariably some desiccation and atomizing of the world in which we live or of ourselves. The outcome has often been made the object of critical attack, as in the case of Locke and the Mills, and, indeed, in much of British thought. It has been rightly pointed out that the logical conclusion is denial of all connection and continuity, terminating in a doctrine of atomistic particularism. But unfortunately these same critics have not been content with the simple act of indicating neglect of context, but have assumed that the conclusion points to the necessity of some over-arching act of organic synthesis on the part of thought or "reason" —a method which, as I shall hope to show later, is the same disease of ignoring context in another form.

It is possible to find fresher straw to thresh than that of the systems of the thinkers just mentioned. Let me take an illustration from a field sufficiently remote from technical philosophical questions as not to arouse at once controversial associations. I have in mind the case of laboratory experimentation in psychology, say with respect to the discrimination of the least distinguishable color or sound, the finest possible discrimination of some sensory quality. Such qualities, when discriminated under conditions of refined control, have been assumed not only to be elements (which they are by definition, an element being only the last product of analysis), but to be original constituents out of which all mental life is built. They have been treated, in other words, as self-sufficient, independent in their isolation, so that all mental life is the result of their compounding.

Any such interpretation illustrates that ignoring of context which is virtually a denial of context. In fact there is present much besides the terminal elements. There is the background of the experimenter. This includes the antecedent state of theory which has given rise to his problem. It takes in his purpose in arranging the apparatus, including the technical knowledge which makes a controlled experiment possible. On the other side, there are the habits and present disposition of the subject, his capacity to give attention and to make verbal responses, etc., etc. Without the phase of context found on the side of the experimenter, there would be no scientific result at all, but an accident without theoretical import. The phase of context supplied from the side of the subject furnishes the causal factor determining the appearance of the quality discriminated. The latter, instead of being an isolated original unit out of which mental life is constructed by external composition, is the last term, for the time being, of an inclusive mental life. The immanent presence of the contextual setting of a moving experience provides connection. It renders unnecessary appeal to synthetic acts of thought, transcendental or otherwise, in order to supply connection. What takes place because of its connections does not require an act of thought to give it connection.

This remark brings me to what I called shortly ago the same disease in another form. The counterpart fallacy to that of analysis (as wrongly interpreted because of denial of context) is that of unlimited extension or universalization. When context is taken into account, it is seen that every generalization occurs under limiting conditions set by the contextual situation. When this fact is passed over or thrown out of court, a principle valid under specifiable conditions is perforce extended without limit. Any genuine case of thinking starts, for example, with considerations which as they stand are fragmentary and discrepant. Thinking then has the task of effecting unification in a single coherent whole. In this sense the goal of all thinking is the attaining of unity. But this unity is unification of just those data and considerations which in that situation are confused and incoherent. The fallacy of unlimited universalization is found when it is asserted, without any such limiting conditions, that the goal of thinking, particularly of philosophic thought, is to bring all things whatsoever into a single coherent and all inclusive whole. Then the idea of unity which has value and import under specifiable conditions is employed with such an unlimited extension that it loses its meaning.

All statements about the universe as a whole, reality as an unconditioned unity, involve the same fallacy. There is genuine meaning in the act of inquiring into the reality of a given situation. It is equivalent to an attempt to discover "the facts of the case," what is actually there or is actually happening— the addition of the adjective "real" to the substantive, "facts," being only for rhetorical emphasis. Within the limits of context found in any valid inquiry, "reality" thus means the confirmed outcome, actual or potential, of the inquiry that is undertaken. There is some specifiable confusion and dispersion which sets the inquiry going, and the latter terminates when the confusion is cleared away and definiteness accrues under conditions of suitable test. When "reality" is sought for at large, it is without intellectual import; at most the term carries the connotation of an agreeable emotional state. A like conclusion holds with reference to the "absolute," the "total," the "unconditioned," and many other terms held sacred on the lips of philosophers.

These statements do not however bring out *why* this fallacy of unlimited extension is the same ailment as that of unbridled analysis, in another form. We may have recourse to the instance already cited, that of mental life. Isolation from context of the distinctions found in a laboratory experiment induces the generalization that all varieties of mental life are compounds of independent units: whether the latter are called sensations, sensa, states of feeling or consciousness, or reflex arcs, or reactions to stimuli, or whatever is the prevailing fashion. This generalization into a sweeping theory is nothing but the logical statement of the conclusion which emerges when the context is suppressed. Given this suppression, elements become absolute, for they have no limiting conditions. Results of inquiry valid within specifiable limits of context are *ipso facto* converted into a sweeping metaphysical doctrine.

Further illustrations, if time permitted would exclude the nature of these two fallacies that tend to haunt philosophizing. I think, for example, that it could be shown that the predilections of many contemporaries for sensa and essences are products of neglect of context. I pass by, however, these possibilities to consider the use made in some aspects of contemporary philosophy of the concept of "events." That all existences are *also* events I do not doubt. For they are qualified by temporal transition. But that existences as such are *only* events strikes me as a proposition that can be maintained in no way except by a wholesale ignoring of context. For, in the first place, every occurrence is a *con*currence. An event is not a self-enclosed, self-executing affair—or it is not save by arbitrary definition. One may easily slip down a hill, but the slipping is not a self-contained entity, even though the *concept* of slipping may be self-contained—a transposition which makes it an essence, not an existence. The actual slide depends upon an interaction of several things, very many in an adequate account. Yet, unless I am mistaken in my interpretation, there is evidence that some contemporary writers tend to treat every existence as if to *be* an existence were to be a slide or a slip.

To escape the difficulty by implying that the context of an event is simply other events is suspiciously like assuming that by putting enough slides together you can make a hill.

There are some cases of interaction which, relatively speaking, are merely displacements: like that which happens when one billiard ball impinges on another. What happens is then —or at least may be so treated for most purposes—merely a rearrangement. There are other transactions in which something happens to which the name interception can be given. In the interaction the product retains as it were something of the qualities of the concurring things. In this case, the event, viewed even as an event, is not merely an event. Such interception and coalescence of qualities hitherto distinct characterize anything that may be called an emergent. Put in a slightly different way, an event is both eventful and an eventuation.

Since every event is also an interaction of different things, it is inherently characterized by something from which and to which. The slide that starts with the slipping of the foot is not the same as that of a propelled sled; and it makes considerable difference to the slide as an event whether it terminates on rocks, water, or a pile of grass. The "from which" and "to which" qualify the event and make it, concretely, the distinctive event which it is. We may, indeed, by legitimate abstraction (legitimate for certain purposes) neglect the characteristic difference and reach the notion of slide in general. But the generalized abstraction would be impossible were there not events having their own qualitative traits. In other words, a *merely* general concept of "event" is undistinguishable from that of ascent, or perpendicular fall, or indeed from the meaning of any other term whatever which is equally treated as indifferent to all qualitative determination.

In the next place, when an event, because of neglect of context, is treated merely as an event, or as self-enclosed instead of as a change which takes place when qualitatively tempered things interact, it at once becomes necessary to invoke essences of eternal objects or some form of static eternal object to give any particular event an assignable character. The statement that interaction is constant and that consequently any existence at every point of its career is also an event, or that an existence may be looked at as *also* a serial set of events, seems to be authorized by the evidence. But to treat this proposition as equivalent to the proposition that every existence (apart from the entrance of an essence) is *merely* a collection of events is an instance of that unlimited extension that is entailed by neglect of context. The appeal to eternal objects has the same root, logically, as the appeal to an act of synthesis when the results of analysis, combined with ignoring of contextual connections, are taken to be the ground for invoking a further act of synthesis. As an added point we may note that a world of self-enclosed events, even when characterized by the entrance of eternal objects, requires something else to hold them together into anything like the semblance of one world. The supplementation takes the form of a framework of space-time—for an event as self-contained can have no change within it. It *is* a beginning and end but it *has* no beginning nor end, and so an outside space-time must be superimposed.

Up to this point the discussion is negative in tone. It is meant to illustrate, though it cannot pretend to prove, that neglect of context is the greatest single disaster which philosophic thinking can incur. If we turn to consideration of the content and scope of the context that philosophizing should take into the reckoning, we approach the positive side of the discussion. Context includes at least those matters which for brevity I shall call background and selective interest. By "background" I mean the whole environment of which philosophy must take account in all its enterprises. A background is implicit in some form and to some degree in all thinking, although as background it does not come into explicit purview; that is, it does not form a portion of the subject matter which is consciously attended to, thought of, examined, inspected, turned over. Background is both temporal and spatial.

When we think, there are some things which we are immediately thinking *of,* considerations that are before us, and that are reflected upon, pondered over, etc. They are that with which we are wrestling, trying to overcome its difficulties and to reduce to order. Surrounding, bathing, saturating, the things of which we are explicitly aware is some inclusive situation which does not enter into the direct material of reflection. It does not come into question; it is taken for granted with respect to the particular question that is occupying the field of thinking. Since it does not come into question, it is stable, settled. To think of it in the sense of making it an object of thought's examination and scrutiny is an irrelevant and confusing distraction. It, or rather some part of it, comes into question, or into the explicit material of reflection, only when we suspect that it exercises such a *differential* effect upon what is consciously thought of as to be responsible for some of the confusion and perplexity we are trying to clear up. Then, of course, it enters into the immediate matter of thinking. But this transfer never disturbs the whole contextual background; it does not all come into question at once. There is always that which continues to be taken for granted, which is tacit, being "understood." If everything were literally unsettled at once, there would be nothing to which to tie those factors that, being unsettled, are in process of discovery and determination.

It was said that this background in thought is both spatial and temporal. The direct material of every reflection proceeds out of some precedent state of affairs in reference to which the existing state is disturbed or problematic or to which it is an "answer" or solution. In the episode related by Malinowski, the particular utterance served to sum up and record a previous struggle which issued in victory for one side. In the instance of the psychological experiment, the temporal background is the prior state of experimenter and subject. Take away the temporal background of the first incident and there is no triumph, nor any other significant happening; take away that of the second, and there is no experiment but merely an incident signifying nothing.

The temporal background of thinking in any case is intellectual as well as existential. That is, in the first cited instance there is a background of culture; in the second, of theory. There is no thinking which does not present itself on a background of tradition, and tradition has an intellectual quality that differentiates it from blind custom. Traditions are ways of interpretation and of observation, of valuation, of everything explicitly thought of. They are the circumambient atmosphere which thought must breathe; no one ever had an idea except as he inhaled some of this atmosphere. Aristotelian physics and Ptolemaic astronomy were for centuries the taken-for-granted background of all special inquiries in those fields. Then came the Newtonian background, for two centuries more imperious than any Tsar. So the fixity of species was the background of biological sciences until the time of Darwinism came; it then reigned so completely (I am speaking of the scientific inquirer) that Mendel's work did not cause even a ripple.

[Emile] Meyerson has remarked that we can explain why medieval thinkers thought as they did and believed as they did, because we are outside their age. We cannot explain why we believe the things which we most firmly hold to because those things are a part of ourselves. We can no more completely escape them when we try to examine into them than we can get outside our physical skins so as to view them from without. Call these regulative traditions apperceptive organs or mental habits or whatever you will, there is no thinking without them. I do not mean, that a philosopher can take account of this context in the sense of making it a complete object of reflection. But he might realize the existence of such a context, and in doing so he would learn humility and would be debarred from a too unlimited and dogmatic universalization of his conclusions. He would not freeze the quotidian truths relevant to the problems that emerge in his own background of culture into eternal truths inherent in the very nature of things.

Spatial background covers all the contemporary setting within which a course of thinking emerges. That which is looked into, consciously scrutinized, has, like a picture, a foreground, middle distance, and a background—and as in some paintings the latter shades off into unlimited space. Demarcations so sharp that they amount to isolations do not occur in nature; their presence in thought is a sure sign that we, for some purpose have taken a certain attitude toward the objective scene. Specify the contextual purpose and no harm arises. Forget it, and the fallacy of misinterpreted analysis ensues. This contextual setting is vague, but it is no mere fringe. It has a solidity and stability not found in the focal material of thinking. The latter denotes the part of the road upon which the spotlight is thrown. The spatial context is the ground through which the road runs and for the sake of which the road exists. It is this setting which gives import to the road and to its consecutive illuminations. The path must be lighted if one is not to lose his way; the remoter territory may be safely left in the dark.

Another aspect of context is that which I have called "selective interest." Every particular case of thinking is what it is because of some attitude, some bias if you will; and no general theory can be framed which is not based upon what happens in particular cases. This attitude is no immediate part of what is consciously reflected upon, but it determines the selection of this rather than that subject matter. The word "interest" may be questioned; it undoubtedly has connotations alien to the point I wish to make. But as to the fact which the word is used to denote, that can hardly be [in] doubt. There is selectivity (and rejection) found in every operation of thought. There is care, concern, implicated in every act of thought. There is some one who has affection for some things over others; when he becomes a thinker he does not leave his characteristic affection behind. As a thinker, he is still differentially sensitive to some qualities, problems, themes. He may at times turn upon himself and inquire into and attempt to discount his individual attitudes. This operation will render some element in his attitude an object of thought. But it cannot eliminate all elements of selective concern; some deeper-lying ones will still operate. No regress will eliminate the attitude of interest that is as much involved in thinking about attitudes as it is in thinking about other things.

The aspect of context which I have called "interest" is known in philosophical terminology as the "subjective." The organism, self, ego, subject, give it whatever name you choose, is implicated in all thinking as in all eating, business, or play. Since it cannot in its entirety be made an explicit object of reflection and yet since it affects all matters thought of, it is legitimately called a phase of context. Subjectivism has a bad name, and as an 'ism it deserves its ill repute. But the subjective as determining attitude is not to be equated to this 'ism. It is not concern which is objectionable even when it takes the form of bias. It is certain kinds of bias that are obnoxious. Bias for impartiality is as much a bias as is partisan prejudice, though it is a radically different quality of bias. To be "objective" in thinking is to have a certain sort of selective interest operative. One can only see from a certain standpoint, but this fact does not make all standpoints of equal value. A standpoint which is nowhere in particular and from which things are not seen at a special angle is an absurdity. But one may have affection for a standpoint which gives a rich and ordered landscape rather than for one from which things are seen confusedly and meagerly.

Interest, as the subjective, is after all equivalent to individuality or uniqueness. There is no reason to limit its presence and operation to the organic and mental, although it is especially exemplified there. Everything which exists may be supposed to have its own unduplicated manner of acting and reacting, even atoms and electrons, although these individual traits are submerged in statistical statement. But in any event that which I have designated selective interest is a unique manner of entering into interaction with other things. It is not a part or constituent of subject matter; but as a manner of action it selects subject matter and leaves a qualitative impress upon it. One may call it genius or originality or give the more neutral and modest name of individuality. One realizes its nature best in thinking of genuine works of art. In the field of fine art, one never objects to that peculiar way of seeing, selecting, and arranging which defines the actual nature of the "subjective." One recognizes that its opposite is not the objective but the academic and mechanical, the merely repetitive. This quality is found in the subject matter of all genuine thinking, for thinking is not the attribute of parrots. Newton may have supposed that he was thinking God's thought after him, but so far as he thought, he thought Newton's thoughts.

Such statements are easily misinterpreted both by those who make them and by those who deny them. They are sometimes taken to signify that the entire subject matter of thought consists of states of consciousness or the material of a thinker's mind. The logical conclusion is then some form of solipsism. But individuality is not, as we have already said, subject matter, but is a mode of selection that determines subject matter. The subject matter of science, physical and mathematical, may at first sight seem to offer an insuperable objection to the statement that subjectivity, in the sense defined, is contextual in all the material of thinking. For in science there is elimination of connection with the mind of any one in particular. Science is science only as far as any especial tie to the mind of its authors can be left out of account. In the objection, however, there resides a confusion of the product of thought with its acceptance and further use. Newtonian conclusions reigned as science just because they were no longer taken as thought, but as given material to be employed in further investigations and interpretations.

One may find an exact enough analogy in the case of coins having an artistic design. The design in its origin bore the impress of individuality. But its further use, its status as legal tender, is not dependent upon that fact. The attitude controlling the selection and arrangement that forms the esthetic pattern is aside from the purposes of trade. Use in exchange is now the significant affair. In devotion to common social use, the design becomes a mere mechanical identifying sign, a mark of fitness to serve in exchange. If we apply the analogy

to science we shall distinguish between science as a conclusion of reflective inquiry, and science as a ready-made body of
organized subject matter. In the first case, it and its status, its
worth, reside in its connection with the quality of the inquiry
of which it is the outcome and this quality bears the impress
of an individual attitude. In the second case, its status and
worth are dependent upon serviceability in the prosecution of
further discovery and interpretation. From this standpoint,
the impress of individuality is negligible because irrelevant;
facility for repeated use is the important matter.

Even so, however, indispensability of reference to context
still holds. It is easy and too usual to convert abstraction from
specific context into abstraction from all context whatsoever:
another instance of the fallacy of unlimited extension. The
fallacy is indulged in whenever the formally logical traits of
organized subject matter are treated as if they were isolated
from all material considerations. One of the necessary characters of subject matter arranged for effective use is internal coherence and economy. When context is ignored this character
is taken to be independent of existential material. But these
formal characteristics have to do with conditions which must
be fulfilled if the given scientific subject matter is to secure
the maximum of applicability in further inquiries and or-
ganizations. Only by a formulation in terms of equivalences
can old subject matter be rendered most effectively available
in new intellectual undertakings. For only subject matter
stated in terms of reciprocal equivalences renders substitution
and free translation possible in an efficient way. This context
of use is ignored when formal traits are regarded as self-
sufficient in their isolation.

It can hardly have escaped notice that my underlying intention in this discussion concerns a desire to make a contribution to the theme of philosophic method. Thinking takes
place in a scale of degrees of distance from the urgencies of
an immediate situation in which something has to be done.
The greater the degree of remoteness, the greater is the danger
that a temporary and legitimate failure of express reference to

context will be converted into a virtual denial of its place and import. Thinking is always thinking, but philosophic thinking is, upon the whole, at the extreme end of the scale of distance from the active urgency of concrete situations. It is because of this fact that neglect of context is the besetting fallacy of philosophical thought.

I should like to take my first example of the harmful working of this fallacy of philosophic method from the history of thought. The context of historic philosophies is too often treated as if it were simply other philosophies, instead of its being the perplexities, the troubles, and the issues of the period in which a philosophy arises. And strangely enough the limited context which is used in interpreting historic philosophy is frequently one which developed after the philosophy in question. I have just read an essay in literary criticism in which the writer remarks that a cursory examination of chronology will show that Aristotle's theory of poetry and tragedy was written subsequent to the production of the great dramatists of Athens, and that it is not likely that they wrote in order to prepare the way for Aristotelian theory. I wonder if the remark does not convey a lesson to interpreters of the history of thought. It may, for example, be reasonably asserted that Locke, Berkeley, and Hume wrote with reference to the intellectual conditions of their own times and not in order to initiate a movement which should find its consummation in Kant.

The significant positive content of this suggestion is the need of study of philosophical writings in their own vital context. I know that there are many persons to whom it seems derogatory to link a body of philosophic ideas to the social life and culture of their epoch. They seem to accept a dogma of immaculate conception of philosophical systems. I cannot argue the point here, but I can at least point to this attitude as an example of what I mean by neglect of context. The only alternative to the doctrine of the virginal birth of philosophies is recourse to the marriage of thinking with a tradition and a culture that are not themselves philosophical in character.

There exists at any period a body of beliefs and of institutions and practices allied to them. In these beliefs there are implicit broad interpretations of life and the world. These interpretations have consequences, often profoundly important. In their actual currency, however, the implications of origin, nature, and consequences are not examined and formulated. The beliefs and their associated practices express attitudes and responses which have operated under conditions of direct and often accidental stress. They constitute, as it seems to me, the *immediate* primary material of philosophical reflection. The aim of the latter is to criticize this material, to clarify it, to organize it, to test its internal coherence, and to make explicit its consequences. At the time of origin of every significant philosophy, this cultural context of beliefs and allied institutions is irretrievably there; reference to it is taken for granted and not made explicit. (I remark in passing, however, that part of the perennial significance of Plato's writings is due to the fact that in his dialogues the implied reference shines through much more than in most philosophic writings.) There are indeed historic philosophies in which reference to such cultural context is hard to detect. But examination will show that they are engaged in filling in chinks in other and more significant systems, or are engaged in a formal reconstruction of the latter.

If one is willing to adopt, even as a hypothesis for the time being, the idea that the immediate subject matter for philosophy is supplied by the body of beliefs, religious, political, scientific, that determines the culture of a people and age, there follow certain conclusions regarding the problem and method of philosophy. The beliefs have their own context of origin, function, and determining interests or attitudes. But they are likely to be potent in the very degree in which these contexts are passed over in silence. Those who are most devoted to them take them as final revelations of truth, as spiritual Melchisedeks, without empirical generation. Moreover they "work"; they have consequences. But *how* they work, the connection of subsequent events and values, with them *as* consequences, is not subjected to examination. It is hardly even noted. Positive values, whatever their source, are treated as proper effects, while failures, evils, are attributed to some external source, even though examination would reveal that they flow directly from accepted beliefs in their institutional operation.

Here is the opportunity for that type of reflection which I should call philosophical. Philosophy is criticism; criticism of the influential beliefs that underlie culture; a criticism which traces the beliefs to their generating conditions as far as may be, which tracks them to their results, which considers the mutual compatibility of the elements of the total structure of beliefs. Such an examination terminates, whether so intended or not, in a projection of them into a new perspective which leads to new surveys of possibilities. This phase of reconstruction through criticism is as marked in justifying and systematizing philosophies as in avowedly skeptical ones, in the work of St. Thomas as of Hume. The clearer and more organized vision of the content of beliefs may have as an immediate outcome an enhanced sense of their worth and greater loyalty to them. But nevertheless the set of beliefs undergoes more than a sea-change in the process. It is dangerous to reflect seriously upon the nature, origin, and consequences of beliefs. The latter are safest when they are taken for granted without reasoned examination. To give reasons, even justifying ones, is to start a train of thoughts—that is, of questionings.

I have referred to religious, political, and scientific beliefs as instances of things that permeate and almost constitute a culture in their institutional accompaniments and their effects. One final example of the indispensability of reference to context will be alluded to, one taken from the relation of philosophy to science. It is sometimes assumed that this relation is exhausted in either an analytic examination of the logical foundations of the sciences, or in a synthesis of their conclusions, or both together. I would not derogate from the importance of such enterprises. But they are at best preparatory. For science itself operates within a context which is, relative to science, raw, crude, and primitive, and yet is pervasive and determining. To work exclusively within the context provided by the sciences themselves is to ignore their vital context. The place of science in life, the place of its peculiar subject matter in the wide scheme of materials we experience, is a more ultimate function of philosophy than is any self-contained reflection upon science as such.

I am, of course, in this brief space of time only setting forth a possible hypothesis for your consideration. But I am confident that those who are willing to let their imaginations tarry with the hypothesis and follow its implications will at least get light upon the importance which some of us attach to "experience." If the finally significant business of philosophy is the disclosure of the context of beliefs, then we cannot escape the conclusion that experience is the name for the last inclusive context. A philosophy does not, of course, veritably acknowledge the significance of context merely by terming itself empirical. Sensational and nominalistic empiricism is perhaps as striking an example as can be found of the fallacy of neglecting context. But its error lay not in insisting upon experience as the basis and the terminus of philosophy but in its inadequate conception of experience. To refute the principle of empiricism by exposing the errors and defects of particular forms that self-avowed empiricisms have assumed is like supposing that when attention has been called to the eccentricities of a planetary orbit, the existence of an orbit has been disproved.

The significance of "experience" for philosophic method is, after all, but the acknowledgment of the indispensability of context in thinking when that recognition is carried to its full term. Let me recur for a moment to the illustration borrowed at the outset from Malinowski. Examination discloses three deepening levels or three expanding spheres of context. The narrowest and most superficial is that of the immediate scene, the competitive race. The next deeper and wider one is that of the culture of the people in question. The widest and deepest is found in recourse to the need of general understanding of

the workings of human nature. We may without undue forcing find here an apt symbol of the necessary course of philosophical thinking.

The first, if most limited consideration, is the range and
vitality of the experience of the thinker himself, that is, his
most direct personal experience—which, however, only
systematic misunderstanding construes to be merely an experience *of* his own person. However widely it reaches out into the
world of things and persons, it is as personal, curtailed, one-
sided, distorted. The remedy, however, is not divorce of
thought from the intimacies of the direct contacts and inter-
courses of life, but a supplementation of limitations and a
correction of biases through acquaintance with the experience
of others, contemporary and as recorded in the history of the
race. Dogmatism, adherence to a school, partisanship, class-
exclusiveness, desire to show off and to impress, are all of
them manifestations of disrespect for experience: for that experience which one makes one's own through sympathetic
intercommunication. They are, as it were, deliberate perpetu-
ations of the restrictions and perversions of personal experience.

Hence, the next wide circle or deepened stratum of context
resides in what I have referred to as culture—in the sense in
which anthropologists use the word. Philosophy proclaims its
devotion to the universal. But as the profession of cosmopoli-
tan philanthropy which is not rooted in neighborly friendli-
ness is suspect, so I distrust the universals that are not reached
by way of profound respect for the significant features and
outcomes of human experience as found in human institutions, traditions, impelling interests, and occupations. A universal which has its home exclusively or predominantly in
philosophy is a sure sign of isolation and artificiality.

Finally, there is the context of the make-up of experience
itself. It is dangerous to begin at this point. Philosophies that
have designated themselves empirical are full of warning to
this effect. But the boundless multiplicity of the concrete experiences of humanity when they are dealt with gently and

humanely, will naturally terminate in some sense of the structure of any and all experience. Biology, psychology, including social psychology and psychiatry, anthropology, all afford indications as to the nature of this structure, and these indications were never so numerous and so waiting for use as now. Those who try to interpret these indications may run the risk of being regarded by some other philosophers as not philosophers at all. They may, however, console themselves with the reflection that they are concerning themselves with that inclusive and pervasive context of experience in which philosophical thinking must, for good or ill, take place, and without reference to which such thinking is in the end but a beating of wings in the void.

V

THE PATTERN OF INQUIRY [1]

In the preface to *Logic: The Theory of Inquiry*, Dewey writes that "this book is a development of ideas regarding the nature of logical theory that were first presented, some forty years ago, in *Studies in Logical Theory*." Many times during that period, Dewey returned to an analysis of the structure or pattern of inquiry. In the following chapter from the *Logic*, which presents Dewey's refined analysis of the common pattern of inquiry, he returns to the central thesis of his theory of inquiry: "Logical forms accrue to subject matter when the latter is subjected to controlled inquiry." This is the heart of Dewey's theory of norms or leading principles in scientific and moral inquiry. Norms are not a priori principles derived from a realm of pure reason or laid down by arbitrary fiat, nor are they simply descriptions of what has occurred in the past. They are learned from experience, and refined and transformed by further experience and inquiry. Dewey, then, questions the sharp dichotomy between the "is" and the "ought." It is certainly true that we cannot learn how men ought to inquire *simply* by observing the ways in which they do inquire. But only by observing inquiries which lead to successful results of warranted judgments and discriminating the general features of these inquiries can we acquire functional norms for further investigations; this is an ongoing and self-corrective process. We also learn from this chapter that "inquiry is the controlled or directed transformation of an indeterminate situation into one that is so determinate in its constituent distinctions and relations as to convert the elements of the original situation into a unified whole." To understand this characterization of inquiry we must appreciate the meaning of "situation" as a context which is more basic than and includes the distinction of subject-object, physical-mental. "*We* are doubtful because the situation is inherently doubtful." The situation or context is the

[1] *Logic: The Theory of Inquiry* (New York: 1938), pp. 101-19.

basic unit of significance. (See "Context and Thought" and "In Defense of the Theory of Inquiry" for further explication of the meaning of "situation," and "Qualitative Thought" for a discussion of the qualitative transformation of an inquiry.)

T HE FIRST chapter set forth the fundamental thesis of this volume: logical forms accrue to subject matter when the latter is subjected to controlled inquiry. It also set forth some of the implications of this thesis for the nature of logical theory. The second and third chapters stated the independent grounds, biological and cultural, for holding that logic is a theory of experiential naturalistic subject matter. The first of the next two chapters developed the theme with reference to the relations of the logic of common sense and science, while the second discussed Aristotelian logic as the organized formulation of the language of Greek life, when that language is regarded as the expression of the meanings of Greek culture and of the significance attributed to various forms of natural existence. It was held throughout these chapters that inquiry, in spite of the diverse subjects to which it applies, and the consequent diversity of its special techniques has a common structure or pattern: that this common structure is applied both in common sense and science, although because of the nature of the problems with which they are concerned, the emphasis upon the factors involved varies widely in the two modes. We now come to the consideration of the common pattern.

The fact that new formal properties accrue to subject matter in virtue of its subjection to certain types of operation is familiar to us in certain fields, even though the idea corresponding to this fact is unfamiliar in logic. Two outstanding instances are provided by art and law. In music, the dance, painting, sculpture, literature, and the other fine arts, subject matters of everyday experience are *trans*formed by the development of forms which render certain products of doing and making objects of fine art. The materials of legal regulations are transactions occurring in the ordinary activities of human beings and groups of human beings; transactions of a sort that are engaged in apart from law. As certain aspects and phases of these transactions are legally formalized, conceptions such as misdemeanor, crime, torts, contracts and so on arise. These formal conceptions arise out of the ordinary transactions; they are not imposed upon them from on high or from any external and *a priori* source. But when they are formed they are also *formative;* they regulate the proper conduct of the activities out of which they develop.

All of these formal legal conceptions are operational in nature. They formulate and define *ways* of operation on the part of those engaged in the transactions into which a number of persons or groups enter as "parties," and the ways of operation followed by those who have jurisdiction in deciding whether established forms have been complied with, together with the existential consequences of failure of observation. The forms in question are not fixed and eternal. They change, though as a rule too slowly, with changes in the habitual transactions in which individuals and groups engage and the changes that occur in the consequences of these transactions. However hypothetical may be the conception that *logical* forms accrue to existential materials in virtue of the control exercised over inquiries in order that they may fulfill their end, the conception is descriptive of something that verifiably exists. The development of forms in consequence of operations is an established fact in some fields; it is not invented *ad hoc* in relation to logical forms.

The existence of inquiries is not a matter of doubt. They enter into every area of life and into every aspect of every area. In everyday living, men examine; they turn things over intellectually; they infer and judge as "naturally" as they reap and sow, produce and exchange commodities. As a mode of conduct, inquiry is as accessible to objective study as are these other modes of behavior. Because of the intimate and decisive way in which inquiry and its conclusions enter into the management of all affairs of life, no study of the latter is adequate save as it is noted how they are affected by the methods and instruments of inquiry that currently obtain. Quite apart, then, from the particular hypothesis about logical forms that is put forth, study of the objective facts of inquiry is a matter of tremendous import, practically and intellectually. These materials provide the theory of logical forms with a subject matter that is not only objective but is objective in a fashion that enables logic to avoid the three mistakes most characteristic of its history.

1. In virtue of its concern with objectively observable subject matter by reference to which reflective conclusions can be tried and tested, dependence upon subjective and "mentalistic" states and processes is eliminated.

2. The distinctive existence and nature of forms is acknowledged. Logic is not compelled, as historic "empirical" logic felt compelled to do, to reduce logical forms to mere transcripts of the empirical materials that antecede the existence of the former. Just as art forms and legal forms are capable of independent discussion and development, so are logical forms, even though the "independence" in question is intermediate, not final and complete. As in the case of these other forms, they originate *out of* experiential material, and when constituted introduce new ways of operating with prior materials, which ways modify the material out of which they develop.

3. Logical theory is liberated from the unobservable, transcendental and "intuitional."

When methods and results of inquiry are studied as objective data, the distinction that has often been drawn between noting and reporting the ways in which men *do* think, and prescribing the ways in which they *ought* to think, takes on a very different interpretation from that usually given. The usual interpretation is in terms of the difference between the psychological and the logical, the latter consisting of "norms" provided from some source wholly outside of and independent of "experience."

The way in which men *do* "think" denotes, as it is *here* interpreted, simply the ways in which men at a given time

carry on their inquiries. So far as it is used to register a difference from the ways in which they *ought* to think, it denotes a
difference like that between good and bad farming or good
and bad medical practice.[2] Men think in ways they should
not when they follow methods of inquiry that experience of
past inquiries shows are not competent to reach the intended
end of the inquiries in question.

Everybody knows that today there are in vogue methods of
farming generally followed in the past which compare very un-
favorably in their results with those obtained by practices that
have already been introduced and tested. When an expert
tells a farmer he *should* do thus and so, he is not setting up
for a bad farmer an ideal drawn from the blue. He is instruct-
ing him in methods that have been tried and that have proved
successful in procuring results. In a similar way we are able
to contrast various kinds of inquiry that are in use or that
have been used in respect to their economy and efficiency in
reaching warranted conclusions. We know that some methods
of inquiry are better than others in just the same way in
which we know that some methods of surgery, farming, road-
making, navigating, or what-not are better than others. It does
not follow in any of these cases that the "better" methods are
ideally perfect, or that they are regulative or "normative" because of conformity to some absolute form. They are the
methods which experience up to the present time shows to be
the best methods available for achieving certain results, while
abstraction of these methods does supply a (relative) norm or
standard for further undertakings.

The search for the pattern of inquiry is, accordingly, not
one instituted in the dark or at large. It is checked and controlled by knowledge of the kinds of inquiry that have and
that have not worked; methods which, as was pointed out
earlier, can be so compared as to yield reasoned or rational
conclusions. For, through comparison-contrast, we ascertain
how and why certain means and agencies have provided warrantably assertible conclusions, while others have not and

2 *Cf.* pp. v and x of Introduction. [*Logic: The Theory of Inquiry.*]

cannot do so in the sense in which "cannot" expresses an intrinsic incompatibility between means used and consequences attained.

We may now ask: What is the *definition* of Inquiry? That is, what is the most highly generalized conception of inquiry which can be justifiably formulated? The definition that will be expanded, directly in the present chapter and indirectly in the following chapters, is as follows: *Inquiry is the controlled or directed transformation of an indeterminate situation into one that is so determinate in its constituent distinctions and relations as to convert the elements of the original situation into a unified whole.*[3]

The original indeterminate situation is not only "open" to inquiry, but it is open in the sense that its constituents do not hang together. The determinate situation on the other hand, *qua* outcome of inquiry, is a closed and, as it were, finished situation or "universe of experience." "Controlled or directed" in the above formula refers to the fact that inquiry is competent in any given case in the degree in which the operations involved in it actually do terminate in the establishment of an objectively unified existential situation. In the intermediate course of transition and transformation of the indeterminate situation, *dis*course through use of symbols is employed as means. In received logical terminology, propositions, or terms and the relations between them, are intrinsically involved.

I. *The Antecedent Conditions of Inquiry: The Indeterminate Situation.* Inquiry and questioning, up to a certain point, are synonymous terms. We inquire when we question; and we inquire when we seek for whatever will provide an answer to a question asked. Thus it is of the very nature of the indeterminate situation which evokes inquiry to be *questionable;* or, in terms of actuality instead of potentiality, to be uncertain, unsettled, disturbed. The peculiar quality of what pervades the given materials, constituting them a situation, is

[3] The word "situation" is to be understood in the sense already expounded, pp. 66-67. [*Logic: The Theory of Inquiry.*]

not just uncertainty at large; it is a unique doubtfulness which makes that situation to be just and only the situation it is. It is this unique quality that not only evokes the particular inquiry engaged in but that exercises control over its special procedures. Otherwise, one procedure in inquiry would be as likely to occur and to be effective as any other. Unless a situation is uniquely qualified in its very indeterminateness, there is a condition of complete panic; response to it takes the form of blind and wild overt activities. Stating the matter from the personal side, we have "lost our heads." A variety of names serves to characterize indeterminate situations. They are disturbed, troubled, ambiguous, confused, full of conflicting tendencies, obscure, etc.

It is the *situation* that has these traits. *We* are doubtful because the situation is inherently doubtful. Personal states of doubt that are not evoked by and are not relative to some existential situation are pathological; when they are extreme they constitute the mania of doubting. Consequently, situations that are disturbed and troubled, confused or obscure, cannot be straightened out, cleared up and put in order, by manipulation of our personal states of mind. The attempt to settle them by such manipulations involves what psychiatrists call "withdrawal from reality." Such an attempt is pathological as far as it goes, and when it goes far it is the source of some form of actual insanity. The habit of disposing of the doubtful as if it belonged only to *us* rather than to the existential situation in which we are caught and implicated is an inheritance from subjectivistic psychology. The biological antecedent conditions of an unsettled situation are involved in that state of imbalance in organic-environmental interactions which has already been described.[4] Restoration of integration can be effected, in one case as in the other, only by operations which actually modify existing conditions, not by merely "mental" processes.

It is, accordingly, a mistake to suppose that a situation is doubtful only in a "subjective" sense. The notion that in

[4] [*Logic: The Theory of Inquiry*, pp. 26-27.]

actual existence everything is completely determinate has been rendered questionable by the progress of physical science itself. Even if it had not been, complete determination would not hold of existences as an *environment*. For Nature is an environment only as it is involved in interaction with an organism, or self, or whatever name be used.[5]

Every such interaction is a temporal process, not a momentary cross-sectional occurrence. The situation in which it occurs is indeterminate, therefore, with respect to its *issue*. If we call it *confused,* then it is meant that its outcome cannot be anticipated. It is called *obscure* when its course of movement permits of final consequences that cannot be clearly made out. It is called *conflicting* when it tends to evoke discordant responses. Even were existential conditions unqualifiedly determinate in and of themselves, they are indeterminate in *significance:* that is, in what they import and portend in their interaction with the organism. The organic responses that enter into the production of the state of affairs that is temporally later and sequential are just as existential as are environing conditions.

The immediate *locus* of the problem concerns, then, what kind of responses the organism shall make. It concerns the interaction of organic responses and environing conditions in their movement toward an existential issue. It is a commonplace that in any troubled state of affairs *things* will come out differently according to what is done. The farmer won't get grain unless he plants and tills; the general will win or lose the battle according to the way he conducts it, and so on. Neither the grain nor the tilling, neither the outcome of the battle nor the conduct of it, are "mental" events. Organic interaction becomes inquiry when existential consequences are anticipated; when environing conditions are examined with

[5] Except of course a purely mentalistic name, like *consciousness.* The alleged problem of "interactionism" versus automatism, parallelism, etc., is a problem (and an insoluble one) because of the assumption involved in its statement—the assumption, namely, that the interaction in question is with something mental instead of with biological-cultural human beings.

reference to their *potentialities;* and when responsive activities are selected and ordered with reference to actualization of some of the potentialities, rather than others, in a final existential situation. Resolution of the indeterminate situation is active and operational. If the inquiry is adequately directed, the final issue is the unified situation that has been mentioned.

II. *Institution of a Problem.* The unsettled or indeterminate situation might have been called a *problematic* situation. This name would have been, however, proleptic and anticipatory. The indeterminate situation becomes problematic in the very process of being subjected to inquiry. The indeterminate situation comes into existence from existential causes, just as does, say, the organic imbalance of hunger. There is nothing intellectual or cognitive in the existence of such situations, although they are the necessary condition of cognitive operations or inquiry. In themselves they are precognitive. The first result of evocation of inquiry is that the situation is taken, adjudged, to be problematic. To see that a situation requires inquiry is the initial step in inquiry.[6]

Qualification of a situation as problematic does not, however, carry inquiry far. It is but an initial step in institution of a problem. A problem is not a task to be performed which a person puts upon himself or that is placed upon him by others—like a so-called arithmetical "problem" in school work. A problem represents the partial transformation by inquiry of a problematic situation into a determinate situation. It is a familiar and significant saying that a problem well put is half-solved. To find out *what* the problem and problems are which a problematic situation presents to be inquired into, is to be well along in inquiry. To mistake the problem involved is to cause subsequent inquiry to be irrelevant or to go astray. Without a problem, there is blind groping in the dark. The

[6] If by "two-valued logic" is meant a logic that regards "true and false" as the sole logical values, then such a logic is necessarily so truncated that clearness and consistency in logical doctrine are impossible. Being the matter of a problem is a primary logical property.

way in which the problem is conceived decides what specific suggestions are entertained and which are dismissed; what data are selected and which rejected; it is the criterion for relevancy and irrelevancy of hypotheses and conceptual structures. On the other hand, to set up a problem that does not grow out of an actual situation is to start on a course of dead work, nonetheless dead because the work is "busy work." Problems that are self-set are mere excuses for seeming to do something intellectual, something that has the semblance but not the substance of scientific activity.

III. *The Determination of a Problem-Solution.* Statement of a problematic situation in terms of a problem has no meaning save as the problem instituted has, in the very terms of its statement, reference to a possible solution. Just because a problem well stated is on its way to solution, the determining of a genuine problem is a *progressive* inquiry; the cases in which a problem and its probable solution flash upon an inquirer are cases where much prior ingestion and digestion have occurred. If we assume, prematurely, that the problem involved is definite and clear, subsequent inquiry proceeds on the wrong track. Hence the question arises: How is the formation of a genuine problem so controlled that further inquiries will move toward a solution?

The first step in answering this question is to recognize that no situation which is *completely* indeterminate can possibly be converted into a problem having definite constituents. The first step then is to search out the *constituents* of a given situation which, as constituents, are settled. When an alarm of fire is sounded in a crowded assembly hall, there is much that is indeterminate as regards the activities that may produce a favorable issue. One may get out safely or one may be trampled and burned. The fire is characterized, however, by some settled traits. It is, for example, located *somewhere.* Then the aisles and exits are at fixed places. Since they are settled or determinate in *existence,* the first step in institution of a problem is to settle them in *observation.* There are other factors which, while they are not as temporally and spatially

ixed, are yet observable constituents; for example, the behavior and movements of other members of the audience. All
of these observed conditions taken together constitute "the
facts of the case." They constitute the terms of the problem,
because they are conditions that must be reckoned with or
taken account of in any relevant solution that is proposed.

A *possible* relevant solution is then suggested by the determination of factual conditions which are secured by observation. The possible solution presents itself, therefore, as an
idea, just as the terms of the problem (which are facts) are instituted by observation. Ideas are anticipated consequences
(forecasts) of what will happen when certain operations are
executed under and with respect to observed conditions.[7] Observation of facts and suggested meanings or ideas arise and
develop in correspondence with each other. The more the
facts of the case come to light in consequence of being subjected to observation, the clearer and more pertinent become
the conceptions of the way the problem constituted by these
facts is to be dealt with. On the other side, the clearer the
idea, the more definite, as a truism, become the operations of
observation and of execution that must be performed in order
to resolve the situation.

An idea is first of all an anticipation of something that may
happen; it marks a *possibility*. When it is said, as it sometimes
is, that science is *prediction,* the anticipation that constitutes
every idea an idea is grounded in a set of controlled observations and of regulated conceptual ways of interpreting them.
Because inquiry is a progressive determination of a problem
and its possible solution, ideas differ in grade according to the

7 The theory of *ideas* that has been held in psychology and epistemology since the time of Locke's successors is completely irrelevant and ob-
structive in logical theory. For in treating them as copies of perceptions
or "impressions," it ignores the prospective and anticipatory character that
defines *being* an idea. Failure to define ideas functionally, in the reference
they have to a solution of a problem, is one reason they have been treated
as merely "mental." The notion, on the other hand, that ideas are fantasies is a derivative. Fantasies arise when the function an idea performs is
ruled out when it is entertained and developed.

stage of inquiry reached. At first, save in highly familiar matters, they are vague. They occur at first simply as suggestions; suggestions just spring up, flash upon us, occur to us. They may then become stimuli to direct an overt activity but they have as yet no logical status. Every idea originates as a suggestion, but not every suggestion is an idea. The suggestion becomes an idea when it is examined with reference to its functional fitness; its capacity as a means of resolving the given situation.

This examination takes the form of reasoning, as a result of which we are able to appraise better than we were at the outset, the pertinency and weight of the meaning now entertained with respect to its functional capacity. But the final test of its possession of these properties is determined when it actually functions—that is, when it is put into operation so as to institute by means of observations facts not previously observed, and is then used to organize them with other facts into a coherent whole.

Because suggestions and ideas are of that which is not present in given existence, the meanings which they involve must be embodied in some symbol. Without some kind of symbol, no idea; a meaning that is completely disembodied cannot be entertained or used. Since an existence (which is an existence) is the support and vehicle of a meaning and is a symbol instead of a merely physical existence only in this respect, embodied meanings or ideas are capable of objective survey and development. To "look at an idea" is not a mere literary figure of speech.

"Suggestions" have received scant courtesy in logical theory. It is true that when they just "pop into our heads," because of the workings of the psycho-physical organism, they are not logical. But they are both the conditions and the primary stuff of logical ideas. The traditional empiristic theory reduced them, as has already been pointed out, to mental copies of physical things and assumed that they were *per se* identical with ideas. Consequently it ignored the function of ideas in directing observation and in ascertaining relevant facts. The rationalistic school, on the other hand, saw clearly that "facts" apart from ideas are trivial, that they acquire import and significance only in relation to ideas. But at the same time it failed to attend to the operative and functional nature of the latter. Hence, it treated ideas as equivalent to the ultimate structure of "Reality." The Kantian formula that apart from each other "perceptions are blind and conceptions empty" marks a profound logical insight. The insight, however, was radically distorted because perceptual and conceptual contents were supposed to originate from different sources and thus required a third activity, that of synthetic understanding, to bring them together. In logical fact, perceptual and conceptual materials are instituted in functional correlativity with each other, in such a manner that the former locates and describes the problem while the latter represents a possible method of solution. Both are determinations in and by inquiry of the original problematic situation whose pervasive quality controls their institution and their contents. Both are finally checked by their capacity to work together to introduce a resolved unified situation. As distinctions they represent logical divisions of labor.

IV. *Reasoning.* The necessity of developing the meaning-contents of ideas in their relations to one another has been incidentally noted. This process, operating with symbols (constituting propositions) is reasoning in the sense of ratiocination or rational discourse.[8] When a suggested meaning is immediately accepted, inquiry is cut short. Hence the conclusion reached is not grounded, even if it happens to be correct. The check upon immediate acceptance is the examination of the meaning as a meaning. This examination consists in noting what the meaning in question implies in relation to other meanings in the system of which it is a member, the formulated relation constituting a proposition. If such and such a relation of meanings is accepted, then we are

8 "Reasoning" is sometimes used to designate *inference* as well as ratiocination. When so used in logic the tendency is to identify inference and implication and thereby seriously to confuse logical theory.

committed to such and such other relations of meanings because of their membership in the same system. Through a series of intermediate meanings, a meaning is finally reached which is more clearly *relevant* to the problem in hand than the originally suggested idea. It indicates operations which can be performed to test its applicability, whereas the original idea is usually too vague to determine crucial operations. In other words, the idea or meaning when developed in discourse directs the activities which, when executed, provide needed evidential material.

The point made can be most readily appreciated in connection with scientific reasoning. An hypothesis, once suggested and entertained, is developed in relation to other conceptual structures until it receives a form in which it can instigate and direct an experiment that will disclose precisely those conditions which have the maximum possible force in determining whether the hypothesis should be accepted or rejected. Or it may be that the experiment will indicate what modifications are required in the hypothesis so that it may be applicable, i.e., suited to interpret and organize the facts of the case. In many familiar situations, the meaning that is most relevant has been settled because of the eventuations of experiments in prior cases so that it is applicable almost immediately upon its occurrence. But, indirectly, if not directly, an idea or suggestion that is not developed in terms of the constellation of meanings to which it belongs can lead only to overt response. Since the latter terminates inquiry, there is then no adequate inquiry into the meaning that is used to settle the given situation, and the conclusion is in so far logically ungrounded.

V. *The Operational Character of Facts-Meanings.* It was stated that the observed facts of the case and the ideational contents expressed in ideas are related to each other, as, respectively, a clarification of the problem involved and the proposal of some possible solution; that they are, accordingly, functional divisions in the work of inquiry. Observed facts in their office of locating and describing the problem are existential; ideational subject matter is nonexistential. How, then, do they co-operate with each other in the resolution of an existential situation? The problem is insoluble save as it is recognized that both observed facts and entertained ideas are operational. Ideas are operational in that they instigate and direct further operations of observation; they are proposals and plans for acting upon existing conditions to bring new facts to light and to organize all the selected facts into a coherent whole.

What is meant by calling facts operational? Upon the negative side what is meant is that they are not self-sufficient and complete in themselves. They are selected and described, as we have seen, for a purpose, namely statement of the problem involved in such a way that its material both indicates a meaning relevant to resolution of the difficulty and serves to test its worth and validity. In regulated inquiry facts are selected and arranged with the express intent of fulfilling this office. They are not merely *results* of operations of observation which are executed with the aid of bodily organs and auxiliary instruments of art, but they are the particular facts and kinds of facts that will link up with one another in the definite ways that are required to produce a definite end. Those not found to connect with others in furtherance of this end are dropped and others are sought for. Being functional, they are necessarily operational. Their function is to serve as evidence and their evidential quality is judged on the basis of their capacity to form an ordered whole in response to operations prescribed by the ideas they occasion and support. If "the facts of the case" were final and complete in themselves, if they did not have a special operative force in resolution of the problematic situation, they could not serve as evidence.

The operative force of facts is apparent when we consider that no fact in isolation has evidential potency. Facts are evidential and are tests of an idea in so far as they are capable of being organized with one another. The organization can be achieved only as they *interact* with one another. When

the problematic situation is such as to require extensive inquiries to effect its resolution, a series of interactions inter-
venes. Some observed facts point to an idea that stands for
a possible solution. This idea evokes more observations. Some
of the newly observed facts link up with those previously observed and are such as to rule out other observed things with
respect to their evidential function. The new order of facts
suggests a modified idea (or hypothesis) which occasions new
observations whose result again determines a new order of
facts, and so on until the existing order is both unified and
complete. In the course of this serial process, the ideas that
represent possible solutions are tested or "proved."

Meantime, the orders of fact, which present themselves in
consequence of the experimental observations the ideas call
out and direct, are *trial* facts. They are provisional. They are
"facts" if they are observed by sound organs and techniques.
But they are not on that account the *facts of the case*. They
are tested or "proved" with respect to their evidential function just as much as ideas (hypotheses) are tested with reference to their power to exercise the function of resolution.
The operative force of both ideas and facts is thus practically
recognized in the degree in which they are connected with
experiment. Naming them "operational" is but a theoretical
recognition of what is involved when inquiry satisfies the conditions imposed by the necessity for experiment.

I recur, in this connection, to what has been said about the
necessity for symbols in inquiry. It is obvious, on the face of
matters, that a possible mode of solution must be carried in
symbolic form since it is a possibility, not an assured present
existence. Observed facts, on the other hand, are existentially
present. It might seem therefore, that symbols are not required for referring to them. But if they are not carried and
treated by means of symbols, they lose their provisional character, and in losing this character they are categorically asserted and inquiry comes to an end. The carrying on of inquiry requires that the facts be taken as *re*presentative and
not just as *pre*-sented. This demand is met by formulating

them in propositions—that is, by means of symbols. Unless they are so represented they relapse into the total qualitative situation.

VI. *Common Sense and Scientific Inquiry.* The discussion up to this point has proceeded in general terms which recognize no distinction between common sense and scientific inquiry. We have now reached a point where the community of pattern in these two distinctive modes of inquiry should receive explicit attention. It was said in earlier chapters that the difference between them resides in their respective subject matters, not in their basic logical forms and relations; that the difference in subject matters is due to the difference in the problems respectively involved; and, finally, that this difference sets up a difference in the ends or objective consequences they are concerned to achieve. Because common sense problems and inquiries have to do with the interactions into which living creatures enter in connection with environing conditions in order to establish objects of use and enjoyment, the symbols employed are those which have been determined in the habitual culture of a group. They form a system but the system is practical rather than intellectual. It is constituted by the traditions, occupations, techniques, interests, and established institutions of the group. The meanings that compose it are carried in the common everyday language of communication between members of the group. The meanings involved in this common language system determine what individuals of the group may and may not do in relation to physical objects and in relations to one another. They regulate *what* can be used and enjoyed and *how* use and enjoyment shall occur.

Because the symbol-meaning systems involved are connected directly with cultural life-activities and are related to each other in virtue of this connection, the specific meanings which are present have reference to the specific and limited environing conditions under which the group lives. Only those things of the environment that are taken, according to custom and tradition, as having connection with and bearing upon this life, enter into the meaning system. There is no such thing as disinterested intellectual concern with either physical or social matters. For, until the rise of science, there were no problems of common sense that called for such inquiry. Disinterestedness existed practically in the demand that group interests and concerns be put above private needs and interests. But there was no intellectual disinterestedness beyond the activities, interests and concerns of the group. In other words, there was no science as such, although, as was earlier pointed out, there did exist information and techniques which were available for the purposes of scientific inquiry and out of which the latter subsequently grew.

In scientific inquiry, then, meanings are related to one another on the ground of their character *as* meanings, freed from direct reference to the concerns of a limited group. Their intellectual abstractness is a product of this liberation, just as the "concrete" is practically identified by directness of connection with environmental interactions. Consequently a new language, a new system of symbols related together on a new basis, comes into existence, and in this new language semantic coherence, as such, is the controlling consideration. To repeat what has already been said, connection with problems of use and enjoyment is the source of the dominant role of qualities, sensible and moral, and of ends in common sense.

In science, since meanings are determined on the ground of their relation as meanings to one another, *relations* become the objects of inquiry and qualities are relegated to a secondary status, playing a part only as far as they assist in institution of relations. They are subordinate because they have an instrumental office, instead of being themselves, as in prescientific common sense, the matters of final importance. The enduring hold of common sense is testified to historically by the long time it took before it was seen that scientific objects are strictly relational. First tertiary qualities were eliminated; it was recognized that moral qualities are not agencies in determining the structure of nature. Then secondary qualities, the wet-dry, hot-cold, light-heavy, which were the explanatory principles of physical phenomena in Greek science, were ejected. But so-called primary qualities took their place, as with Newton and the Lockian formulation of Newtonian existential postulates. It was not until the threshold of our time was reached that scientific inquiries perceived that their own problems and methods required an interpretation of "primary qualities" in terms of relations, such as position, motion, and temporal span. In the structure of distinctively scientific objects these relations are indifferent to qualities.

The foregoing is intended to indicate that the different objectives of common sense and of scientific inquiry demand different subject matters and that this difference in subject matters is not incompatible with the existence of a common pattern in both types. There are, of course, secondary logical forms which reflect the distinction of properties involved in the change from qualitative and teleological subject matter to nonqualitative and nonteleological relations. But they occur and operate within the described community of pattern. They are explicable, and explicable only, on the ground of the distinctive problems generated by scientific subject matter. The independence of scientific objects from limited and fairly direct reference to the environment as a factor in activities of use and enjoyment, is equivalent, as has already been intimated, to their *abstract* character. It is also equivalent to their *general* character in the sense in which the generalizations of science are different from the generalizations with which common sense is familiar. The generality of *all* scientific subject matter as such means that it is freed from restriction to conditions which present themselves at particular times and places. Their reference is to *any* set of time and place conditions—a statement which is not to be confused with the doctrine that they have no reference to actual existential occasions. Reference to time-place of existence is necessarily involved, but it is reference to whatever set of existences fulfils the general relations laid down in and by the constitution of the scientific object.[9]

Summary. Since a number of points have been discussed, it will be well to round up conclusions reached about them in a summary statement of the structure of the common pattern of inquiry. Inquiry is the directed or controlled transformation of an indeterminate situation into a determinately unified one. The transition is achieved by means of operations of two kinds which are in functional correspondence with each other. One kind of operations deals with ideational or conceptual subject matter. This subject matter stands for possible ways and ends of resolution. It anticipates a solution, and is marked off from fancy because, or, in so far as, it becomes operative in instigation and direction of new observations yielding new factual material. The other kind of operations is made up of activities involving the techniques and organs of observation. Since these operations are existential they modify the prior existential situation, bring into high relief conditions previously obscure, and relegate to the background other aspects that were at the outset conspicuous. The ground and criterion of the execution of this work of emphasis, selection, and arrangement is to delimit the problem in such a way that existential material may be provided with which to test the ideas that represent possible modes of solution. Symbols, defining terms and propositions, are necessarily required in order to retain and carry forward both ideational and existential subject matters in order that they may serve their proper functions in the control of inquiry. Otherwise the problem is taken to be closed and inquiry ceases.

One fundamentally important phase of the transformation

---

[9] The consequences that follow are directly related to the statement in Ch. IV [*Logic: The Theory of Inquiry*] that the elimination of qualities and ends is intermediate; that, in fact, the construction of purely relational objects has enormously liberated and expanded common-sense uses and enjoyments by conferring control over production of qualities, by enabling new ends to be realistically instituted, and by providing competent means for achieving them.

of the situation which constitutes inquiry is central in the treatment of judgment and its functions. The transformation is existential and hence temporal. The pre-cognitive unsettled situation can be settled only by modification of its constituents. Experimental operations change existing conditions. Reasoning, as such, can provide means for effecting the change of conditions but by itself cannot effect it. Only execution of existential operations directed by an idea in which ratiocination terminates can bring about the reordering of environing conditions required to produce a settled and unified situation. Since this principle also applies to the meanings that are elaborated in science, the experimental production and rearrangement of physical conditions involved in natural science is further evidence of the unity of the pattern of inquiry. The temporal quality of inquiry means, then, something quite other than that the process of inquiry takes time. It means that the objective subject matter of inquiry undergoes temporal modification.

Terminological. Were it not that knowledge is related to inquiry as a product to the operations by which it is produced, no distinctions requiring special differentiating designations would exist. Material would merely be a matter of knowledge or of ignorance and error; that would be all that could be said. The content of any given proposition would have the values "true" and "false" as final and exclusive attributes. But if knowledge is related to inquiry as its warrantably assertible product, and if inquiry is progressive and temporal, then the material inquired into reveals distinctive properties which need to be designated by distinctive names. As *undergoing* inquiry, the material has a different logical import from that which it has as the *outcome* of inquiry. In its first capacity and status, it will be called by the general name *subject matter.* When it is necessary to refer to subject matter in the context of either observation or ideation, the name *content* will be used, and, particularly on account of its *representative* character, content of propositions.

The name *objects* will be reserved for subject matter so far as it has been produced and ordered in settled form by means of inquiry; proleptically, objects are the *objectives* of inquiry. The apparent ambiguity of using "objects" for this purpose (since the word is regularly applied to things that are observed or thought of) is only apparent. For things exist *as* objects for us only as they have been previously determined as outcomes of inquiries. When used in carrying on new inquiries in new problematic situations, they are known as objects in virtue of prior inquiries which warrant their assertibility. In the new situation, they are *means* of attaining knowledge of something else. In the strict sense, they are part of the *contents* of inquiry as the word content was defined above. But retrospectively (that is, as products of prior determination in inquiry) they are objects.

✒️ VI ✒️

IN DEFENSE OF THE THEORY
OF INQUIRY[1]

At the age of ninety, Dewey was still ready to answer his
critics and defend his philosophy. The following letter was
written in response to a letter by Albert Balz in which some
penetrating questions concerning the doctrine of possibility
in *Logic: The Theory of Inquiry* were raised. (Both letters
appeared in the *Journal of Philosophy,* Vol. XLVI, 1949.)
Dewey in reply presents "a fresh statement of some of the
fundamentals of my position," which is one of the clearest
and most eloquent descriptions of what he sought to achieve
in his theory of inquiry. "I tried the experiment of transferring the old well-known figures from the stage of ontology to the stage of inquiry. As a consequence of this transfer, the scene as it presented itself to me was not only more
coherent, but indefinitely more instructive and humanly
dramatic." Dewey once again stresses the significance of
"situation," which cuts across the subject-object distinction,
and of the "problematic," which initiates inquiry. He also
clears up a number of confusions surrounding the instrumentalist view of scientific abstraction and mathematics.
Abstract scientific theories are the most powerful instruments of explanation. Mathematics, which carries abstraction to its limit, is not a source of embarrassment for the
instrumentalist theory of inquiry. On the contrary, recent
progress in mathematical inquiry has shaken mathematics
free from a restrictive ontological setting. This letter, then,
presents us with the unique opportunity of reviewing, with
Dewey as our guide, the essentials of his theory of inquiry.

[1] Originally published as part of "A Letter to Mr. Dewey concerning
John Dewey's Doctrine of Possibility, published together with his Reply,"
by Albert G. A. Balz and John Dewey, *Journal of Philosophy,* XLVI
(1949), 313-42.

I

Discovery Bay,
Jamaica

MY DEAR A——:

In sending you this letter I can not do otherwise than begin with expressing my appreciation of the spirit in which you have written. I also wish to express my gratitude to you for affording me this opportunity to restate the position which, as you suggest, has occasioned difficulties to others as well as to yourself.

When, however, I began to write to you in reply, I found myself in a quandary; in fact, on the horns of a dilemma. On the one hand it seemed obligatory for me to take up each one of your difficulties one by one, and do what I could to clarify each point. The more, however, I contemplated that course, the more I became doubtful of its success in attaining the desired end of clarification. If, I thought, I had not been able to make my position clear in the course of several hundred pages, how can I expect to accomplish that end in the course of a small number of pages devoted to a variety of themes? The other horn of the dilemma was that failure to take up all your points might seem to show a disrespect for your queries and criticism which I am very far from feeling. While I was pondering this matter, I received a letter from a younger fellow student of philosophy. In this letter, written naturally in ignorance of our proposed discussion, he quoted some words written by me some thirty years or more ago. The passage reads: "As philosophers, our disagreements with one another as to conclusions are trivial in comparison with our disagreements as to problems; to see the problem another sees, in the same perspective and at the same angle—that amounts to something. Agreement as to conclusions is in comparison perfunctory."

When I read this sentence it was as if a light dawned. It then occurred to me that I should proceed by trying to show that what is said by me in the book which is the source of your intellectual difficulties, is set forth in a context which is determined, entirely and exclusively, by problems that arise in connection with a development of a Theory of Inquiry; that is, in the context of problems that arise in undertaking an inquiry into the facts of inquiry. Accordingly, I concluded that I might best accede to your request for clarification of the difficulties you have experienced by means of a fresh statement of some of the fundamentals of my position. Since your difficulties and questions hang together, I am sure you will find no disrespect in my treating them as a systematic whole instead of as if they were scattered, independent, and fragmentary. There is also no disrespect in the belief that their systematic nature is due to the fact that you read what was actually written in the context of connection with the conduct of *inquiry* as if it were written in an *ontological* context—especially as this latter context is classic, in comparison with which that set forth in my *Theory of Inquiry* is an upstart.

I hope, accordingly, dear A——, that you will understand why what is here said delays in coming to a direct answer to specific questions you raise. In order to make my position clear as a whole I have to begin at the beginning, which in the present case lies far back of your questions. I think, for example, that the importance in my writings of what is designated by the words "situation" and "problematic" must have escaped you. Whether this be so or not, we have right here at hand what seems to be an excellent example of their meaning. "Situation" stands for something inclusive of a large number of diverse elements existing across wide areas of space and long periods of time, but which, nevertheless, have their own unity. This discussion which we are here and now carrying on is precisely part of a situation. Your letter to me and what I am writing in response are evidently parts of that to which I have given the name "situation"; while these items are conspicuous features of the situation they are far from being the only or even the chief ones. In each case there is prolonged prior study: into this study have entered teachers, books, articles, and all the contacts which have shaped the views that now find themselves in disagreement with each other. It is this complex of the fact that determines also the applicability of "problematic" to the present situation. That word stands for the existence of something questionable, and hence provocative of investigation, examination, discussion—in short, inquiry. However, the word "problematic" covers such a great variety of occasions for inquiry that it may be helpful to specify a number of them. It covers the features that are designated by such adjectives as confusing, perplexing, disturbed, unsettled, indecisive; and by such nouns as jars, hitches, breaks, blocks—in short, all incidents occasioning an interruption of the smooth, straightforward course of behavior and that deflect it into the kind of behavior constituting inquiry.

The foregoing, as I quite recognize, my dear friend, is an indirect approach to the questions you raise. Perhaps I can render it somewhat more direct by calling attention to the fact that the unsettled, indecisive character of the situation with which inquiry is compelled to deal affects all of the subject matters that enter into all inquiry. It affects, on the one hand, the observed existing facts that are taken to locate and delimit the problem; on the other side, it affects all of the suggestions, surmises, ideas that are entertained as possible solutions of the problem. There is, of course, nothing at all sacred in employing the words "potentiality" and "possibility" to designate the subject matters in inquiry that stand for progress made in determining, respectively, the problem and its solution. What is important, and from the standpoint of my position, all important, is that the tentative, on-trial nature of the subject matters involved in each case be recognized; while that recognition can hardly be attained unless some names are given. The indecisive and tentative nature of the subject matters involved might have been expressed by using either the word "potentiality" or the word "possibility" for the subject matters of both the problem and solution. But in that case, it would have been at once necessary to find sub-terms to designate the distinctive places held and the specific offices or functions performed by subject matters constituting what is taken during the conduct of inquiry, as on the one hand the problem to be dealt with and on the other hand the solution suggested: both of them, let it be recalled, being tentative on-trial since both are equally implicated in doubt and inquiry.

From the standpoint of conduct of inquiry it directly follows that the nature of the problem as well as of the solution to be reached is *under* inquiry; failure in solution is sure to result if the problem has not been properly located and described. While this fact is not offered as a justification of the use of the particular words "potentiality" and "possibility," given the standpoint of connection with inquiry, it does imperatively demand the use of two different words as *names* and as names for two disparate but complementary uses.

In any case, dear friend, what has been said has a much wider application than simply to the meaning to be assigned to these two words. For it indicates how and why meaning assigned to *any* phase or aspect of my position which puts what is said in an ontological context instead of that of inquiry is sure to go amiss in respect to understanding. And when I say this, I say it in full recognition of the fact that exclusion of the need of ontological backing and reference of any kind may quite readily convert your difficulty and doubt into outright rejection. But, after all, rejection based upon understanding is better than apparent agreement based on misunderstanding. I should be happy indeed, dear A——, to obtain your assent to my view, but failing that, I shall be quite content if I can obtain an understanding of what it is that my theory of inquiry is trying to do if and when it is taken to be, wholly and exclusively, a theory of knowledge.

II

I hardly need remind you that there is nothing new in recognizing that both observed facts and ideas, theories, rational principles, have entered in fundamental ways into historic discussion of philosophical theories of knowledge. There is nothing new to be found in the fact that I have made them the subject matter of a problem. Whatever relative novelty may be found in my position consists in regarding the *problem* as belonging in the context of the conduct of inquiry and not in either the traditional ontological or the traditional epistemological context. I shall, accordingly, in the interest of elucidation attempt another line of approach: one in terms of familiar historical materials.

One outstanding problem of modern philosophy of knowledge is found in its long preoccupation with the controversy between empiricism and rationalism. Even today, when the controversy has receded at least temporarily into the background, it can not be denied by one who surveys the course of the historical discussion that important statements were made with respect both to what was called experience and what was called reason, and this in spite of the fact that the controversy never reached the satisfactory conclusion constituted by the two parties arriving at agreement. It is not a mere biographical fact, accordingly, if I call attention to the fact that I am in no way an inventor of the problem in a theory of knowledge of the relation to each other of observed factual material on one side and ideational or theoretical material on the other side. The failure of the controversy.to arrive at solution through agreement is an important ground of the idea that it is worth while to take these constituents of controversy out of an ontological context, and note how they look when they are placed in the context of the use they perform and the service they render in the context of *inquiry*. The net product of this way of viewing the two factors in the old controversy is expressed in the phrase "The Autonomy of Inquiry." That phrase does more than merely occur in the book that is the source of the discussion in which we are now engaged, since its use there was intended to serve as a key to understanding its contents. The elimination of ontological reference that at first sight may seem portentous actually amounts to the simple matter of saying that whatever claims to be or to convey knowledge has to be found in the context of inquiry; and that this thesis applies to *every* statement which is put forth in the theory of knowledge, whether the latter deals with its origin, its nature, or its possibility.

III

In approaching the special topic of mathematical subject matter and mathematical inquiry, I find it necessary, as well as advisable, to begin with the topic of Abstraction. According to the standpoint taken in *The Theory of Inquiry*, something of the nature of abstraction is found in the case of *all* ideas and of all theories. Abstraction from assured and certain existential reference belongs to *every* suggestion of a possible solution; otherwise inquiry comes to an end and positive assertion takes its place. But subject matters constituting during the course of inquiry what is taken to be the *problem* are also held in suspense. If they are not so maintained, then, to repeat, inquiry comes automatically to an end. It *terminates* even though the termination is not, with respect to inquiry, a *conclusion.* A flight away from what there and then exists does not of itself accomplish anything. It may take the form of day-dreaming or building castles in the air. But when the flight lands upon what for the purpose of inquiry is an idea, it at once becomes the point of departure for instigating and directing new observations serving to bring to light facts the use of which will develop further use and which thereby develop awareness of the problem to be dealt with, and consequently serve to indicate an improved mode of solution; which in turn instigates and directs new observation of existential material, and so on and on till both problem and solution take on a determinate form. In short, unless it is clearly recognized that in *every* case of obstructed ongoing behavior "*ideas*" are temporary deviations and escapes, what I have called their functional and operational standing will not be understood. Every *idea* is an *escape,* but escapes are saved from being *evasions* so far as they are put to use in evoking and directing observations of further factual material.

I am reasonably confident, dear A——, that in this one point at least we shall find ourselves in agreement. I do not believe that either of us is in sympathy with the wholesale attacks upon abstractions that are now being made in some quarters. Theories as they are used in scientific inquiry are themselves matters of systematic abstraction. Like ideas, they get away from what may be called the immediately given facts in order to be applicable to a much fuller range of relevant facts. A scientific theory differs from the ideas which, as we say, "pop into our heads," only in its vast and systematic range of applicability. The peculiarity of *scientific* abstraction lies in the degree of its freedom from *particular* existential adhesions.

It follows as a matter of course that abstraction is carried on indefinitely further in scientific inquiry than there is occasion for carrying it on in connection with the affairs of everyday life. For, in the latter case, an abstraction loses its serviceability if it is carried beyond applicability to the *specific* difficulty then and there encountered. In the case of scientific inquiry, theory is carried to a point of abstraction which renders it available in dealing with a maximum variety of possible uses. What we call *comprehensiveness* in the case of a theory is not a matter of its own content, but of the serviceability in range of application of that content. It is perhaps worth while to notice that the Newtonian theory was, for a long time, believed to be completely comprehensive in respect to all astronomical subject matter; not merely that which had already been observed but to all that ever could possibly be observed. Finally, there occurred what in the case of an everyday affair of life would be called a *hitch* or *block*. Instead of the discrepancy being accepted as a finality it was, however, at once *put to use* in suggesting further development upon the side of theory as abstraction. The outcome constitutes what is known as "The Relativity Theory." Newton had carried *his* abstraction to a point which was shocking to many of his contemporaries. They felt that it took away the reality which gave point and zest to the affairs of life, moral and esthetic as well as practical in a utilitarian sense. In so doing they made the same mistake that professional philosophers made after them. They treated a use, function, and service rendered in conduct of inquiry as if it had ontological reference apart from inquiry.

When viewed from the standpoint of its position in the conduct of inquiry, the relativity theory rendered space and time themselves subject matters of inquiry instead of its fixed limits. In the Newtonian theory they had been treated as an *Ultima Thule* beyond which scientific inquiry could not possibly go. These considerations may be used, dear A——, as an example of how submitting inquiry to ontological reference obstructs it. But here they are mentioned on account of their bearing on the question of mathematical subject matter. No matter how far physical theory carries its abstractions, it would contradict the very intent of the latter if they went beyond possibility of application to every kind of *observable* existential materials. The privilege of *that* use and office is reserved for mathematical inquiry. The story of the development of mathematical inquiry shows that its advances have usually been occasioned by something which struck some inquirer as a hitch or block in the previous state of its subject matter. But in the course of the last one or two generations, mathematicians have arrived at the point at which they see that the heart of the work they are engaged in is the method of free postulation. It is hardly necessary to note how the constructions in which the interior angles of a triangle are, as the case may be, either less or more than two right angles, have removed the ontological obstructions that inhered in Euclidean geometry. While in most respects I am compelled to admit that important features of my position are incompatible with philosophical theories that have received authoritative and, so to say, official formulations, in this matter of mathematics, I believe, Mr. A——, that I am "on the side of the angels." At all events, I did not invent the position that I have taken in the foregoing statements. I took it over almost bodily from what the mathematicians have said who have brought about the recent immense advances in that subject. It is the progress of mathematical inquiry *as* mathematical which has profoundly shaken the ontological rigidity once belonging to the circle and the triangle as their own immutable "essences." I can not, accordingly, refrain from mentioning the role that considerations similar to those just mentioned have played in inducing me to undertake an attempt to convert all the *ontological,* as prior to inquiry, into the *logical* as occupied wholly and solely with what takes place in the conduct of inquiry as an evergoing concern.

IV

In the hope that it may further a clarified understanding of my position, I shall now take up another outstanding problem of modern epistemological philosophy. It is a familiar fact that the historical systems of epistemological philosophy did their best to make ontological conclusions depend upon prior investigation of the conditions and nature of knowledge. A fact which is not so familiar, which indeed is often ignored, is that this attempt was itself based upon an ontological assumption of literally tremendous import; for it was assumed that whatever else knowledge is or is not, it is dependent upon the independent existence of a *knower* and of something *to be known;* occurring, that is, between mind and the world; between self and not-self; or, in words made familiar by use, between subject and object. The assumption consisted in holding that the subject matters designated by these antithetical terms are separate and independent; hence the problem of problems was to determine some method of harmonizing the status of one with the status of the other with respect to the possibility and nature of knowledge. Controversy on this topic, as is the case with the other historic problem already mentioned, has now receded into the background. It cannot be affirmed, however, that the problem is settled by means of reaching an agreed-upon solution. It is rather as if t had been discovered that the competing theories of the various kinds of realism, idealism, and dualism had finally so covered the ground that nothing more could be found to say.

In this matter also it accordingly occurred to me that it might be a good idea to try the experiment of placing in the context of inquiry whatever matters were of moment and weight in what was urged by the various parties to the controversy. For observed and observable facts of inquiry are readily available: there is a mass of fact extending throughout the whole recorded intellectual history of man, in which are manifest for study and investigation both failures and successes— much as is the case in the story of any important human art. In this transfer of matters at issue from their prior ontological setting into a context that is set *wholly and only* by conditions of the conduct of inquiry, what had been taken to be inherent ontological demands were seen to be but arbitrary assumptions from their own standpoint, but important distinctions of use and office in the progressive carrying on of inquiry.

In pursuing this line of inquiry, it proved to be a natural affair to take as a point of departure the physiological connection and distinction of organism and environment as the *most readily observable* instance of the *principle* involved in the matter of the connection and distinction of "subject and object." Consideration of the simpler physiological activities which significantly enough already bore the name "functions" served to indicate that a life-activity is not anything going on *between* one thing, the organism, and another thing, the environment, but that, *as* life-activity, it is a simple event over and across that distinction (not to say separation). Anything that can be entitled to either of these names has first to be located and identified as it is incorporated, engrossed, in life-activity. Hence there was presented in an acute form the following problem: Under what conditions of life-activity and to what consequences in the latter is the distinction relevant?

The issue involved in this question coalesced, almost of itself, with the point of view independently reached in regard to knowing as inquiry with respect to its origin in the event of a hitch, blockage, or break, in the ongoing of an active situation. The coalescence worked both ways. With respect to the distinction within the course of physiological life-activity, the obvious suggestion was that the subject matters to which the names "organism" and "environment," respectively, apply are distinguished when some function, say digestion, is disturbed, unsettled, and it is necessary, *in order to do something about it* which will restore the normal activity (in which organs and foods work together in a single unified process) to *locate* the source of the trouble. Is there something wrong inside? Or is the source of the disturbance located in water or in food that has been taken into the system? When such a distinction is once clearly made there are those who devote themselves especially to inquiry into the structures and processes that can be *referred* distinctively to the organisms, (although they could not take place and be capable of such reference without continuous partnership in a single transaction), while others study the relations of air, climate, foods water, etc., to the maintenance of health—that is, of unified functionings.

What happens when distinctions which are indispensable to form and use in an efficient conduct of inquiry—that is to say, one which meets its own conditions *as* inquiry— are converted into something ontological, that is to say, into something taken to exist on its own account prior to inquiry and to which inquiry must conform, is exhibited, I submit, my dear questioner, in the epistemological phase of modern philosophy; and yet the new science could not have accomplished its revolution in astronomy, physics, and physiology if it had not *in the course of its own development* of method been able by means of such distinctions as those to which theory gave the names "subject" and "object," "mind" and "the world," etc., to slough off the vast mass of irrelevant preconceptions which kept ancient and medieval cosmology from attaining scientific standing.

It is not implied, however, that what has just been said covers the whole scope of the problem. There remains the question of why at a particular time the distinction between knower and the subject matter to be known became so conspicuous and so central as to be for two centuries or more one of *the outstanding* philosophical issues. No such problem was urgent in either ancient or medieval philosophy. The idea that most directly suggests itself as an indication of a solution of this problem is that the rather sudden and certainly striking emergence of the "subject-object" problem is intimately connected with the cultural conditions that mark the transition of the medieval period into that age that is called *modern*. This view of the matter is, I believe, an interesting and even important hypothesis; it is one which in another connection might be followed out with advantage. It is introduced here, however, solely for whatever service it may render in understanding a position which, like that set forth in *The Theory of Inquiry,* transfers what had been taken to be ontological separations into distinctions that serve a useful, indeed necessary, function in conduct of inquiry.

Before leaving this endeavor to clarify my position through reference to well-known events in the history of philosophy, I shall mention a third matter which, unlike the two already mentioned, is still more or less actively pursued in contemporary philosophical discussion. I refer here to the extraordinary contrast that exists beyond peradventure between the subject matters that are known in science and those known in the course of our everyday and common living—common not only in the sense of the usual but of that which is shared by large numbers of human beings in the conduct of the affairs of their life. To avoid misunderstanding it should be observed that the word "practical" has a much fuller meaning when used to designate these affairs than it has when it is used in a narrow utilitarian way, since it includes the moral, the political, and the artistic. A simple but fairly typical example of the undeniable contrast between the subject matters of this common life and the knowings that are appropriate to it, and the subject matter and method of scientific knowing, is found in the radical unlikeness of the water we drink, wash with, sail boats upon, use to extinguish fires, etc., etc., and the H_2O of scientific subject matter.

It would appear dogmatic were I to say that the problem involved in this radical unlikeness of subject matters is insoluble if its terms are placed in an ontological context. But the differences between, say, a spiritualistic and a materialistic ontological solution remind us how far away we are from any agreed-upon solution. It hardly seems unreasonable to suggest that parties to the controversy are lined up on the basis of preferences which are external to the terms of the issue rather than on grounds which are logically related to it. When the issue pertaining to and derived from this contrast is placed and treated in the context of different types of *problems* demanding different methods of treatment and different types of subject matter, the problem involved assumes a very different shape from that which it has when it is taken to concern the ontological "reality." It would be irrelevant to the present issue were I to attempt to tell just what form the problem and its solution assume when they are seen and treated in the context of inquiry. It is relevant, however, to the understanding of the point of view to say that it demands statement on the ground of types of problems so different that they are capable of solution only in terms of types of subject matter as unlike one another as are those exemplified in the case of "*water*." I may, however, at least point out that a thirsty man seeking water to drink in a dry land would hardly be furthered in the emergency in which he finds himself by calling upon H_2O as his subject matter; while, on the other hand, the physicist engaged in his type of problem and inquiry would soon be brought to a halt if he could not treat water as H_2O. For it is on account of *that* mode of treatment that water is taken out of isolation as a subject of knowledge and brought into vital and intimate connection with an indefinitely extensive range of other matters qualitatively and immediately of radically different kinds from water and from one another.

It seems pertinent at this point, my dear A——, to refer to that aspect of my theory of knowledge to which I gave the name "instrumentalism." For it was intended to deal with the problem just mentioned on the basis of the idea or hypothesis that scientific subject matter grows out of and returns into the subject matter of the everyday kind—the kind of subject matter to which *on the basis of ontological interpretation* it is totally and unqualifiedly opposed. Upon the basis of this view the metaphysical problem which so divided Berkeley from Sir Isaac Newton, and which has occupied such a prominent place in philosophy ever since the rise of new physical science, is not so much resolved as dissolved. Moreover, new construction accrues to the subject matter of physical science just because of its extreme unlikeness to the subject matters which for the sake of brevity may be called those of common sense. There is presented in this unlikeness a striking example of the view of the function of thoroughgoing abstraction mentioned shortly ago. The extreme remoteness of the subject matter of physical science from the subject matter of everyday living is precisely that which renders the former applicable to an immense variety of the occasions that present themselves in the course of everyday living. Today there is probably no case of everyday living in which physical conditions hold a place that is beyond the reach of being effectively dealt with on the ground of available *scientific* subject matter. A similar statement is now coming to hold regarding matters which are specifically physiological! Note, in evidence, the revolution that is taking place in matters relating to illness and health. Negative illustration, if not confirmation, may be supplied by the backward state of both knowledge and practice in matters that are distinctively human and moral. The latter in my best judgment will continue to be a matter of customs and of conflict of customs until inquiry has found a method of abstraction which, because of its degree of remoteness from established customs, will bring them into a light in which their nature will be indefinitely more clearly seen than is now the case.

As I see the matter, what marks the scientific movement that began a few centuries ago and that has accomplished a veritable revolution in the methods and the conclusions of natural science are its *experimental* conduct and the fact that even the best established theories retain *hypothetical* status. Moreover, these two traits hang together. Theories as hypotheses are developed and tested through being put to use in the conducting of experimental activities which bring to the light of observation new areas of fact. Before the scientific revolution some theories were taken to be inherently settled beyond question because they dealt with Being that was eternal and immutable. During that period the word "hypothesis" meant that which *was placed under* subject matters so firmly as to be beyond the possibility of doubt or question. I do not know how I could better exemplify what I mean to be understood by the functional and operational character of ideational subject matter than by the radical change that in the development of scientific inquiry has taken place in the working position now attached to hypothesis, and to *theory* as hypothetical.

Let me say, my friend, that I have engaged in this fairly long, even if condensed, historical exposition solely for the sake of promoting understanding of my position. As I have already indicated, I did not originate the main figures that play their parts in my theory of knowing. I tried the experiment of transferring the old well-known figures from the stage of ontology to the stage of inquiry. As a consequence of this transfer, the scene as it presented itself to me was not only more coherent but indefinitely more instructive and humanly dramatic.

In any event the various factors, ancient and modern, of historical discussion and controversy were precipitated in the book whose subject matter is the occasion of this present exchange of views. I am aware that I have not made the kind of reply which in all probability you felt you had a right to anticipate. At the same time, while I have taken advantage of considerations that have occurred to me since the text in question was written, I do not believe that I have departed from its substantial intent and spirit. Yet I am bound to acknowledge that the occasion of precipitating historical materials into the treatise under discussion was the great variety of works on logical theory that appeared during the nineteenth century. As I look back I am led to the conclusion that the attempt conscientiously to do my full duty by these treatises is accountable for a certain cloudiness which obscures clear vision of what the book was trying to do. The force of the word "Logic," in all probability, has overshadowed for the reader the import of what in my intention was the significant expression, *The Theory of Inquiry*. For that source of misapprehension I accept full responsibility. I am, accordingly, the more grateful to you, my dear friendly critic, for affording me this opportunity for restatement, which, I venture to hope, is free from some of the encumbrances that load down the text. I shall be content if I have succeeded in this response to your request for clarification in conveying a better understanding of the *problem* that occupied me. As I reflect upon the historical course of philosophy I am unable to find its course marked by notable successes in the matter of conclusions attained. I yield to none, however, in admiring appreciation of the liberating work it has accomplished in opening new perspectives of vision through its sensitivity to problems it has laid hold of in ways which, over and over again, have loosened the hold upon us exerted by predispositions that owe their strength to conformities which became so habitual as not to be questioned, and which in all probability would still be unquestioned were it not for the debt we owe to philosophers.

Very sincerely yours,

JOHN DEWEY

ᦵ VII ᦵ

HAVING AN EXPERIENCE[1]

In *Art as Experience,* Dewey not only treated problems in the philosophy of art, he rethought his entire philosophy of experience. Earlier in his career, Dewey had stressed the conflicts within experience, the obstacles to be overcome, and the problems to be solved. Consequently, Dewey had created the impression that man is always caught in a struggle, striving for a future that never seems to come. In *Art as Experience,* he deliberately sought to correct this false impression and present a more balanced view of experience. Dewey analyzes, in the chapter selected, the meaning of *"an* experience." "An experience is a whole and carries with it its own individualizing quality. . . . " *An* experience is a consummation or fulfillment where the pervading or aesthetic quality binds the constituents into an integral whole. At first, it may appear as if Dewey is talking about a special type of experience which is called aesthetic, but it soon becomes clear that aesthetic quality is a characteristic of anything which is distinctively *an* experience. Thus, for example, *"an* experience of thinking has its own esthetic quality." In fact, "esthetic cannot be sharply marked off from intellectual experience since the latter must bear an esthetic stamp to be itself complete." The continuity of the aesthetic and the intellectual can be seen from another perspective. It is a mere prejudice to believe that artistic creation excludes and is opposed to thinking. "To think effectively in terms of relations of qualities is as severe a demand upon thought as to think in terms of symbols, verbal and mathematical." This selection, then, in addition to discussing the nature of art, recasts Dewey's entire philosophy of experience.

E XPERIENCE occurs continuously, because the interaction of live creature and environing conditions is involved in the very process of living. Under conditions of resistance and conflict, aspects and elements of the self and the world that are implicated in this interaction qualify experi-

[1] *Art as Experience* (New York: 1934), pp. 35-57.

ence with emotions and ideas so that conscious intent emerges.
Oftentimes, however, the experience had is inchoate. Things
are experienced but not in such a way that they are composed
into an experience. There is distraction and dispersion; what
we observe and what we think, what we desire and what we
get, are at odds with each other. We put our hands to the
plow and turn back; we start and then we stop, not because
the experience has reached the end for the sake of which it
was initiated but because of extraneous interruptions or of
inner lethargy.

In contrast with such experience, we have *an* experience
when the material experienced runs its course to fulfillment.
Then and then only is it integrated within and demarcated
in the general stream of experience from other experiences.
A piece of work is finished in a way that is satisfactory; a
problem receives its solution; a game is played through; a situation, whether that of eating a meal, playing a game of chess,
carrying on a conversation, writing a book, or taking part in
a political campaign, is so rounded out that its close is a consummation and not a cessation. Such an experience is a whole
and carries with it its own individualizing quality and self-
sufficiency. It is *an* experience.

Philosophers, even empirical philosophers, have spoken for
the most part of experience at large. Idiomatic speech, however, refers to experiences each of which is singular, having
its own beginning and end. For life is no uniform uninter-
rupted march or flow. It is a thing of histories, each with its
own plot, its own inception and movement toward its close,
each having its own particular rhythmic movement; each with
its own unrepeated quality pervading it throughout. A flight
of stairs, mechanical as it is, proceeds by individualized steps,
not by undifferentiated progression, and an inclined plane is
at least marked off from other things by abrupt discreteness.

Experience in this vital sense is defined by those situations
and episodes that we spontaneously refer to as being "real
experiences"; those things of which we say in recalling them,
"that *was* an experience." It may have been something of

tremendous importance—a quarrel with one who was once an intimate, a catastrophe finally averted by a hair's breadth. Or it may have been something that in comparison was slight—and which perhaps because of its very slightness illustrates all the better what is to be an experience. There is that meal in a Paris restaurant of which one says "that *was* an experience." It stands out as an enduring memorial of what food may be. Then there is that storm one went through in crossing the Atlantic—the storm that seemed in its fury, as it was experienced, to sum up in itself all that a storm can be, complete in itself, standing out because marked out from what went before and what came after.

In such experiences, every successive part flows freely, without seam and without unfilled blanks, into what ensues. At the same time there is no sacrifice of the self-identity of the parts. A river, as distinct from a pond, flows. But its flow gives a definiteness and interest to its successive portions greater than exist in the homogeneous portions of a pond. In an experience, flow is from something to something. As one part leads into another and as one part carries on what went before, each gains distinctness in itself. The enduring whole is diversified by successive phases that are emphases of its varied colors.

Because of continuous merging, there are no holes, mechanical junctions, and dead centers when we have *an* experience. There are pauses, places of rest, but they punctuate and define the quality of movement. They sum up what has been undergone and prevent its dissipation and idle evaporation. Continued acceleration is breathless and prevents parts from gaining distinction. In a work of art, different acts, episodes, occurrences melt and fuse into unity, and yet do not disappear and lose their own character as they do so—just as in a genial conversation there is a continuous interchange and blending, and yet each speaker not only retains his own character but manifests it more clearly than is his wont.

An experience has a unity that gives it its name, *that* meal, that storm, that rupture of friendship. The existence of this unity is constituted by a single *quality* that pervades the entire experience in spite of the variation of its constituent parts. This unity is neither emotional, practical, nor intellectual, for these terms name distinctions that reflection can make within it. In discourse *about* an experience, we must make use of these adjectives of interpretation. In going over an experience in mind *after* its occurrence, we may find that one property rather than another was sufficiently dominant so that it characterizes the experience as a whole. There are absorbing inquiries and speculations which a scientific man and philosopher will recall as "experiences" in the emphatic sense. In final import they are intellectual. But in their actual occurrence they were emotional as well; they were purposive and volitional. Yet the experience was not a sum of these different characters; they were lost in it as distinctive traits. No thinker can ply his occupation save as he is lured and rewarded by total integral experiences that are intrinsically worth while. Without them he would never know what it is really to think and would be completely at a loss in distinguishing real thought from the spurious article. Thinking goes on in trains of ideas, but the ideas form a train only because they are much more than what an analytic psychology calls ideas. They are phases, emotionally and practically distinguished, of a developing underlying quality; they are its moving variations, not separate and independent like Locke's and Hume's so-called ideas and impressions, but are subtle shadings of a pervading and developing hue.

We say of an experience of thinking that we reach or draw a conclusion. Theoretical formulation of the process is often made in such terms as to conceal effectually the similarity of "conclusion" to the consummating phase of every developing integral experience. These formulations apparently take their cue from the separate propositions that are premises and the proposition that is the conclusion as they appear on the printed page. The impression is derived that there are first two independent and ready-made entities that are then manipulated so as to give rise to a third. In fact, in an experience of thinking, premises emerge only as a conclusion becomes manifest. The experience, like that of watching a storm reach its height and gradually subside, is one of continuous movement of subject matters. Like the ocean in the storm, there are a series of waves; suggestions reaching out and being broken in a clash, or being carried onwards by a co-operative wave. If a conclusion is reached, it is that of a movement of anticipation and cumulation, one that finally comes to completion. A "conclusion" is no separate and independent thing; it is the consummation of a movement.

Hence *an* experience of thinking has its own esthetic quality. It differs from those experiences that are acknowledged to be esthetic, but only in its materials. The material of the fine arts consists of qualities; that of experience having intellectual conclusion are signs or symbols having no intrinsic quality of their own, but standing for things that may in another experience be qualitatively experienced. The difference is enormous. It is one reason why the strictly intellectual art will never be popular as music is popular. Nevertheless, the experience itself has a satisfying emotional quality because it possesses internal integration and fulfillment reached through ordered and organized movement. This artistic structure may be immediately felt. In so far, it is esthetic. What is even more important is that not only is this quality a significant motive in undertaking intellectual inquiry and in keeping it honest, but that no intellectual activity is an integral event (is *an* experience), unless it is rounded out with this quality. Without it, thinking is inconclusive. In short, esthetic cannot be sharply marked off from intellectual experience since the latter must bear an esthetic stamp to be itself complete.

The same statement holds good of a course of action that is dominantly practical, that is, one that consists of overt doings. It is possible to be efficient in action and yet not have a conscious experience. The activity is too automatic to permit of a sense of what it is about and where it is going. It comes to an end but not to a close or consummation in consciousness. Obstacles are overcome by shrewd skill, but they

do not feed experience. There are also those who are waver-
ing in action, uncertain, and inconclusive like the shades in
classic literature. Between the poles of aimlessness and mechanical efficiency, there lie those courses of action in which
through successive deeds there runs a sense of growing meaning conserved and accumulating toward an end that is felt
as accomplishment of a process. Successful politicians and gen-
erals who turn statesmen like Caesar and Napoleon have something of the showman about them. This of itself is not art,
but it is, I think, a sign that interest is not exclusively, perhaps
not mainly, held by the result taken by itself (as it is in the
case of mere efficiency), but by it as the outcome of a process.
There is interest in completing an experience. The experience
may be one that is harmful to the world and its consummation undesirable. But it has esthetic quality.

The Greek identification of good conduct with conduct
having proportion, grace, and harmony, the *kalon-agathon,*
is a more obvious example of distinctive esthetic quality in
moral action. One great defect in what passes as morality is
its anesthetic quality. Instead of exemplifying wholehearted
action, it takes the form of grudging piecemeal concessions to
the demands of duty. But illustrations may only obscure the
fact that any practical activity will, provided that it is integrated and moves by its own urge to fulfillment, have esthetic
quality.

A generalized illustration may be had if we imagine a stone,
which is rolling down hill, to have an experience. The activity
is surely sufficiently "practical." The stone starts from somewhere, and moves, as consistently as conditions permit, toward
a place and state where it will be at rest—toward an end. Let
us add, by imagination, to these external facts, the ideas that
it looks forward with desire to the final outcome; that it is
interested in the things it meets on its way, conditions that
accelerate and retard its movement with respect to their bearing on the end; that it acts and feels toward them according
to the hindering or helping function it attributes to them;
and that the final coming to rest is related to all that went be-

fore as the culmination of a continuous movement. Then the stone would have an experience, and one with esthetic quality.

If we turn from this imaginary case to our own experience, we shall find much of it is nearer to what happens to the actual stone than it is to anything that fulfills the conditions fancy just laid down. For in much of our experience we are not concerned with the connection of one incident with what went before and what comes after. There is no interest that controls attentive rejection or selection of what shall be organized into the developing experience. Things happen, but they are neither definitely included nor decisively excluded; we drift. We yield according to external pressure, or evade and compromise. There are beginnings and cessations, but no genuine initiations and concludings. One thing replaces another, but does not absorb it and carry it on. There is experience, but so slack and discursive that it is not *an* experience. Needless to say, such experiences are anesthetic.

Thus the esthetic [2] lies within two limits. At one pole is the loose succession that does not begin at any particular place and that ends—in the sense of ceasing—at no particular place. At the other pole is arrest, constriction, proceeding from parts having only a mechanical connection with one another. There exists so much of one and the other of these two kinds of experience that unconsciously they come to be taken as norms of all experience. Then, when the esthetic appears, it so sharply contrasts with the picture that has been formed of experience, that it is impossible to combine its special qualities with the features of the picture and the esthetic is given an outside place and status. The account that has been given of experience dominantly intellectual and practical is intended to show that there is no such contrast involved in having an experience; that, on the contrary, no experience of whatever sort is a unity unless it has esthetic quality.

The enemies of the esthetic are neither the practical nor the intellectual. They are the humdrum; slackness of loose

---

[2] [The original text has "non-esthetic," which seems obviously to be a typographical error.—Ed.]

ends; submission to convention in practice and intellectual procedure. Rigid abstinence, coerced submission, tightness on one side and dissipation, incoherence, and aimless indulgence on the other, are deviations in opposite directions from the unity of an experience. Some such considerations perhaps induced Aristotle to invoke the "mean proportional" as the proper designation of what is distinctive of both virtue and the esthetic. He was formally correct. "Mean" and "proportion" are, however, not self-explanatory, nor to be taken over in a prior mathematical sense, but are properties belonging to an experience that has a developing movement toward its own consummation.

I have emphasized the fact that every integral experience moves toward a close, an ending, since it ceases only when the energies active in it have done their proper work. This closure of a circuit of energy is the opposite of arrest, of *stasis*. Maturation and fixation are polar opposites. Struggle and conflict may be themselves enjoyed, although they are painful, when they are experienced as means of developing an experience; members in that they carry it forward, not just because they are there. There is, as will appear later, an element of undergoing, of suffering in its large sense, in every experience. Otherwise there would be no taking in of what preceded. For "taking in" in any vital experience is something more than placing something on the top of consciousness over what was previously known. It involves reconstruction which may be painful. Whether the necessary undergoing phase is by itself pleasurable or painful is a matter of particular conditions. It is indifferent to the total esthetic quality, save that there are few intense esthetic experiences that are wholly gleeful. They are certainly not to be characterized as amusing, and as they bear down upon us they involve a suffering that is none the less consistent with, indeed a part of, the complete perception that is enjoyed.

I have spoken of the esthetic quality that rounds out an experience into completeness and unity as emotional. The reference may cause difficulty. We are given to thinking of emotions as things as simple and compact as are the words by which we name them. Joy, sorrow, hope, fear, anger, curiosity, are treated as if each in itself were a sort of entity that enters full-made upon the scene, an entity that may last a long time or a short time, but whose duration, whose growth and career, is irrelevant to its nature. In fact emotions are qualities, when they are significant, of a complex experience that moves and changes. I say, when they are *significant,* for otherwise they are but the outbreaks and eruptions of a disturbed infant. All emotions are qualifications of a drama and they change as the drama develops. Persons are sometimes said to fall in love at first sight. But what they fall into is not a thing of that instant. What would love be were it compressed into a moment in which there is no room for cherishing and for solicitude? The intimate nature of emotion is manifested in the experience of one watching a play on the stage or reading a novel. It attends the development of a plot; and a plot requires a stage, a space, wherein to develop and time in which to unfold. Experience is emotional but there are no separate things called emotions in it.

By the same token, emotions are attached to events and objects in their movement. They are not, save in pathological instances, private. And even an "objectless" emotion demands something beyond itself to which to attach itself, and thus it soon generates a delusion in lack of something real. Emotion belongs of a certainty to the self. But it belongs to the self that is concerned in the movement of events toward an issue that is desired or disliked. We jump instantaneously when we are scared, as we blush on the instant when we are ashamed. But fright and shamed modesty are not in this case emotional states. Of themselves they are but automatic reflexes. In order to become emotional they must become parts of an inclusive and enduring situation that involves concern for objects and their issues. The jump of fright becomes emotional fear when there is found or thought to exist a threatening object that must be dealt with or escaped from. The blush becomes the emotion of shame when a person connects, in thought, an action he has performed with an unfavorable reaction to himself of some other person.

Physical things from far ends of the earth are physically transported and physically caused to act and react upon one another in the construction of a new object. The miracle of mind is that something similar takes place in experience without physical transport and assembling. Emotion is the moving and cementing force. It selects what is congruous and dyes what is selected with its color, thereby giving qualitative unity to materials externally disparate and dissimilar. It thus provides unity in and through the varied parts of an experience. When the unity is of the sort already described, the experience has esthetic character even though it is not, dominantly, an esthetic experience.

Two men meet; one is the applicant for a position, while the other has the disposition of the matter in his hands. The interview may be mechanical, consisting of set questions, the replies to which perfunctorily settle the matter. There is no experience in which the two men meet, nothing that is not a repetition, by way of acceptance or dismissal, of something which has happened a score of times. The situation is disposed of as if it were an exercise in bookkeeping. But an interplay may take place in which a new experience develops. Where should we look for an account of such an experience? Not to ledger entries nor yet to a treatise on economics or sociology or personnel psychology, but to drama or fiction. Its nature and import can be expressed only by art, because there is a unity of experience that can be expressed only as an experience. The *experience* is of material fraught with suspense and moving toward its own consummation through a connected series of varied incidents. The primary emotions on the part of the applicant may be at the beginning hope or despair, and elation or disappointment at the close. These emotions qualify the experience as a unity. But as the interview proceeds, secondary emotions are evolved as variations of the primary underlying one. It is even possible for each attitude and gesture, each sentence, almost every word, to produce more than a fluctuation in the intensity of the basic emotion; to produce, that is, a change of shade and tint in its quality. The employer sees by means of his own emotional reactions the character of the one applying. He projects him imaginatively into the work to be done and judges his fitness by the way in which the elements of the scene assemble and either clash or fit together. The presence and behavior of the applicant either harmonize with his own attitudes and desires or they conflict and jar. Such factors as these, inherently esthetic in quality, are the forces that carry the varied elements of the interview to a decisive issue. They enter into the settlement of every situation, whatever its dominant nature, in which there are uncertainty and suspense.

There are, therefore, common patterns in various experiences, no matter how unlike they are to one another in the details of their subject matter. There are conditions to be met without which an experience cannot come to be. The outline of the common pattern is set by the fact that every experience is the result of interaction between a live creature and some aspect of the world in which he lives. A man does something; he lifts, let us say, a stone. In consequence he undergoes, suffers, something: the weight, strain, texture of the surface of the thing lifted. The properties thus undergone determine further doing. The stone is too heavy or too angular, not solid enough; or else the properties undergone show it is fit for the use for which it is intended. The process continues until a mutual adaptation of the self and the object emerges and that particular experience comes to a close. What is true of this simple instance is true, as to form, of every experience. The creature operating may be a thinker in his study and the environment with which he interacts may consist of ideas instead of a stone. But interaction of the two constitutes the total experience that is had, and the close which completes it is the institution of a felt harmony.

An experience has pattern and structure, because it is not

just doing and undergoing in alternation, but consists of them in relationship. To put one's hand in the fire that consumes it is not necessarily to have an experience. The action and its consequence must be joined in perception. This relationship is what gives meaning; to grasp it is the objective of all intelligence. The scope and content of the relations measure the significant content of an experience. A child's experience may be intense, but because of lack of background from past experience, relations between undergoing and doing are slightly grasped, and the experience does not have great depth or breadth. No one ever arrives at such maturity that he perceives all the connections that are involved. There was once written (by Mr. Hinton) a romance called "The Unlearner." It portrayed the whole endless duration of life after death as a living over of the incidents that happened in a short life on earth, in continued discovery of the relationships involved among them.

Experience is limited by all the causes which interfere with perception of the relations between undergoing and doing. There may be interference because of excess on the side of doing or of excess on the side of receptivity, of undergoing. Unbalance on either side blurs the perception of relations and leaves the experience partial and distorted, with scant or false meaning. Zeal for doing, lust for action, leaves many a person, especially in this hurried and impatient human environment in which we live, with experience of an almost incredible paucity, all on the surface. No one experience has a chance to complete itself because something else is entered upon so speedily. What is called experience becomes so dispersed and miscellaneous as hardly to deserve the name. Resistance is treated as an obstruction to be beaten down, not as an invitation to reflection. An individual comes to seek, unconsciously even more than by deliberate choice, situations in which he can do the most things in the shortest time.

Experiences are also cut short from maturing by excess of receptivity. What is prized is then the mere undergoing of this and that, irrespective of perception of any meaning. The crowding together of as many impressions as possible is thought to be "life," even though no one of them is more than a flitting and a sipping. The sentimentalist and the daydreamer may have more fancies and impressions pass through their consciousness than has the man who is animated by lust for action. But his experience is equally distorted, because nothing takes root in mind when there is no balance between doing and receiving. Some decisive action is needed in order to establish contact with the realities of the world and in order that impressions may be so related to facts that their value is tested and organized.

Because perception of relationship between what is done and what is undergone constitutes the work of intelligence, and because the artist is controlled in the process of his work by his grasp of the connection between what he has already done and what he is to do next, the idea that the artist does not think as intently and penetratingly as a scientific inquirer is absurd. A painter must consciously undergo the effect of his every brush stroke or he will not be aware of what he is doing and where his work is going. Moreover, he has to see each particular connection of doing and undergoing in relation to the whole that he desires to produce. To apprehend such relations is to think, and is one of the most exacting modes of thought. The difference between the pictures of different painters is due quite as much to differences of capacity to carry on this thought as it is to differences of sensitivity to bare color and to differences in dexterity of execution. As respects the basic quality of pictures, difference depends, indeed, more upon the quality of intelligence brought to bear upon perception of relations than upon anything else—though of course intelligence cannot be separated from direct sensitivity and is connected, though in a more external manner, with skill.

Any idea that ignores the necessary role of intelligence in production of works of art is based upon identification of thinking with use of one special kind of material, verbal signs and words. To think effectively in terms of relations of qualities is as severe a demand upon thought as to think in terms of symbols, verbal and mathematical. Indeed, since words are easily manipulated in mechanical ways, the production of a work of genuine art probably demands more intelligence than does most of the so-called thinking that goes on among those who pride themselves on being "intellectuals."

I have tried to show in these chapters that the esthetic is no intruder in experience from without, whether by way of idle luxury or transcendent ideality, but that it is the clarified and intensified development of traits that belong to every normally complete experience. This fact I take to be the only secure basis upon which esthetic theory can build. It remains to suggest some of the implications of the underlying fact.

We have no word in the English language that unambiguously includes what is signified by the two words "artistic" and "esthetic." Since "artistic" refers primarily to the act of production and "esthetic" to that of perception and enjoyment, the absence of a term designating the two processes taken together is unfortunate. Sometimes, the effect is to separate the two from each other, to regard art as something superimposed upon esthetic material, or, upon the other side, to an assumption that, since art is a process of creation, perception and enjoyment of it have nothing in common with the creative act. In any case, there is a certain verbal awkwardness in that we are compelled sometimes to use the term "esthetic" to cover the entire field and sometimes to limit it to the receiving perceptual aspect of the whole operation. I refer to these obvious facts as preliminary to an attempt to show how the conception of conscious experience as a perceived relation between doing and undergoing enables us to understand the connection that art as production and perception and appreciation as enjoyment sustain to each other.

Art denotes a process of doing or making. This is as true of fine as of technological art. Art involves molding of clay, chipping of marble, casting of bronze, laying on of pigments, construction of buildings, singing of songs, playing of instruments, enacting roles on the stage, going through rhythmic movements in the dance. Every art does something with some physical material, the body or something outside the body, with or without the use of intervening tools, and with a view to production of something visible, audible, or tangible. So marked is the active or "doing" phase of art, that the dictionaries usually define it in terms of skilled action, ability in execution. The Oxford Dictionary illustrates by a quotation from John Stuart Mill: "Art is an endeavor after perfection in execution," while Matthew Arnold calls it "pure and flawless workmanship."

The word "esthetic" refers, as we have already noted, to experience as appreciative, perceiving, and enjoying. It denotes the consumer's rather than the producer's standpoint. It is Gusto, taste; and, as with cooking, overt skillful action is on the side of the cook who prepares, while taste is on the side of the consumer, as in gardening there is a distinction between the gardener who plants and tills and the householder who enjoys the finished product.

These very illustrations, however, as well as the relation that exists in having an experience between doing and undergoing, indicate that the distinction between esthetic and artistic cannot be pressed so far as to become a separation. Perfection in execution cannot be measured or defined in terms of execution; it implies those who perceive and enjoy the product that is executed. The cook prepares food for the consumer and the measure of the value of what is prepared is found in consumption. Mere perfection in execution, judged in its own terms in isolation, can probably be attained better by a machine than by human art. By itself, it is at most technique, and there are great artists who are not in the first ranks as technicians (witness Cézanne), just as there are great performers on the piano who are not great esthetically, and as Sargent is not a great painter.

Craftmanship to be artistic in the final sense must be "loving"; it must care deeply for the subject matter upon which skill is exercised. A sculptor comes to mind whose busts are marvelously exact. It might be difficult to tell in the presence of a photograph of one of them and of a photograph of the original which was of the person himself. For virtuosity they are remarkable. But one doubts whether the maker of the busts had an experience of his own that he was concerned to have those share who look at his products. To be truly artistic, a work must also be esthetic—that is, framed for enjoyed receptive perception. Constant observation is, of course, necessary for the maker while he is producing. But if his perception is not also esthetic in nature, it is a colorless and cold recognition of what has been done, used as a stimulus to the next step in a process that is essentially mechanical.

In short, art, in its form, unites the very same relation of doing and undergoing, outgoing and incoming energy, that makes an experience to be an experience. Because of elimination of all that does not contribute to mutual organization of the factors of both action and reception into one another, and because of selection of just the aspects and traits that contribute to their interpenetration of each other, the product is a work of esthetic art. Man whittles, carves, sings, dances, gestures, molds, draws and paints. The doing or making is artistic when the perceived result is of such a nature that *its* qualities *as perceived* have controlled the question of production. The act of producing that is directed by intent to produce something that is enjoyed in the immediate experience of perceiving has qualities that a spontaneous or uncontrolled activity does not have. The artist embodies in himself the attitude of the perceiver while he works.

Suppose, for the sake of illustration, that a finely wrought object, one whose texture and proportions are highly pleasing in perception, has been believed to be a product of some primitive people. Then there is discovered evidence that proves it to be an accidental natural product. As an external thing, it is now precisely what it was before. Yet at once it ceases to be a work of art and becomes a natural "curiosity." It now belongs in a museum of natural history, not in a museum of art. And the extraordinary thing is that the difference that is thus made is not one of just intellectual classification. A difference is made in appreciative perception and in a direct way. The esthetic experience—in its limited sense—is thus seen to be inherently connected with the experience of making.

The sensory satisfaction of eye and ear, when esthetic, is so because it does not stand by itself but is linked to the activity of which it is the consequence. Even the pleasures of the palate are different in quality to an epicure than [to] one who merely "likes" his food as he eats it. The difference is not of mere intensity. The epicure is conscious of much more than the taste of the food. Rather, there enter into the taste, as directly experienced, qualities that depend upon reference to its source and its manner of production in connection with criteria of excellence. As production must absorb into itself qualities of the product as perceived and be regulated by them, so, on the other side, seeing, hearing, tasting, become esthetic when relation to a distinct manner of activity qualifies what is perceived.

There is an element of passion in all esthetic perception. Yet when we are overwhelmed by passion, as in extreme rage, fear, jealousy, the experience is definitely non-esthetic. There is no relationship felt to the qualities of the activity that has generated the passion. Consequently, the material of the experience lacks elements of balance and proportion. For these can be present only when, as in the conduct that has grace or dignity, the act is controlled by an exquisite sense of the relations which the act sustains—its fitness to the occasion and to the situation.

The process of art in production is related to the esthetic in perception organically—as the Lord God in creation surveyed his work and found it good. Until the artist is satisfied in perception with what he is doing, he continues shaping and reshaping. The making comes to an end when its result is experienced as good—and that experience comes not by mere intellectual and outside judgment but in direct perception. An artist, in comparison with his fellows, is one who is not only specially gifted in powers of execution but in unusual sensitivity to the qualities of things. This sensitivity also directs his doings and makings.

As we manipulate, we touch and feel; as we look, we see; as we listen, we hear. The hand moves with etching needle or with brush. The eye attends and reports the consequence of what is done. Because of this intimate connection, subsequent doing is cumulative and not a matter of caprice nor yet of routine. In an emphatic artistic-esthetic experience, the relation is so close that it controls simultaneously both the doing and the perception. Such vital intimacy of connection cannot be had if only hand and eye are engaged. When they do not, both of them, act as organs of the whole being, there is but a mechanical sequence of sense and movement, as in walking that is automatic. Hand and eye, when the experience is esthetic, are but instruments through which the entire live creature, moved and active throughout, operates. Hence the expression is emotional and guided by purpose.

Because of the relation between what is done and what is undergone, there is an immediate sense of things in perception as belonging together or as jarring; as re-enforcing or as interfering. The consequences of the act of making as reported in sense show whether what is done carries forward the idea being executed or marks a deviation and break. In as far as the development of an experience is *controlled* through reference to these immediately felt relations of order and fulfillment, that experience becomes dominantly esthetic in nature. The urge to action becomes an urge to that kind of action which will result in an object satisfying in direct perception. The potter shapes his clay to make a bowl useful for holding grain; but he makes it in a way so regulated by the series of perceptions that sum up the serial acts of making, that the bowl is marked by enduring grace and charm. The general situation remains the same in painting a picture or molding a bust. Moreover, at each stage there is anticipation of what is to come. This anticipation is the connecting link between the next doing and its outcome for sense. What is done and what

is undergone are thus reciprocally, cumulatively, and continu
ously instrumental to each other.

The doing may be energetic, and the undergoing may b
acute and intense. But unless they are related to each other t
form a whole in perception, the thing done is not full
esthetic. The making for example may be a display of tech
nical virtuosity, and the undergoing a gush of sentiment of
revery. If the artist does not perfect a new vision in h
process of doing, he acts mechanically and repeats some ol
model fixed like a blueprint in his mind. An incredibl
amount of observation and of the kind of intelligence that
exercised in perception of qualitative relations characterize
creative work in art. The relations must be noted not onl
with respect to one another, two by two, but in connectio
with the whole under construction; they are exercised i
imagination as well as in observation. Irrelevancies arise tha
are tempting distractions; digressions suggest themselves in th
guise of enrichments. There are occasions when the grasp c
the dominant idea grows faint, and then the artist is move
unconsciously to fill in until his thought grows strong agaii
The real work of an artist is to build up an experience that
coherent in perception while moving with constant change i
its development.

When an author puts on paper ideas that are already clearl
conceived and consistently ordered, the real work has bee
previously done. Or, he may depend upon the greater pe
ceptibility induced by the activity and its sensible report t
direct his completion of the work. The mere act of transcrip
tion is esthetically irrelevant save as it enters integrally int
the formation of an experience moving to completeness. Eve
the composition conceived in the head and, therefore, phys
cally private, is public in its significant content, since it
conceived with reference to execution in a product that
perceptible and hence belongs to the common world. Othei
wise it would be an aberration or a passing dream. The urg
to express through painting the perceived qualities of
landscape is continuous with demand for pencil or brusl

Without external embodiment, an experience remains incomplete; physiologically and functionally, sense organs are motor organs and are connected, by means of distribution of energies in the human body and not merely anatomically, with other motor organs. It is no linguistic accident that "building," "construction," "work," designate both a process and its finished product. Without the meaning of the verb that of the noun remains blank.

Writer, composer of music, sculptor, or painter can retrace, during the process of production, what they have previously done. When it is not satisfactory in the undergoing or perceptual phase of experience, they can to some degree start fresh. This retracing is not readily accomplished in the case of architecture—which is perhaps one reason why there are so many ugly buildings. Architects are obliged to complete their idea before its translation into a complete object of perception takes place. Inability to build up simultaneously the idea and its objective embodiment imposes a handicap. Nevertheless, they too are obliged to think out their ideas in terms of the medium of embodiment and the object of ultimate perception unless they work mechanically and by rote. Probably the esthetic quality of medieval cathedrals is due in some measure to the fact that their constructions were not so much controlled by plans and specifications made in advance as is now the case. Plans grew as the building grew. But even a Minerva-like product, if it is artistic, presupposes a prior period of gestation in which doings and perceptions projected in imagination interact and mutually modify one another. Every work of art follows the plan of, and pattern of, a complete experience, rendering it more intensely and concentratedly felt.

It is not so easy in the case of the perceiver and appreciator to understand the intimate union of doing and undergoing as it is in the case of the maker. We are given to supposing that the former merely takes in what is there in finished form, instead of realizing that this taking in involves activities that are comparable to those of the creator. But receptivity is not passivity. It, too, is a process consisting of a series of responsive acts that accumulate toward objective fulfillment. Otherwise, there is not perception but recognition. The difference between the two is immense. Recognition is perception arrested before it has a chance to develop freely. In recognition there is a beginning of an act of perception. But this beginning is not allowed to serve the development of a full perception of the thing recognized. It is arrested at the point where it will serve some *other* purpose, as we recognize a man on the street in order to greet or to avoid him, not so as to see him for the sake of seeing what is there.

In recognition we fall back, as upon a stereotype, upon some previously formed scheme. Some detail or arrangement of details serves as a cue for bare identification. It suffices in recognition to apply this bare outline as a stencil to the present object. Sometimes in contact with a human being we are struck with traits, perhaps of only physical characteristics, of which we were not previously aware. We realize that we never knew the person before; we had not seen him in any pregnant sense. We now begin to study and to "take in." Perception replaces bare recognition. There is an act of reconstructive doing, and consciousness becomes fresh and alive. *This* act of seeing involves the co-operation of motor elements even though they remain implicit and do not become overt, as well as co-operation of all funded ideas that may serve to complete the new picture that is forming. Recognition is too easy to arouse vivid consciousness. There is not enough resistance between new and old to secure consciousness of the experience that is had. Even a dog that barks and wags his tail joyously on seeing his master return is more fully alive in his reception of his friend than is a human being who is content with mere recognition.

Bare recognition is satisfied when a proper tag or label is attached, "proper" signifying one that serves a purpose outside the act of recognition—as a salesman identifies wares by a sample. It involves no stir of the organism, no inner commotion. But an act of perception proceeds by waves that extend serially throughout the entire organism. There is, therefore, no such thing in perception as seeing or hearing *plus* emotion. The perceived object or scene is emotionally pervaded throughout. When an aroused emotion does not permeate the material that is perceived or thought of, it is either preliminary or pathological.

The esthetic or undergoing phase of experience is receptive. It involves surrender. But adequate yielding of the self is possible only through a controlled activity that may well be intense. In much of our intercourse with our surroundings we withdraw; sometimes from fear, if only of expending unduly our store of energy; sometimes from preoccupation with other matters, as in the case of recognition. Perception is an act of the going-out of energy in order to receive, not a withholding of energy. To steep ourselves in a subject matter we have first to plunge into it. When we are only passive to a scene, it overwhelms us and, for lack of answering activity, we do not perceive that which bears us down. We must summon energy and pitch it at a responsive key in order to *take* in.

Every one knows that it requires apprenticeship to see through a microscope or telescope, and to see a landscape as the geologist sees it. The idea that esthetic perception is an affair for odd moments is one reason for the backwardness of the arts among us. The eye and the visual apparatus may be intact; the object may be physically there, the cathedral of Notre Dame, or Rembrandt's portrait of Hendrik Stoeffel. In some bald sense, the latter may be "seen." They may be looked at, possibly recognized, and have their correct names attached. But for lack of continuous interaction between the total organism and the objects, they are not perceived, certainly not esthetically. A crowd of visitors steered through a picture gallery by a guide, with attention called here and there to some high point, does not perceive; only by accident is there even interest in seeing a picture for the sake of subject matter vividly realized.

For to perceive, a beholder must *create* his own experience. And his creation must include relations comparable to those which the original producer underwent. They are not the same in any literal sense. But with the perceiver, as with the artist, there must be an ordering of the elements of the whole that is in form, although not in details, the same as the process of organization the creator of the work consciously experienced. Without an act of recreation the object is not perceived as a work of art. The artist selected, simplified, clarified, abridged and condensed according to his interest. The beholder must go through these operations according to his point of view and interest. In both, an act of abstraction, that is of extraction of what is significant, takes place. In both, there is comprehension in its literal signification—that is, a gathering together of details and particulars physically scattered into an experienced whole. There is work done on the part of the percipient as there is on the part of the artist. The one who is too lazy, idle, or indurated in convention to perform this work will not see or hear. His "appreciation" will be a mixture of scraps of learning with conformity to norms of conventional admiration and with a confused, even if genuine, emotional excitation.

The considerations that have been presented imply both the community and the unlikeness, because of specific emphasis, of *an* experience, in its pregnant sense, and esthetic experience. The former has esthetic quality; otherwise its materials would not be rounded out into a single coherent experience. It is not possible to divide in a vital experience the practical, emotional, and intellectual from one another and to set the properties of one over against the characteristics of the others. The emotional phase binds parts together into a single whole; "intellectual" simply names the fact that the experience has meaning; "practical" indicates that the organism is interacting with events and objects which surround it. The most elaborate philosophic or scientific inquiry and the most ambitious industrial or political enterprise has, when its different in-

redients constitute an integral experience, esthetic quality.
'or then its varied parts are linked to one another, and do
not merely succeed one another. And the parts through their
xperienced linkage move toward a consummation and close,
not merely to cessation in time. This consummation, moreover, does not wait in consciousness for the whole undertaking
o be finished. It is anticipated throughout and is recurrently
avored with special intensity.

Nevertheless, the experiences in question are dominantly
ntellectual or practical, rather than *distinctively* esthetic, be-
ause of the interest and purpose that initiate and control
hem. In an intellectual experience, the conclusion has value
on its own account. It can be extracted as a formula or as a
'truth," and can be used in its independent entirety as factor
and guide in other inquiries. In a work of art there is no such
ingle self-sufficient deposit. The end, the terminus, is significant not by itself but as the integration of the parts. It has no
other existence. A drama or novel is not the final sentence,
even if the characters are disposed of as living happily ever
after. In a distinctively esthetic experience, characteristics that
are subdued in other experiences are dominant; those that are
subordinate are controlling—namely, the characteristics in
virtue of which the experience is an integrated complete experience on its own account.

In every integral experience there is form because there is
dynamic organization. I call the organization dynamic because
it takes time to complete it, because it is a growth. There is
inception, development, fulfillment. Material is ingested and
digested through interaction with that vital organization of
the results of prior experience that constitutes the mind of the
worker. Incubation goes on until what is conceived is brought
forth and is rendered perceptible as part of the common
world. An esthetic experience can be crowded into a moment
only in the sense that a climax of prior long-enduring
processes may arrive in an outstanding movement which so
sweeps everything else into it that all else is forgotten. That

which distinguishes an experience as esthetic is conversion of resistance and tensions, of excitations that in themselves are temptations to diversion, into a movement toward an inclusive and fulfilling close.

Experiencing like breathing is a rhythm of intakings and outgivings. Their succession is punctuated and made a rhythm by the existence of intervals, periods in which one phase is ceasing and the other is inchoate and preparing. William James aptly compared the course of a conscious experience to the alternate flights and perchings of a bird. The flights and perchings are intimately connected with one another; they are not so many unrelated lightings succeeded by a number of equally unrelated hoppings. Each resting place in experience is an undergoing in which is absorbed and taken home the consequences of prior doing, and, unless the doing is that of utter caprice or sheer routine, each doing carries in itself meaning that has been extracted and conserved. As with the advance of an army, all gains from what has been already effected are periodically consolidated, and always with a view to what is to be done next. If we move too rapidly, we get away from the base of supplies—of accrued meanings—and the experience is flustered, thin, and confused. If we dawdle too long after having extracted a net value, experience perishes of inanition.

The *form* of the whole is therefore present in every member. Fulfilling, consummating, are continuous functions, not mere ends, located at one place only. An engraver, painter, or writer is in process of completing at every stage of his work. He must at each point retain and sum up what has gone before as a whole and with reference to a whole to come. Otherwise there is no consistency and no security in his successive acts. The series of doings in the rhythm of experience give variety and movement; they save the work from monotony and useless repetitions. The undergoings are the corresponding elements in the rhythm, and they supply unity; they save the work from the aimlessness of a mere succession of excitations. An object is peculiarly and dominantly esthetic, yielding the enjoyment characteristic of esthetic perception, when the factors that determine anything which can be called *an* experience are lifted high above the threshold of perception and are made manifest for their own sake.

VIII

QUALITATIVE THOUGHT[1]

One of the most original and basic features of Dewey's philosophy is his theory of quality. Qualities per se are *had* or directly experienced. Qualities are not simply located in a subject or object: they are "in" a situation or context. There are tertiary or pervasive qualities which bind together the constituents of a situation and set it off from the rest of experience. And in a developing situation, a pervasive and underlying quality exerts a regulative influence on the direction of its development. The theory of quality is the key to understanding Dewey's contextualism; it is a pervasive quality that unifies an experiential situation and makes it more than an aggregate of discrete entities and something less than an all-encompassing Absolute. The theory of quality is also the basis of Dewey's critique of the subject-object dichotomy; qualities in their existential occurrence are neither subjective nor objective. The theory is also at the heart of his criticism of the doctrine of immediate knowledge which confuses *having*, i.e., directly experiencing a quality, and *knowing*. Quality is essential, too, for understanding the "problematic situation"; in such a situation there is an underlying quality of indeterminateness which guides the direction of the inquiry and is transformed in a successful inquiry. Dewey's theory of value, including ethical, aesthetic, and religious values, is based on this concept of a quality which can pervade and condition our experiences. In the following article Dewey explores the ramifications of "the logic of qualitative thinking."

THE WORLD in which we immediately live, that in which we strive, succeed, and are defeated is pre-eminently a qualitative world. What we act for, suffer, and enjoy are things in their qualitative determinations. This world forms the field of characteristic modes of thinking, characteristic in

[1] Originally published in *The Symposium*, I (1930), 5-32.

that thought is definitely regulated by qualitative considerations. Were it not for the double and hence ambiguous sense of the term "common sense," it might be said that common-sense thinking, that concerned with action and its consequences, whether undergone in enjoyment or suffering, is qualitative. But since "common-sense" is also used to designate accepted traditions and is appealed to in support of them, it is safe at the outset to refer simply to that thought which has to do with objects involved in the concerns and issues of living.

The problem of qualitative objects has influenced metaphysics and epistemology but has not received corresponding attention in logical theory. The propositions significant in physical science are oblivious of qualitative considerations as such; they deal with "primary qualities" in distinction from secondary and tertiary; in actual treatment, moreover, these primary qualities are not qualities but relations. Consider the difference between movement as qualitative alteration, and motion as $F = ma$; between stress as involving effort and tension, and as force per unit surface; between the red of the blood issuing from a wound, and red as signifying 400 trillion vibrations per time unit. Metaphysics has been concerned with the existential status of qualitative objects as contrasted with those of physical science, while epistemology, having frequently decided that qualities are subjective and psychical, has been concerned with their relation in knowing to the properties of "external" objects defined in non-qualitative terms.

But a logical problem remains. What is the relation or lack of relations between the two types of propositions, one which refers to objects of physical science and the other to qualitative objects? What, if any, are the distinguishing logical marks of each kind? If it were true that things as things, apart from interaction with an organism, are qualityless, the logical problem would remain. For the truth would concern the mode of production and existence of qualitative things. It is irrelevant to their logical status. Logic can hardly admit that it is concerned only with objects having one special mode of production and existence, and yet claim universality. And it would be fatal to the claims of logic to say that because qualities are psychical—supposing for the moment that they are—therefore logical theory has nothing to do with forms of thought characteristic of qualitative objects. It is even possible that some of the difficulties of metaphysical and epistemological theory about scientific and ordinary objects spring from neglect of a basic logical treatment.

A preliminary introduction to the topic may be found in the fact that Aristotelian logic, which still passes current nominally, is a logic based upon the idea that qualitative objects are existential in the fullest sense. To retain logical principles based on this conception along with the acceptance of theories of existence and knowledge based on an opposite conception is not, to say the least, conductive to clearness—a consideration that has a good deal to do with the existing dualism between traditional and the newer relational logics. A more obviously pertinent consideration is the fact that the interpretation of classic logic treats qualitative determinations as fixed properties of objects, and thus is committed to either an attributive or a classificatory doctrine of the import of propositions. Take the proposition: "The red Indian is stoical." This is interpreted either as signifying that the Indian in question is characterized by the property of stoicism in addition to that of redness, or that he belongs to the class of stoical objects. The ordinary direct sense of the proposition escapes recognition in either case. For this sense expresses the fact that the indigenous American was permeated throughout by a certain quality, instead of being an object possessing a certain quality along with others. He lived, acted, endured stoically.

If one thinks that the difference between the two meanings has no logical import, let him reflect that the whole current subject-predication theory of propositions is affected by the "property" notion, whether the theory speaks in the language of attribution or classification. A subject is "given"—ultimately apart from thinking—and then thought adds to what is given a further determination or else assigns it to a ready-made class of things. Neither theory can have any place for the integral development and reconstruction of subject matter effected by the thought expressed in propositions. In effect it excludes thought from any share in the determination of the subject matter of knowledge, confining it to setting forth the results (whether conceived as attributive or classificatory) of knowledge already attained in isolation from the method by which it is attained.

Perhaps, however, the consideration that will appeal to most people is the fact that the neglect of qualitative objects and considerations leaves thought in certain subjects without any logical status and control. In esthetic matters, in morals and politics, the effect of this neglect is either to deny (implicitly at least) that they have logical foundation or else, in order to bring them under received logical categories, to evacuate them of their distinctive meaning—a procedure which produces the myth of the "economic man" and the reduction of esthetics and morals, as far as they can receive any intellectual treatment at all, to quasi-mathematical subjects.

Consider for example a picture that is a work of art and not just a chromo or other mode of mechanical product. Its quality is not a property which it possesses in addition to its other properties. It is something which externally demarcates it from other paintings, and which internally pervades, colors, tones, and weights every detail and every relation of the work of art. The same thing is true of the "quality" of a person or of historic events. We follow, with apparently complete understanding, a tale in which a certain quality or character is ascribed to a certain man. But something said causes us to interject, "Oh, you are speaking of Thomas Jones, I supposed you meant John Jones." Every detail related, every distinction set forth remains just what it was before. Yet the significance, the color and weight, of every detail is altered. For the quality that runs through them all, that gives meaning to each and binds them together, is transformed.

Now my point is that unless such underlying and pervasive qualitative determinations are acknowledged in a distinct logical formulation, one or other of two results is bound to follow. Either thought is denied to the subject matter in question and the phenomena are attributed to "intuition" or "genius" or "impulse" or "personality" as ultimate and unanalyzable entities; or, worse yet, intellectual analysis is reduced to a mechanical enumeration of isolated items or "properties." As a matter of fact, such intellectual definiteness and coherence as the objects and criticisms of esthetic and moral subjects possess is due to their being controlled by the quality of subject matter as a whole. Consideration of the meaning of regulation by an underlying and pervasive quality is the theme of this article.

What is intended may be indicated by drawing a distinction between something called a "situation" and something termed an "object." By the term situation in this connection is signified the fact that the subject matter ultimately referred to in existential propositions is a complex existence that is held together, in spite of its internal complexity, by the fact that it is dominated and characterized throughout by a single quality. By "object" is meant some element in the complex whole that is defined in abstraction from the whole of which it is a distinction. The special point made is that the selective determination and relation of objects in thought is controlled by reference to a situation—to that which is constituted by a pervasive and internally integrating quality, so that failure to acknowledge the situation leaves, in the end, the logical force of objects and their relations inexplicable.

Now in current logical formulations, the beginning is always made with "objects." If we take the proposition "the stone is shaly," the logical import of the proposition is treated as if something called "stone" had complete intellectual import in and of itself and then some property, having equally a fixed content in isolation, "shaly" is attributed to it. No such self-sufficient and self-enclosed entity can possibly lead anywhere nor be led to; connection among such entities is mechanical and arbitrary, not intellectual. Any proposition about "stone" or "shaly" would have to be analytic in the Kantian sense, merely stating part of the content already known to be contained in the meaning of the terms. That a tautological proposition is a proposition only in name is well recognized. In fact, "stone," "shaly" (or whatever are subject and predicate) are determinations or distinctions instituted within the total subject matter to which thought refers. When such propositions figure in logical textbooks, the actual subject matter referred to is some branch of logical theory which is exemplified in the proposition.

This larger and inclusive subject matter is what is meant by the term "situation." Two further points follow. The situation as such is not and cannot be stated or made explicit. It is taken for granted, "understood," or implicit in all propositional symbolization. It forms the universe of discourse of whatever is expressly stated or of what appears as a term in a proposition. The situation cannot present itself as an element in a proposition any more than a universe of discourse can appear as a member of discourse within that universe. To call it "implicit" does not signify that it is implied. It is present throughout as that of which whatever is explicitly stated or propounded is a distinction. A quart bowl cannot be held within itself or in any of its contents. It may, however, be contained in another bowl, and similarly what is the "situation" in one proposition may appear as a term in *another* proposition—that is, in connection with some *other* situation to which thought now refers.

Secondly, the situation controls the terms of thought; for they are *its* distinctions, and applicability to it is the ultimate test of their validity. It is this phase of the matter which is suggested by the earlier use of the idea of a pervasive and underlying quality. If the quart container affected the import of everything held within it, there would be a physical analogy; a consideration that may be awkwardly hinted at by the case of a person protesting to a salesman that he has not received a full quart; the deficiency affects everything that he has purchased. A work of art provides an apter illustration. In it, as we have already noted, the quality of the whole permeates, affects, and controls every detail. There are paintings, buildings, novels, arguments, in which an observer notes an inability of the author to sustain a unified attention throughout. The details fall to pieces; they are not distinctions of one subject matter, because there is no qualitative unity underlying them. Confusion and incoherence are always marks of lack of control by a single pervasive quality. The latter alone enables a person to keep track of what he is doing, saying, hearing, reading, in whatever explicitly appears. The underlying unity of qualitativeness regulates pertinence or relevancy and force of every distinction and relation; it guides selection and rejection and the manner of utilization of all explicit terms. This quality enables us to keep thinking about one problem without our having constantly to stop to ask ourselves what it is after all that we are thinking about. We are aware of it not by itself but as the background, the thread, and the directive clue in what we do expressly think of. For the latter things are *its* distinctions and relations.[2]

If we designate this permeating qualitative unity in psychological language, we say it is felt rather than thought. Then, if we hypostatize it, we call it *a* feeling. But to term it a feeling is to reverse the actual state of affairs. The existence of unifying qualitativeness in the subject matter defines the meaning of "feeling." The notion that "a feeling" designates a ready-made independent psychical entity is a product of a reflection which presupposes the direct presence of quality as such. "Feeling" and "felt" are names for a *relation* of quality. When, for example, anger exists, it is the pervading tone, color, and quality of persons, things, and circumstances, or of

[2] The "fringe" of James seems to me to be a somewhat unfortunate way of expressing the role of the underlying qualitative character that constitutes a situation—unfortunate because the metaphor tends to treat it as an additional element instead of an all-pervasive influence in determining other contents.

a situation. When angry we are not aware of anger but of these objects in their immediate and unique qualities. In another situation, anger may appear as a distinct term, and analysis may then call it a feeling or emotion. But we have now shifted the universe of discourse, and the validity of the terms of the latter one depends upon the existence of the direct quality of the whole in a former one. That is, in saying that something was *felt,* not thought of, we are analyzing, in a new situation having its own immediate quality, the subject matter of a prior situation; we are making anger an object of analytic examination, not being angry.

When it is said that I have a feeling, or impression, or "hunch," that things are thus and so, what is actually designated is primarily the presence of a dominating quality in a situation as a whole, not just the existence of a feeling as a psychical or psychological fact. To say I have a feeling or impression that so and so is the case is to note that the quality in question is not yet resolved into determinate terms and relations; it marks a conclusion without statement of the reasons for it, the grounds upon which it rests. It is the first stage in the development of explicit distinctions. All thought in every subject begins with just such an unanalyzed whole. When the subject matter is reasonably familiar, relevant distinctions speedily offer themselves, and sheer qualitativeness may not remain long enough to be readily recalled. But it often persists and forms a haunting and engrossing problem. It is a commonplace that a problem *stated* is well on its way to solution, for statement of the nature of a problem signifies that the underlying quality is being transformed into determinate distinctions of terms and relations or has become an object of articulate thought. But something presents itself as problematic before there is recognition of *what* the problem is. The problem is had or experienced before it can be stated or set forth; but it is had as an immediate quality of the whole situation. The sense of something problematic, of something perplexing and to be resolved, marks the presence of something pervading all elements and considerations.

Thought is the operation by which it is converted into pertinent and coherent terms.

The word "intuition" has many meanings. But in its popular, as distinct from refined philosophic usage, it is closely connected with the single qualitativeness underlying all the details of explicit reasoning. It may be relatively dumb and inarticulate and yet penetrating; unexpressed in definite ideas which form reasons and justifications and yet profoundly right. To my mind, Bergson's contention that intuition precedes conception and goes deeper is correct. Reflection and rational elaboration spring from and make explicit a prior intuition. But there is nothing mystical about this fact, and it does not signify that there are two modes of knowledge, one of which is appropriate to one kind of subject matter, and the other mode to the other kind. Thinking and theorizing about physical matters set out from an intuition, and reflection about affairs of life and mind consists in an ideational and conceptual transformation of what begins as an intuition. Intuition, in short, signifies the realization of a pervasive quality such that it regulates the determination of relevant distinctions or of whatever, whether in the way of terms or relations, becomes the accepted object of thought.

While some ejaculations and interjections are merely organic responses, there are those which have an intellectual import, though only context and the total situation can decide to which class a particular ejaculation belongs. "Alas," "Yes," "No," "Oh" may each of them be the symbol of an integrated attitude toward the quality of a situation as a whole; that it is thoroughly pitiful, acceptable, to be rejected, or is a matter of complete surprise. In this case, they characterize the existent situation and as such have a cognitive import. The exclamation "Good!" may mark a deep apprehension of the quality of a piece of acting on the stage, of a deed performed, or of a picture in its wealth of content. The actual judgment may find better expression in these symbols than in a long-winded disquisition. To many persons there is something artificial and repellent in discoursing about any consummatory event or object. It speaks so completely for itself that words are poor substitutes—not that thought fails, but that thought so completely grasps the dominant quality that translation into explicit terms gives a partial and inadequate result.

Such ejaculatory judgments supply perhaps the simplest example of qualitative thought in its purity. While they are primitive, it does not follow that they are always superficial and immature. Sometimes, indeed, they express an infantile mode of intellectual response. But they may also sum up and integrate prolonged previous experience and training, and bring to a unified head the results of severe and consecutive reflection. Only the situation symbolized and not the formal and propositional symbol can decide which is the case. The full content of meaning is best apprehended in the case of the judgment of the esthetic expert in the presence of a work of art. But they come at the beginning and at the close of every scientific investigation. These open with the "Oh" of wonder and terminate with the "Good" of a rounded-out and organized situation. Neither the "Oh" nor the "Good" expresses a mere state of personal feeling. Each characterizes a subject matter. "How beautiful" symbolizes neither a state of feeling nor the supervening of an external essence upon a state of existence but marks the realized appreciation of a pervading quality that is now translated into a system of definite and coherent terms. Language fails not because thought fails, but because no verbal symbols can do justice to the fullness and richness of thought. If we are to continue talking about "data" in any other sense than as reflective distinctions, the original datum is always such a qualitative whole.

The logic of artistic construction is worth more than a passing notice, whether its product be a painting, a symphony, a statue, a building, a drama, or a novel. So far as it is not evidence of conceit on the part of a specialized class, refusal to admit thought and logic on the part of those who make these constructions is evidence of the breakdown of traditional logic. There are (as we previously noted) alleged works of art in which parts do not hang together and in which the quality of one part does not reinforce and expand the quality of every other part. But this fact is itself a manifestation of the defective character of the thought involved in their production. It illustrates by contrast the nature of such works as are genuine intellectual and logical wholes. In the latter, the underlying quality that defines the work, that circumscribes it externally and integrates it internally, controls the thinking of the artist; his logic is the logic of what I have called qualitative thinking.

Upon subsequent analysis, we term the properties of a work of art by such names as symmetry, harmony, rhythm, measure, and proportion. These may, in some cases at least, be formulated mathematically. But the apprehension of these formal relationships is not primary for either the artist or the appreciative spectator. The subject matter formulated by these terms is primarily qualitative, and is apprehended qualitatively. Without an independent qualitative apprehension, the characteristics of a work of art can be translated into explicit harmonies, symmetries, etc., only in a way which substitutes mechanical formulae for esthetic quality. The value of any such translation in esthetic criticism is measured, moreover, by the extent to which the propositional statements return to effect a heightening and deepening of a qualitative apprehension. Otherwise, esthetic appreciation is replaced by judgment of isolated technique.

The logic of artistic construction and esthetic appreciation is peculiarly significant because they exemplify in accentuated and purified form the control of selection of detail and of mode of relation, or integration, by a qualitative whole. The underlying quality demands certain distinctions, and the degree in which the demand is met confers upon the work of art that necessary or inevitable character which is its mark. Formal necessities, such as can be made explicit, depend upon the material necessity imposed by the pervasive and underlying quality. Artistic thought is not however unique in this respect but only shows an intensification of a characteristic of all thought. In a looser way, it is a characteristic of all non-technical, non-"scientific" thought. Scientific thought is, in its turn, a specialized form of art, with its own qualitative control. The more formal and mathematical science becomes, the more it is controlled by sensitiveness to a special kind of qualitative considerations. Failure to realize the qualitative and artistic nature of formal scientific construction is due to two causes. One is conventional, the habit of associating art and esthetic appreciation with a few popularly recognized forms. The other cause is the fact that a student is so concerned with the mastery of symbolic or propositional forms that he fails to recognize and to repeat the creative operations involved in their construction. Or, when they are mastered, he is more concerned with their further application than with realization of their intrinsic intellectual meaning.

The foregoing remarks are intended to suggest the significance to be attached to the term "qualitative thought." But as statements they are propositions and hence symbolic. Their meaning can be apprehended only by going beyond them, by using them as clues to call up qualitative situations. When an experience of the latter is had and they are relived, the realities corresponding to the propositions laid down may be had. Assuming that such a realization has been experienced, we proceed to consider some further questions upon which qualitative thought throws light.

First as to the nature of the predication. The difficulties connected with the problem of predication are of long standing. They were recognized in Greek thought, and the skepticism they induced was a factor in developing the Platonic theory of the same-and-the-other and the Aristotelian conception of potentiality-and-actuality. The skeptical difficulty may be summed up in the statement that predication is either tautological and so meaningless, or else falsifying or at least arbitrary. Take the proposition, "that thing is sweet." If "sweet" already qualifies the meaning of "that thing," the predication is analytic in the Kantian sense, or forms a trivial proposition in the sense of Locke. But if "sweet" does not already qualify "that thing" what ground is there for tacking it on? The most that can be said is that some one who did not know before that it was sweet has now learned it. But such a statement refers only to an episode in the some one's intellectual biography. It has no logical force; it does not touch the question of predication that has objective reference and possible validity.

When, however, it is recognized that predication—any proposition having subject-predicate form—marks an attempt to make a qualitative whole which is directly and nonreflectively experienced into an object of thought for the sake of its own development, the case stands otherwise. What is "given" is not an object by itself nor a term having a meaning of its own. The "given," that is to say the existent, is precisely an undetermined and dominant complex quality. "Subject" and "predicate" are correlative determinations of this quality. The "copula" stands for the fact that one term is predicated of the other, and is thus a sign of the development of the qualitative whole by means of their distinction. It is, so to speak, the assertion of the fact that the distinctions designated in subject and predicate are correlative and work together in a common function of determination.

A certain quality is experienced. When it is inquired into or thought (judged), it differentiates into "that thing" on the one hand, and "sweet" on the other. Both "that thing" and "sweet" are analytic of the quality, but are additive, synthetic, ampliative, with respect to each other. The copula "is" marks just the effect of this distinction upon the correlative terms. They mark something like a division of labor, and the copula marks the function or work done by the structures that exhibit the division of labor. To say that "that thing is sweet" means "that thing" will *sweeten* some other object, say coffee, or a batter of milk and eggs. The intent of sweetening something formed the ground for converting a dumb quality into an articulate object of thought.

The logical force of the copula is always that of an active verb. It is merely a linguistic peculiarity, not a logical fact, that we say "that is red" instead of "that reddens," either in the sense of growing, becoming, red, or in the sense of making something else red. Even linguistically our "is" is a weakened form of an active verb signifying "stays" or "stands." But the nature of any act, (designated by the true verbal form) is best apprehended in its effect and issue; we say "is sweet" rather than "sweetens," "is red" rather than "reddens" because we define the active change by its anticipated or attained outcome. To say "the dog is ugly" is a way of setting forth what he is likely to *do,* namely to snarl and bite. "Man is mortal" indicates what man does or what actively is done to him, calling attention to a consequence. If we convert its verbal form into "men die," we realize the transitive and additive force of predication and escape the self-made difficulties of the attributive theory.

The underlying pervasive quality in the last instance, when it is put in words, involves care or concern for human destiny. But we must remember that this exists as a dumb quality until it is symbolized in an intellectual and propositional form. Out of this quality there emerges the idea of man and of mortality and of their existential connection with each other. No one of them has any meaning apart from the others, neither the distinctions, the terms, nor their relation, the predication. All the difficulties that attend the problem of predication spring from supposing that we can take the terms and their connection as having meaning by themselves. The sole alternative to this supposition is the recognition that the object of thought, designated propositionally, is a quality that is first directly and unreflectively experienced or had.

One source of the difficulty and the error in the classic theory lies in a radical misconception of the treacherous idea of the "given." The only thing that is unqualifiedly given is the total pervasive quality; and the objection to calling it "given" is that the word suggests something *to* which it is given, mind or thought or consciousness or whatever, as well possibly as something that gives. In truth "given" in this connection signifies only that the quality immediately exists, or is brutely there. In this capacity, it forms that to which all objects of thought refer, although, as we have noticed, it is never part of the manifest subject matter of thought. In itself, it is the big, buzzing, blooming confusion of which James wrote. This expresses not only the state of a baby's experience but the first stage and background of all thinking on any subject. There is, however, no inarticulate quality which is merely buzzing and blooming. It buzzes to some effect; it blooms toward some fruitage. That is, the quality, although dumb, has as a part of its complex quality a movement or transition in some direction. It can, therefore, be intellectually symbolized and converted into an object of thought. This is done by statement of limits and of direction of transition between them. "That" and "sweet" define the limits of the moving quality, the copula "tastes" (the real force of "is") defines the direction of movement between these limits. Putting the nature of the two limits briefly and without any attempt to justify the statement here, the subject represents the pervasive quality as means or condition and the predicate represents it as outcome or end.

These considerations define not only the subject-predicate structure of categorical propositions but they explain why the selective character of all such propositions with respect to the fullness of existence is not falsifying in character. Idealistic logicians, in calling attention to the partial or selective character of particular judgments, have used the fact to cast logical aspersion upon them, and to infer their need of correction first by transformation into conditional propositions and then finally into a judgment coextensive with the whole universe, arguing that only the latter can be truly true. But enough is always enough, and the underlying quality is itself the test of the "enough" for any particular case. All that is needed is to determine this quality by indicating the limits between which it moves and the direction or tendency of its movement. Sometimes the situation is simple and the most meager indications serve, like the "safe" or "out" of a baseball umpire. At other times, a quality is complex and pro-

longed, and a multitude of distinctions and subordinate relations are required for its determinate statement. It would
have been logically vicious on one occasion to propound more
than "my kingdom for a horse," while under other circumstances it may need a volume to set forth the quality of the
situation so as to make it comprehensible. Any proposition
that serves the purpose for which it is made is logically adequate; the idea that it is inadequate until the whole universe
has been included is a consequence of giving judgment a
wrong office—an error that has its source in failure to see the
domination of every instance of thought by a qualitative
whole needing statement in order that it may function.

At this point a reference to what is termed association of
ideas is in place. For while the subject is usually treated as
psychological in nature, thinking as an existential process
takes place through association; existentially, thinking *is*
association as far the latter is controlled. And the mechanics
of thinking can hardly be totally irrelevant to its *logical*
structure and function. I shall assume without much argument that "ideas" here signify objects, not psychical entities;
objects, that is to say, as meanings to which reference may be
made. When one, seeing smoke, thinks of fire he is associating
objects, not just states in his own mind. And so when thinking
of a hand, one thinks of grasping or of an organism. Thus,
when association takes the form of thought, or is controlled
and not loose day-dreaming, association is a name for a connection of objects or their elements in the total situation having a qualitative unity. This statement signifies something
different than does a statement that associated objects are
physical parts of a physical whole. It happens to hold in the
case of "hand-organism" and with some qualifications in the
case of "smoke-fire." But a philosophical student might be led
by the thought of hand to the thought of Aristotle on the
ground of a remark made by Aristotle.

In any case an original contiguity (or similarity) is not
the cause of an association. We do not associate *by* contiguity,
for recognition of a whole in which elements are juxtaposed

in space or in temporal sequence is the *result* of suggestion. The absurdity of the preposition "by" when applied to similarity is still more obvious. It is the reason why some writers reduce similarity to identity in differences, a position that will be examined later. That by which association is effected, by which suggestion and evocation of a distinct object of thought is brought about, is some acquired modification of the organism, usually designated habit. The conditioning mechanism may not be known at present in detail, but it cannot be an original contiguity because that contiguity is apprehended only in consequence of association. It may well be an organic attitude formed in consequence of a responsive act to things once coexistent or sequential. But this act was unitary; reference to it only accentuates the fact that the quality attending it was spread over and inclusive of the two things in question. That is, it was a response to a *situation* within which objects were related in space or time.

Given the conditions, the real problem is to say why objects once conjoined in a whole are now distinguished as two objects, one that which suggests, and the other that which is suggested. If I think of a chiffonier, the thought does not call up that of drawers as a distinct idea. For the drawers are a part of the object thought of. So when I originally saw, say a bird-in-a-nest, I saw a single total object. Why then does the sight or thought of a bird now call up that of a nest as a distinct idea? In general, the reason is that I have so often seen birds without seeing a nest and nests without birds. Moreover, it must be remembered that a person often sees a bird or nest, and instead of thinking of any other object, he reacts to it directly, as a man does when shooting at a bird or a boy climbing a tree to get the nest. While there is no association without habit, the natural tendency of habit is to produce an immediate reaction, not to evoke another distinct object of thought or idea. As the *dis*association of birds and nests in experience shows, this additional factor is some resistance to the attitude formed by the sight of nest-with-a-bird-in-it. Otherwise we should have the case over again of chiffonier and its drawers, or any object and its constitutive parts. Without the resistant or negative factor, there would be no tension to effect the change from a direct response, an immediate act, to an indirect one, a distinct object of thought.

Not only then is there no association *by* contiguity, but association is not *of* two objects separated yet contiguous in a prior experience. Its characteristic nature is that it presents as distinct but connected objects what originally were either two parts of one situational object, or (in the case that a man had previously always seen birds and nests separately from each other) that it presents in coexistence or sequence with one another objects previously separated in space and time. This consideration is fatal to the notion that the associated objects account by themselves or in their own isolated nature for association. It indicates that coexistence or sequence as a physical existential fact is not the ground of association. What alternative remains save that the quality of a situation as a whole operates to produce a functional connection? Acceptance of this alternative implies that association is an *intellectual* connection, thus aligning association with thought, as we shall now see.

There is nothing intellectual or logical in contiguity, in mere juxtaposition in space and time. If association were, then, either *of* or *by* contiguity, association would not have any logical force, any connection with thought.[3] But in fact association of bare contiguities is a myth. There is an indefinite number of particulars contiguous to one another in space and time. When I think of a nest why does a bird come into my mind? As a matter of contiguity, there are multitudinous leaves and twigs which are more frequently and more obviously juxtaposed than is a bird. When I think of a hammer, why is the idea of nail so likely to follow? Such questions suggest, I hope, that even in seemingly casual cases of associa-

[3] The assumption that in the case of contiguity association is of a merely *de facto* or existential nature is the root of Lotze's (and others') theory that *a priori* logical forms are necessary in order to change juxtaposition of things into coherence of meaning.

tion, there is an underlying quality which operates to control the connection of objects thought of. It takes something else than contiguity to effect association; there must be relevancy of both ideas to a situation defined by unity of quality. There is coherence of some sort because of mutual pertinency of both ideas, (or of all ideas in train) to a basis beyond any of them and beyond mere juxtaposition of objects in space and time.

The usual notion that association is merely *de facto* receives a still more obvious shock in the case of similarity. When I associate bird with nest, there may have been at least some previous conjunction in experience of the two objects, even though that conjunction is not by itself a sufficient condition of the later association. But when troublesome thought suggests the sting of an insect, or when change of fortune suggests the ebb and flow of the sea, there is *no* physical conjunction in the past to which appeal can be made. To try to explain the matter by saying that two objects are associated *because* they are similar is either to offer the problem as a solution or to attribute causal efficacy to "similarity"—which is to utter meaningless words. So-called association "by" similarity is a striking example of the influence of an underlying pervasive quality in determining the connection essential in thought.

There is, as far as I am aware, but one serious attempt to explain such association on some other basis. This is found in the view that there is in what is called similarity an actual existential identity among differences and that this identity works and then reinstates differences by contiguity. I fail to see how the explanation applies in many cases—such as that of the troublesome thought and the sting of an insect, or Socrates and a gadfly. "Identity" seems to be the result rather than the antecedent of the association. But I shall confine the discussion to instances in which it is claimed to work. Bradley has stated the theory in question most clearly and I shall use his illustration.[4]

4 Logic, Book II, Part 2, Ch. I, Sec. 30. [1883.]

Walking on the shore of England, one sees a promontory and remarks how like it is to one in Wales. Bradley's explanation is that there is an actual identity of form in both and that this identical form suggests by contiguity in space certain elements which cannot be referred to the promontory now seen (size, color, etc., being incompatible) and thus constitutes in connection with identical form the content of the idea of the promontory in Wales. The seeming plausibility of this explanation is shattered by the fact that form is not one isolated element among others, but is an arrangement or pattern of elements. Identity of pattern, arrangement of form is something that can be apprehended only *after* the other promontory has been suggested, by comparison of the two objects.

The only way that form or pattern can operate as an immediate link is by the mode of a directly experienced *quality,* something present and prior to and independent of all reflective analysis, something of the same nature which controls artistic construction. In psychological language, it is felt, and the feeling is made explicit or a term of thought in the idea of another promontory. What operates is not an external existential identity between two things, but a present immediate quality—an explanation which is the only one applicable to some cases already cited, and to being reminded of blotting paper by a certain voice. The priority of regulative quality of the situation as a whole is especially obvious in the case of esthetic judgments. A man sees a picture and says at first sight that it is by Goya or by some one influenced by him. He passes the judgment long before he has made any analysis or any explicit identification of elements. It is the quality of the picture as a whole that operates. With a trained observer such a judgment based on pervasive quality may lead later to definite analysis of elements and details; the result of the analysis may confirm or may lead to rejection of the original ascription. But the basic appreciation of quality as a whole is a more dependable basis of such point by point analysis and its conclusion than is an external analysis performed by a critic who knows history and mechanical points of brush-work but who is lacking in sensitiveness to pervasive quality.

Another instance of Bradley's refers to Mill's denial that the suggestion of another triangle by a given triangle can be reduced to contiguity. For, Mill says, "the form of a triangle is not one single feature among others." Bradley thinks such a view absurd; he cannot, he says, even tell what is meant. The use of the term "feature" may be unfortunate. For when we speak of a nose as a feature of a face, we have in mind one element or part among others. Now triangularity is not such an isolable element. It is a characteristic of the disposition, arrangement, or pattern of all elements, and it must be capable of immediate realization. Even a nose as a feature of a man's face is not completely isolable. For it is characterized by the whole face as well as characterizing that face. A better instance is found, however, when we speak of a man's *expression*. That assuredly is a total effect of all elements in their relation to one another, not a "single feature among others." And so is triangularity. Family resemblances are often detected, and yet one is totally unable to specify the points of resemblance. Unanalyzed quality of the whole accounts for the identification as a *result,* and it is a radically different thing from identification of a man by fingerprints.

The outcome of this brief discussion, in revealing the significance of dominant qualitativeness in suggestion and connection of ideas, shows why thinking as an existential process is all one with controlled association.[5] For the latter is not explained by any merely external conjunction or any external identity in things. If it were, association would itself be merely another case of existential sequence, coexistence, or identity

[5] Were I to venture into speculative territory, I might apply this conception to the problem of "thinking" in animals, and what the *Gestalt* psychologists call "insight." That total quality operates with animals and sometimes secures, as with monkeys, results like those which we obtain by reflective analysis cannot, it seems to me, be doubted. But that this operation of quality in effecting results then goes out into symbolization and analysis is quite another matter.

and would be lacking in intellectual and logical import. But selection and coherence determined by an immediate quality that constitutes and delimits a situation are characteristics of "association." These traits are different in kind from existential conjunction and physical sameness, and identical with those of thought. The case of similarity or resemblance is almost uniquely significant. The problem of its nature is a crux of philosophies. The difficulty of dealing with it leads one on the one hand to thinking of it as purely psychical in nature, and, on the other hand, to the idealistic identification of the ontological and the logical *via* the principle of identity in difference. The recognition of pervasive quality enables us to avoid both extremes. By its means a voice is assimilated to blotting paper, and in more serious intellectual matters analogy becomes a guiding principle of scientific thought. On the basis of *assimilation* a further explicit recognition of similarity takes place. For assimilation is not itself the perception or judgment of similarity; the latter requires a further act made possible by symbols. It involves a proposition. The saying that there is a "tide in the affairs of men, etc.," does not of itself involve any direct comparison of human affairs with the ocean and an explicit judgment of likeness. A pervasive quality has resulted in an assimilation. If symbols are at hand, this assimilation may lead to a further act—the judgment of similarity. But *de facto* assimilation comes first and need not eventuate in the express conception of resemblance.[6]

"Assimilation" denotes the efficacious operation of pervasive quality; "similarity" denotes a *relation*. Sheer assimilation results in the presence of a single object of apprehension. To identify a seen thing *as* a promontory is a case of assimilation. By some physiological process, not exactly understood at present but to which the name "habit" is given, the net outcome of prior experiences gives a dominant quality, designated "promontory," to a perceived existence. Passage from

[6] Thus, to recur to Bradley's example, one may pass directly from the promontory in England to one in Wales and become absorbed in the latter without any judgment of the likeness of the two.

this object to some other implies resistance to mere assimilation and results in making distinctions. The pervasive quality is differentiated while at the same time these differentiations are connected. The result is an explicit statement or proposition.

I have touched, as I am well aware, only upon the fringes of a complex subject. But in view of the general neglect of the subject, I shall be satisfied if I have turned the attention of those interested in thought and its workings to an overlooked field. Omitting reference to ramifications, the gist of the matter is that the immediate existence of quality, and of dominant and pervasive quality, is the background, the point of departure, and the regulative principle of all thinking. Thought which denies the existential reality of qualitative things is therefore bound to end in self-contradiction and in denying itself. "Scientific" thinking, that expressed in physical science, never gets away from qualitative existence. Directly, it always has its own qualitative background; indirectly, it has that of the world in which the ordinary experience of the common man is lived. Failure to recognize this fact is the source of a large part of the artificial problems and fallacies that infect our theory of knowledge and our metaphysics, or theories of existence. With this general conclusion goes another that has been emphasized in the preceding discussion. Construction that is artistic is as much a case of genuine thought as that expressed in scientific and philosophical matters, and so is all genuine esthetic appreciation of art, since the latter must in some way, to be vital, retrace the course of the creative process. But the development of this point in its bearing upon esthetic judgment and theory is another story.

IX

PEIRCE'S THEORY OF QUALITY[1]

Peirce's influence on Dewey is a curious story in intellectual history. Dewey was a graduate student at Johns Hopkins during the brief period in the early 1880's when Peirce lectured on logic. By that time, Peirce had already formulated the outlines of pragmatism, but Dewey, who had just discovered Hegel, was influenced by neither Peirce's pragmatism nor his logic. When Dewey was developing his instrumentalism at the turn of the century, he was only obliquely influenced by Peirce. Peirce even severely criticized Dewey's view of logic in his review of the *Studies in Logical Theory* (1903). The real affinity with Peirce is evidenced in Dewey's later writings. It is as if Dewey discovered in Peirce's theory of inquiry and investigation of the ultimate categories, confirmation and support for his own basic theses, which he had discovered by a different path. In this article, which is more technical than most of the other selections, Dewey closely examines Peirce's theory of quality or Firstness. It was written in response to Thomas A. Goudge's "The Views of Charles Peirce on the Given in Experience." [2] The significance of Peirce's views on quality is suggested when Dewey says, "I am quite sure that he, above all modern philosophers, has opened the road which permits a truly experiential philosophy to be developed which does not, like traditional empirical philosophies, cut experience off from nature." One can add that this is a road which Dewey himself continued to follow.

THE QUESTIONS raised in Mr. Goudge's criticism of Peirce [3] on the nature of the "given," are of high importance in the contemporary state of philosophy in which the problems of the given, on one hand, and of universals and essences, on the other, bulk so large. The problems themselves

[1] *Journal of Philosophy*, XXXII (1935), 701-8.

[2] *Journal of Philosophy*, XXXII (1935), 533-44. Goudge wrote a reply to Dewey's criticism in the following volume.

[3] *Journal of Philosophy*, XXXII (1935), 533-44.

far transcend, of course, the question of the internal con
sistency of Peirce's own views on the subject. But their im
portance also renders it highly important that Peirce's own
contribution be correctly apprehended. Hence I propose to
point out some fundamental misconceptions in Mr. Goudge'
rendering of Peirce's ideas.

Peirce is considering, in the passages of which Mr. Goudge
treats, phenomenology, or the matter of experience as ex
perienced. While he introduces at times (and rather unfortu
nately in my opinion) his predilection for panpsychic meta
physics, he is not writing on a metaphysical or cosmologica
basis, but is giving a logical analysis of experience; an analysi
based on what he calls Firstness, or sheer totality and pervad
ing unity of quality in *every*thing experienced, whether it b
odor, the drama of King Lear, or philosophic or scientifi
systems; Secondness, existentiality, or singular occurrence; and
Thirdness, mediation, or continuity.

Now Mr. Goudge finds an inconsistency in Peirce's treat
ment of Firstness on the ground that the latter holds both tha
it is brutely given as qualities of feeling and that it consists o
"logical possibilities or universals" (p. 538). Now I submit tha
a careful reading of Peirce shows (i) that when he uses th
word "possibility" he means by it material potentiality o
power, not logical possibility, and (ii) that he does *not* hold
that Firstness as such, that is, as the given permeating tota
quality of anything experienced is, strictly speaking, eve
potentiality. I begin with the latter point. Mr. Goudge quote
the following: "Firstness . . . is perfectly simple and withou
parts. . . . The word *possibility* fits it." [4] Very unfortunately
Mr. Goudge terminates his quotation in the middle of th
sentence quoted, and thereby omits a point that is necessar
to the correct understanding of Peirce's point. Here is th
passage as it stands in the original text: "The word poss
bility fits it, *except* that possibility implies a relation to wha

[4] Page 537 of Mr. Goudge's article; *Collected Papers of Charles Sande*
Peirce, I, 531. [1933-1935. All quotations from the *Collected Papers* refe
to the volume and paragraph number.]

xists, while universal Firstness is the mode of being of itself.
hat is why a new word was required for it. *Otherwise,* pos-
bility would have answered the purpose." [5]

I am not suggesting that Mr. Goudge omitted the qualifying
lause and the additional sentences in order to make out his
oint. Doubtless he thought them irrelevant. But they are not;
ley are the meat of the matter as far as quality as possibility
concerned. In his analysis, which is logical not psychological,
f a phenomenon, of anything as experienced, he finds it
ecessary to consider Firstness, or the quality of an experience,
oth as it is in itself and as it is in relation to the other
spects of a phenomenon. What he is saying in the passage
uoted is that while quality is possibility in relation to
econdness, or existence, it is *not* possibility in and of itself.
econdness, or existence, he defines elsewhere in terms of re-
ction and interaction, of resistance or brute self-assertion. It
actuality in the literal sense. It is also strictly individual.
n reference to existence so defined quality is both possibility
nd generality. A pervasive unity of quality is a condition to
e satisfied in connection with the existential aspect of any
henomenon. Existence, he says, is "just when and where it
akes place . . . and, therefore, different Secondnesses, strictly
peaking, have no common quality." [6] But experiences do
ave common qualities; therefore Secondness is *logically* con-
litioned by quality. Generality does not belong to any
henomenon *in its occurrence,* but the *matter* of the experi-

[5] Italics not in original text. [The entire Section I, 531, is as follows:
A Firstness is exemplified in every quality of a total feeling. It is per-
ectly simple and without parts; and everything has its quality. Thus the
ragedy of King Lear has its Firstness, its flavor *sui generis.* That wherein
ll such qualities agree is universal Firstness, the very being of Firstness.
he word *possibility* fits it, except that possibility implies a relation to
vhat exists, while universal Firstness is the mode of being of itself. That
s why a new word was required for it. Otherwise, "possibility" would
ave answered the purpose."]

[6] *Collected Papers,* I, 532. [The original text is as follows: "Secondness,
trictly speaking, is just when and where it takes place, and has no other
eing; and therefore different Secondnesses, strictly speaking, have in
hemselves no quality in common."]

ence gets generality because of co-presence of Firstness or total
undivided quality. Quality or Firstness *per se* is neither in
dividual nor general. But *as* the Firstness *of* Secondness it
provides generality to the latter. Unless the fact is clearly
recognized that Peirce deals with Firstness both by itself-
indicating its denotation—and as the Firstness *of* Secondness
(as well as of Thirdness) what he says is more than incon
sistent. It has no point.

I come now to the other point. "Possibility" in isolation
from a context is an ambiguous word. It means both logical
possibility and material potentiality. While Peirce is con
cerned to indicate that quality is Firstness because it is a
logical condition of what he terms existence (and of Third
ness, continuity or rationality), yet when he says "the word
possibility fits it," he is speaking of power, of material po
tentiality, not of quality as logical possibility. This fact had
been made clear by the time Peirce arrived at the passage
quoted. As early as 422-25 (where he is expressly discuss
ing quality) he makes this point evident in a fairly extended
discussion from which I quote some typical passages. Quality-

> is not anything dependent upon the *mind*. It is not any
> thing which is dependent, in its being, upon mind, whether
> in the form of sense or thought. Nor is it dependent, in its
> *being*, upon the fact that some material things possess it
> That quality is dependent upon sense is the great error of
> the conceptualists. A quality is a mere abstract *potentiality*
> and the error of these schools lies in holding that the po
> tential, or possible, is nothing but what the actual makes
> it to be.[7]

[7] Italics mine. [The entire original text is as follows: "What, then, is a
quality? Before answering this, it will be well to say what it is not. It is
not anything which is dependent, in its being, upon mind, whether in the
form of sense or in that of thought. Nor is it dependent, in its being
upon the fact that some material thing possesses it. That quality is de
pendent upon sense is the great error of the conceptualists. That it is
dependent upon the subject in which it is realized is the great error of all
nominalistic schools. A quality is a mere abstract potentiality; and the
error of those schools lies in holding that the potential, or possible, is

The concrete illustrations that Peirce goes on to use prove incontestably that his use of the word "potentiality" is not accidental. He criticizes those who claim that a thing does not have the *quality* of red in the dark, or that iron does not have the quality of resistance when not actually exerting pressure. "Do you mean to say that a piece of iron not actually under pressure has lost its *power* of resisting pressure?" (I, 422). [Dewey's italics.] This power is actualized only under conditions of interaction with something, but it is there as a power nevertheless. Quality *per se,* in itself, is precisely and exclusively, according to Peirce, this potentiality; it is like potential energy in relation to kinetic, the latter involving resistance and hence actuality or existence. "It is impossible to hold consistently that a quality only exists when it actually inheres in a body." [I, 422] A quality is what *"might* happen," and since every law, indeed every description of an event, involves something that *may* happen, but is not now happening, it involves quality as potentiality. The same analysis applies to generality. Capacity or power to resist pressure is actualized on particular or individual occasions. But *qua* power it is general, for it is a *way of* behaving. So he criticizes the nominalists for denying, by implication if not explicitly, that things have *ways* of being. In Peirce's scheme, the potentiality and generality he is talking about are so far from being *"logical* possibilities or universals" that they provide the cosmological or physical basis for logical possibilities and universals. Peirce's theory of "leading principles" as universals has no meaning except as a carrying over into the field of inquiry ways of behaving that are characteristic of things. What in my opinion is Peirce's most characteristic philosophical contribution, namely, his original theory of the relation between the existential and the logical, is wholly mean-

___

nothing but what the actual makes it to be." Section I, 422.] Compare this passage with a prior statement, 419, "The qualities, in so far as they are general, are somewhat vague and potential. But an occurrence is perfectly individual. It [happens] here and now. . . . Qualities are concerned in facts but they do not make up facts."

ingless if it is not seen that he is speaking of possibility and generality as ways or modes that with respect to actualization are potential and general, being actualized only under individualized conditions of interaction with other things.

Peirce even goes so far as to question the generally accepted theory that such actualized qualities as those of different colors are connected simply with *quantitative* differences of vibrations. They "will not make such a difference as that between deep vermillion and violet blue. . . . It is doubtless our imperfect knowledge of these vibrations that has led us to represent them abstractly as differing only in quantity," [8] so that increased knowledge of electrons will enable us to find in them different ways of behaving, or potentialities, that correspond to different qualities of sense.[9]

It should now be evident that what Mr. Goudge thinks is an inconsistency consists simply of the fact that in his analysis Peirce takes Firstness, or quality, in two aspects; once as it is in itself and once as it is in relation to Secondness or existence; and that potentiality and generality attach to it exclusively and necessarily in the latter connection. Moreover, he gives the reader explicit notice that this is just what he is doing. He does it in the clause and sentences Mr. Goudge omitted, and he has done it earlier in the following passage:

> We see that the idea of a quality is the idea of a phenomenon or partial phenomenon considered as a monad, without reference to its parts or components and *without reference to anything else*. We must not consider whether it exists or is only imaginary, because *existence* depends upon having a place in the general [system] of the universe. An

8 [I, 311. The original text is as follows: "It seems at first glance unaccountable that a mere slight difference in the speed of vibration should make such a difference of quality as that between deep vermillion and violet blue. But then it is to be remembered that it is doubtless our imperfect knowledge of those vibrations which has led us to represent them abstractly as differing only in quantity."]

9 At this point Peirce brings in his panpsychic metaphysics. But he expressly calls his reference a *guess,* and in any case his logical analysis is independent of this particular metaphysical interpretation.

t.lement separated from everything else and in no world but itself, may be said, *when we come to reflect upon [its isolation]*, to be merely potential. But we must not even attend to any determinate [aspect] of other things; we are to consider the total as a unit.[10]

And almost as if to guard against such a misconception as that of Mr. Goudge, he says:

When we say that qualities are general, are partial determinations, etc., all that is true of qualities *reflected upon;* but these things do *not belong* to the quality-element of experience.[11]

Considered in itself, quality is that which totally and intimately pervades a phenomenon or experience, rendering it just the one experience which it is. Of course, then it is "ineffable." Mr. Peirce or any one can only call attention to it and invite others to note its presence in any and every experience they have a mind to take. When it is described, even when it is denotatively mentioned, there is another and new experience having its own, so to say, totalizing unifying quality—and so on *ad infinitum*. When such quality is reflected upon in relation to existence, it is seen to be a potentiality and to be general. As Peirce points out, a quality does not *resist,* while existence involves reaction and resistance. Hence the experience of anything purely imaginary, say, centaurs, has its own pervading and unifying quality, just as much as does that of horses in the barn. But this quality, while having no evidential value with respect to existence, is a condition of there being *any* experience and hence of an experience or phenomenon ("phaneron").

The distinction involved in the clause "or *partial* phenomenon" is also important. What is true of the experience of the drama of *King Lear* as a whole is true of every act, scene, and line in it so far as that experience has its own unity. It would be a complete mistake to confine the application of quality as Firstness to such things as red and hard and

[10] *Collected Papers,* I, 424; italics mine.
[11] [I, 425; Dewey's italics.]

sweet, although it applies to them as partial phenomena. It is something which characterizes any and every experienced subject matter, as far as that experience has unity and totality, wholly independent of the complexity of its "components" and of the place of these components in the existential world. Hence where we recall a prior experience, the experience of recall is a new experience having its own pervasive unifying quality.

Up to a point, therefore, Peirce in what he says about ineffability and undescribability is simply generalizing the commonplace that in order to *have* red as a quality you have to have direct experience of it; that while a blind man can understand the theory of color and the place of what is designated red in the theory, red as an immediate quality can not be present in his experience. This is not a matter of dialectic or argument, but is something which is either so or not so, and the only way of finding out whether or no it is so, is denotative, not dialectical. In addition to generalization of the commonplace in question, he is saying that no matter how complex the constituents of any unitary experience and whether the constituents are existential or imaginary, the unity and totality of the experience is that of quality, and conversely.

When Mr. Goudge, then, says that quality or Firstness in Peirce is the *given* in the sense of being "broadly synonymous with the 'ideas' of Locke and Berkeley, the 'impressions' of Hume, the *Vorstellungen* of Kant, and the 'sensa' and 'presentations' of contemporary [philosophical discussion]," he is far off the track.[12] It would be nearer the fact to say that he is engaging in deliberate, even if implicit, criticism of the basis and implications of all such theories. For he is pointing out that any *experience* of "ideas, impressions, sensa, presentations," etc., has its own unity, its own unique and unreduplicable quality. This statement holds, for example, of Locke's experiences when thinking and writing about *ideas* and of the experiences of anyone reading Locke's *Essay* or reflecting upon it. Moreover, what are called ideas by Locke

12 P. 534 of his article.

are taken by him to have *existence* (at least in or before the mind), and the whole point about *Vorstellungen* and *sensa* is that some kind of existence is attributed to them, whether psychical or otherwise. But, as the foregoing should have made evident, Firstness or quality is something in itself wholly independent of existence, the latter being a matter of "struggle," of action-reaction. Any problems that arise about ideas, impressions, etc., are in Peirce's theory affairs of *components,* of their place in the scheme of existence as determined by actual reaction and resistance. If what Peirce means by Firstness resembled in any way, to say nothing of being "broadly synonymous with," the givens of various modern philosophers, it would have been sheer nonsense to call them ineffable, or to apply to them any of the characterizations Peirce employs. But it is not nonsense to say that every experience which has Lockian ideas or Humean impressions for its subject matter or components has its own quality, and that any description of this quality that may occur takes place in another and new experience having its own unity and totality of quality.

When Mr. Goudge suggests some rough similarity between Peirce's qualities and Santayana's sense-data as essences, he is following the same wrong road still further.[13] Anything that can be termed essence, meaning, subsistence, belongs in the domain which Peirce calls Thirdness. Similarly, when he discusses Peirce's view that quality as such is indescribable, he says: "Peirce's view that the act of describing must alter the *nature* of the given would entail a denial of the possibility of real knowledge, and is therefore self-contradictory," and uses the multiplication table as an instance of the givenness in question.[14] It is completely overlooked that this conception of *nature* is a conception belonging to the domain of Thirdness, not of Firstness. It belongs, by description, to the domain of knowledge, while quality belongs to the domain of the occurrences of any single and total experience wholly irrespective of any cognitive or reflective reference. Peirce does not hold that

13 P. 543 of his article.
14 P. 539 of his article.

the act of describing alters the quality of what is described, but that the experience occurring in an act of describing the quality of another experience, of the multiplication-table, or anything else, itself has another quality. The quality of the original experience has become a *component* of this further experience, which has its own quality. Quality, as Peirce says, is "first, present [immediate, fresh], new, initiative, original, spontaneous, free, vivid, conscious, and evanescent." [15] But it is such just because it is of a different dimension from any content or component of either existent or rational objects.

I wish to add a few words about Peirce's *psychological* identifications and descriptions of Firstness, Secondness, and Thirdness, respectively. In this psychological universe of discourse, Quality (including sensations as barely *had* and not referred) represents feeling; Secondness represents existence as conative (since involving effort-resistance); and Thirdness, as cognitive thought, represents rationality. Now these psychological descriptions can be interpreted in two ways. As far as Peirce's panpsychic predilections are concerned, they are doubtless to be taken rather literally. That is, in his metaphysical cosmology Peirce was inclined to believe that *apart* from experience and phenomenology, the universe is constituted out of relations between something very like feelings and acts of effort-resistance, while natural continuity is inherently assimilable to what presents itself in experience as reflective thought. But, as I have already pointed out, his logical analysis of a phenomenon, or any experience, is logically independent of this cosmological interpretation, and stands or falls on its own merits.

Moreover, the matter in question is incapable of another interpretation. Whether "feelings," for example, are or are not constituents of the natural world, it can be affirmed that, *psychologically,* it is through feeling (including sensation as such) that qualities present themselves in *experience;* that it is through volitional experiences that existence, as a matter of action-reaction, is actualized in experience, and it is through

15 [I, p. 357.]

thought that continuities are experienced. All that is required on the ontological side is that existence itself is qualitative, not merely quantitative, is marked by stress and strain, and by continuities. That much, but only that much, of ontological interpretation is postulated in Peirce's logical analysis of experience.

Mr. Goudge quotes a passage from Peirce which is highly significant in this connection; "Feeling is the true *psychical representative* of the immediate as it is in its immediacy, of the present in its direct, positive presentness." [16] This idea that feeling is the psychical representative of that immediacy of being which characterizes, according to Peirce, everything in the natural world, is all that is essential to his theory. The rest is supernumerary; as he repeatedly says, with unusual frankness for a philosopher, it is a *guess*. If what is suggested in such a passage is followed out, we do not define or identify quality in terms of feeling. The reverse is the case. Anything that can be called feeling is objectively defined by reference to immediate quality: anything that is a feeling, whether of red or of a noble character, or of *King Lear,* is of some immediate quality when that is present as *experience*. Personally, I believe this to be sound doctrine. But whether it is or is not, it is all that is implied in Peirce's logical analysis. I do not wish to minimize Peirce's own inclination toward a panpsychic interpretation which makes the immediate quality of *things* to be of the nature of feelings. But I do emphasize the fact, which he himself repeatedly emphasizes, that this interpretation is optional so far as the analysis of experience is concerned.

I do not profess, to end with a personal word, to agree completely with Peirce's analysis, for I do not think that I have fully mastered it. But I am quite sure that he, above all

---

[16] *Collected Papers,* V, 44; italics mine. The passage as printed in Peirce makes even a closer connection with the Firstness of the passages taken from Vol. I. It actually reads as follows: "The quality of feeling is the true psychical representative of the first category of the immediate as it is, etc."

modern philosophers, has opened the road which permits a truly experiential philosophy to be developed which does not, like traditional empirical philosophies, cut experience off from nature, a road which if followed leads out of the impasse into which Locke's "ideas" and the contemporary theory of sensa and of essences alike conduct philosophy. For this reason, it is important that Peirce's theory should be understood for what it is.

X

THE SUBJECT MATTER OF METAPHYSICAL INQUIRY[1]

In this early article, Dewey outlines a program for a naturalistic metaphysics which he was to pursue in a systematic fashion ten years later in *Experience and Nature.* Two senses of "ultimate" are distinguished: that which is beyond all possible experiential contexts, "ultimate origins and ends"; and that which is basic and irreducible in all existence. Dewey claims, as Kant did, that the metaphysics which searches after ultimates in the former sense is a futile discipline, but that it is a legitimate and important inquiry to study "the generic traits of existence." Such a metaphysics is descriptive and hypothetical. It does not purport to deal with a realm of ultimate reality which is inaccessible to the special sciences. It studies "certain irreducible traits found in any and every scientific inquiry." Dewey's concept of the nature and domain of metaphysics resembles Peirce's when the latter described metaphysics as resting "upon kinds of phenomena with which every man's experience is so saturated that he usually pays no particular attention to them." (See "Nature in Experience" for a further discussion of these issues.)

A NUMBER of biologists holding to the adequacy of the mechanistic conception in biology have of late expressed views not unlike those clearly and succinctly set forth in the following quotation: "If we consider the organism simply as a system forming a part of external nature, we find no evidence that it possesses properties that may not eventually be satisfactorily analyzed by the methods of physico-chemical science; but we admit also that those peculiarities of ultimate constitution which have in the course

[1] *Journal of Philosophy,* XII (1915), 337-45.

of evolution led to the appearance of living beings in nature are such that we can not well deny the possibility or even legitimacy of applying a vitalistic or biocentric conception to the cosmic process [considered] as a whole." [2]

The problems connected with the organism as a part of external nature are referred to in the context of the quotation as scientific problems; those connected with the peculiarities of ultimate constitution as metaphysical. The context also shows that ultimate constitution is conceived in a temporal sense. Metaphysical questions are said to be those having to do with "ultimate origins." Such questions lie quite beyond the application of scientific method. "Why it [nature] exhibits certain apparently innate potentialities and modes of action which have caused it to evolve in a certain way is a question which really lies beyond the sphere of natural science." [3] These "apparently innate potentialities and modes of action" which have caused nature as a whole to evolve in the direction of living beings are identified with "ultimate peculiarities"; and it is with reference to them that the biocentric idea has a possible legitimate application. The argument implies that when we insist upon the adequacy of the physico-chemical explanation of living organisms, we are led, in view of the continuity of evolution of organisms from nonliving things, to recognize that the world out of which life developed "held latent or potential within itself the possibility of life." In considering such a world and the nature of the potentiality which caused it to evolve living beings, we are forced, however, beyond the limits of scientific inquiry. We pass the boundary which separates it from metaphysics.

Thus is raised the question as to the nature of metaphysical inquiry. I wish to suggest that while one may accept as a preliminary demarcation of metaphysics from science the more "ultimate traits" with which the former deals, it is not neces-

2 Professor Ralph S. Lillie, *Science*, XL (1914), 846. See also the references given in the article, which is entitled "The Philosophy of Biology—Vitalism *vs.* Mechanism."

3 [*Ibid.*, p. 846.]

sary to identify these ultimate traits with temporally original traits—that, in fact, there are good reasons why we should not do so. We may also mark off the metaphysical subject matter by reference to certain irreducible traits found in any and every subject of scientific inquiry. With reference to the theme of evolution of living beings, the distinctive trait of metaphysical reflection would not then be its attempt to discover some temporally original feature which caused the development, but the irreducible traits of a world in which at least some changes take on an evolutionary form. A world where some changes proceed in the direction of the appearance of living and thinking creatures is a striking sort of a world. While science would trace the conditions of their occurrence in detail, connecting them in their variety with their antecedents, metaphysics would raise the question of the sort of world which *has* such an evolution, not the question of the sort of world which causes it. For the latter type of question appears either to bring us to an *impasse* or else to break up into just the questions which constitute scientific inquiry.

Any intelligible question as to causation seems to be a wholly scientific question. Starting from any given existence, be it a big thing like a solar system or a small thing like a rise of temperature, we may ask how it came about. We account for the change by linking up the thing in question with other specific existences acting in determinate ways—ways which collectively are termed physico-chemical. When we have traced back a present existence to the earlier existences with which it is connected, we may ask a like question about the occurrence of the earlier things, viewed as changes from something still earlier. And so on indefinitely; although, of course, we meet practical limits in our ability to push such questions beyond a certain indefinite point. Hence it may be said that a question about ultimate origin or ultimate causation is either a meaningless question, or else the words are used in a relative sense to designate the point in the past at which a particular inquiry breaks off. Thus we might inquire as to the "ultimate" origin of the French language. This would take us back to certain definite antecedent existences, such as persons speaking the Latin tongue, others speaking barbarian tongues; the contact of these peoples in war, commerce, political administration, education, etc. But the term "ultimate" has meaning only in relation to the particular existence in question: French speech. We are landed in another historic set of existences, having their own specific antecedents. The case is not otherwise if we ask for the ultimate origin of human speech in general. The inquiry takes us back to animal cries, gestures, etc., certain conditions of intercourse, etc. The question is, how one set of specific existences gradually passed into another. No one would think of referring to latent qualities of the Latin speech as the cause of the evolution of French; one tries to discover actual and overt features which, *interacting* with other equally specific existences, brought about this particular change. If we are likely to fall into a different mode of speech with reference to human language in general, it is because we are more ignorant of the specific circumstances under which the transition from animal cries to articulate speech with a meaning took place. Upon analysis, reference to some immanent law or cause which forced the evolution will be found to be a lazy cloak for our ignorance of the specific facts needed in order to deal successfully with the question.

Suppose we generalize the situation still more. We may ask for the ultimate origin of the entire present state of things. Taken *en masse,* such a question is meaningless. Taken in detail, it means that we may apply the same procedure distributively to each and any of the things which now exist. In each case we may trace its history to an earlier state of things. But in each case, *its* history is what we trace, and the history always lands us at some state of things in the past, regarding which the same question might be asked. That scientific inquiry does not itself deal with any question of ultimate origins, except in the purely relative sense already indicated, is, of course, recognized. But it also seems to follow from what has been said that scientific inquiry does not generate, or leave over, such a question for some other discipline, such as metaphysics, to deal with. The contrary conception with respect to the doctrine of evolution is to be explained, I think, by the fact that theology used to have the idea of ultimate origin in connection with creation, and that at a certain juncture it was natural to regard the theory of evolution as a substitute or rival of the theological idea of creation.

If all questions of causation and origin are specific scientific questions, is there any place left for metaphysical inquiry at all? If its theme can not be ultimate origin and causation, is metaphysics anything but a kind of pseudo-science whose illusory character is now to be recognized? This question takes us to the matter of whether there are ultimate, that is, irreducible, traits of the very existences with which scientific reflection is concerned. In all such investigations as those referred to above we find at least such traits as the following: Specifically diverse existences, interaction, change. Such traits are found in any material which is the subject matter of inquiry in the natural science. They are found equally and indifferently whether a subject matter in question be dated 1915 or ten million years B.C. Accordingly, they would seem to deserve the name of ultimate, or irreducible, traits. As such they may be made the object of a kind of inquiry differing from that which deals with the genesis of a particular group of existences, a kind of inquiry to which the name metaphysical may be given.[4]

[4] The name at least has the sanction of the historical designation given to Aristotle's consideration of existence as existence. But it should be noted that we also find in Aristotle the seeds (which, moreover, have at places developed into flourishing growths in his own philosophy) of the conception of metaphysics rejected above. For he expressly gives the more general traits of existence the eulogistic title "divine" and identifies his first philosophy with theology, and so makes this kind of inquiry "superior" to all others, because it deals with the "highest of existing things." While he did not himself seek for this higher or supreme real in time, but rather located it, in its fullness of reality, just beyond space, this identification of existence as such with the divine led to such an identifi-

It may well seem as if the fact that the subject matter of science is always a plurality of diverse interacting and changing existences were too obvious and commonplace to invite or reward investigation. Into this point I shall not go, beyond pointing out, in connection with the present theme, that certain negative advantages in the economizing of intellectual effort would at least accrue from the study. Bare recognition of the fact just stated would wean men from the futility of concern with ultimate origins and laws of causation with which the "universe" is supposed to have been endowed at the outset. For it would reveal that, whatever the date of the subject matter which may be successfully reflected upon, we have the same situation that we have at present: diversity, specificity, change. These traits have to be begged or taken in any case. If we face this fact without squeamishness we shall be saved from the recurrent attempts to reduce heterogeneity to homogeneity, diversity to sheer uniformity, quality to quantity, and so on. That considerations of quantity and mathematical order are indispensable to the successful prosecution of researches into particular occurrences is a precious fact. It exhibits certain irreducible traits *of* the irreducible traits we have mentioned, but it does not replace them. When it tries to do so it cuts the ground out from under its own feet.

Let me emphasize this point by comment on a further quotation. "If we assume constancy of the elementary natural processes, and constancy in the modes of connection between them—as exact observation forces us to do—there seems no avoiding the conclusion that—given an undifferentiated universe at the start—only one course of evolution can ever have

---

cation the moment theology became supremely interested in "creation." But unless one approaches the study of the most general traits of the matter of scientific inquiry with theological presuppositions, there is, of course, no ground for the application to them of eulogistic predicates. There is no ground for thinking that they are any better or any worse, any higher or any lower, than other traits, or that any peculiar dignity attaches to a study of them.

been possible. Laplace long ago perceived this consequence of the mechanistic view of nature, and the inevitability of [his] conclusion has never been seriously disputed by scientific men. Nevertheless, this is a very strange result, and to many has seemed a *reductio ad absurdum* of the scientific view as applied to the whole of nature." [5]

Note that the inevitable conclusion as to the predetermined course of evolution and the apparent incredibility of the conclusion both depend upon the premise "given an undifferentiated universe at the start." Now this is precisely a premise which a scientific view can not admit, for science deals with any particular existence only by tracing its occurrence to a plurality of prior changing interacting things. Any Laplacean formula would, in any case, be a formula for the structure of *some* existence *in* the world, not for the world as a "whole." The scientific grounds which made it impossible to take the world *en masse* at the present time and to give a comprehensive formula for it in its entirety apply even more strongly, if possible, to some earlier state of affairs. For such a formula can be reached only by tracing back a specific present phenomenon to its specific antecedents.

A curious illusion exists as to formulae for the ancient states of nature. It is frequently assumed that they denote not merely some absolute original (which is impossible), but also one from which later events unroll in a mathematically predetermined fashion. We seem to be passing in a one-sided way from the earlier to the later. The illusion vanishes when we ask where the formula came from. How was it obtained? Evidently, by beginning with some present existence and tracing its earlier course, till at some time (relevant to the object of the inquiry) we stop and condense the main features of the course into a formula for the structure of the state of things at the date where we stop. Instead of really deducing or deriving the course \of subsequent events from an original state, we are simply taking out of a formula the traits which we have put into it on the basis of knowledge of subsequent

[5] [*Op. cit.*, p. 845.]

events. Let the present state be anything you please, as different as may be from what is actually found, and it will still be true that we could (theoretically) construct a comprehensive formula for its earlier estate. In short, as a matter of fact, a Laplacean formula merely summarizes what the actual course of events has been with respect to some selected features. How then can it be said to describe an original state of nature in virtue of which just such and such things have necessarily happened? A statement that the world is thus and so can not be tortured into a statement of how and why it must be as it is. The account of how a thing came to be as it is always starts and comes back to the fact that it *is* thus and so. How then can this fact be derived according to some law of predestination from the consideration of its own prior history? For, I repeat, this history is *its* history.[6]

This discussion, however, oversimplifies matters. It overlooks the extent to which inference as to a prior state of affairs is dependent upon the diversity and complexity of what is now observed. We should be in a hard case in trying to fix upon the structure of the Latin language if our sole datum were, say, the French language. As a matter of fact, in considering the growth of the French tongue we have other Romance languages to fall back upon. Above all, we have independent evidence as to the characteristics of Latin speech. If we had not, we should be reasoning in a circle. Science is rightly suspicious of accounts of things in terms of a hypothesis for whose existence nothing can be alleged save that if it existed it would or might account for something which is actually found. Independent evidence of the existence of such an object is required. This consideration has an interesting application to the question in hand. It brings out clearly the absurdity involved in supposing that any formula, of the Laplacean type, about some earlier state of existence, however comprehensive, is comprehensive enough to cover the whole scope of existence of that earlier time.

[6] Compare Woodbridge, "Evolution," *Philosophical Review*, XXI (1912), 137.

Let us suppose the formula to be descriptive of a primitive state of the solar system. Not only must it start from and be framed in terms of what *now* exists, but the present datum must be larger than the existing solar system if we are to escape reasoning in a circle. In such cosmological constructions, astronomers and geologists rely upon observation of what is going on outside of the solar system. Without such data, the inquiry would be hopelessly crippled. The stellar field now presents, presumably, systems in all stages of formation. Is there any reason for supposing that a like state of affairs did not present itself at any and every prior time? Whatever formula is arrived at for the beginning of our present solar system describes, therefore, only one structure existing amid a vaster complex. A state of things adequately and inclusively described by the formula would be, by conception, a state of things in which nothing could happen. To get change we have to assume other structures which interact with it, existences not covered by the formula.

As a matter of fact, the conception of a solar system seems to have exercised an hypnotic influence upon Newton's successors. The gathering together of sun, planets, and their satellites, etc., into a system which might be treated as an individual having its own history was a wonderful achievement, and it impressed men's imaginations. It served for the time as a kind of symbol of the "universe." But as compared with the entire stellar field, the solar system is, after all, only a "right little, tight little island." Yet unless its complex context be ignored the idea of "an undifferentiated universe" which, by some immanent potential force, determined everything which has happened since, could hardly arise.[7] That the French language did not evolve out of Latin because of some immanent causality in the latter we have already noted. It is equally true that the contact and interaction of those speaking Latin with those speaking barbaric tongues were not due to

[7] One who turns to Spencer's chapter on the "Instability of the Homogeneous" [*First Principles*, Part II, Ch. 19] will perceive that his proof of its instability consists in showing that it was really already heterogeneous.

the fact that they spoke Latin, but to independent variables. Internal diversity is as much a necessity as something externally heterogeneous.[8]

The consideration throws light, I think, upon the meaning of potentiality with reference to any state of things. We never apply the term except where there *is* change or a process of becoming. But we have an unfortunate tendency to conceive a fixed state of affairs and then appeal to a latent or potential something or other to effect change. But in reality the term refers to a characteristic of change. Anything changing might be said to exhibit potentiality with respect to two facts: first, that the change exhibits (in connection with interaction with new elements in its surroundings) qualities it did not show till it was exposed to them and, secondly, that the changes in which these qualities are shown run a certain course. To say that an apple has the potentiality of decay does not mean that it has latent or implicit within it a causal principle which will some time inevitably display itself in producing decay, but that its existing changes (in interaction with its surroundings) will take the form of decay, *if* they are exposed or subjected to certain conditions not now operating upon them. Potentiality thus signifies a certain limitation of present powers, due to the limited number of conditions with which they are in interaction plus the fact of the manifestation of new powers under different conditions. To generalize the idea, we have to add the fact that the very changes now going on have a tendency to expose the thing in question to these different conditions which will call out new modes of behavior, in other words, further changes of a different kind. Potentiality thus implies not merely diversity, but a progres-

---

[8] Some contemporary metaphysical theories attempt to start from pure "simple" entities and then refer change exclusively to "complexes." This overlooks the fact that without internal diversification in the alleged simple entity, a complex entity would no more exhibit change than a simple one. The history of the doctrine of atoms is instructive. Such a metaphysics transgresses the conditions of intelligent inquiry in exactly the same way as the metaphysics of ultimate origins.

sively increasing diversification of a specific thing in a particular direction. So far is it from denoting a causal force immanent within a homogeneous something and leading it to change.

We may say then that an earlier condition of our earth was potential with life and mind. But this means that it was changing in a certain way and direction. Starting where we must start, with the present, the fact or organization shows that the world is of a certain kind. In spots, it *has* organization. Reference to the evolution of this organization out of an earlier world in which *such* organization was not found, means something about that earlier condition—it means that it was characterized by a change having direction—that is, in the direction of vital and intelligent organization. I do not see that this justifies the conclusion that that earlier world was biocentric or vitalistic or psychic. Yet two conclusions seem to follow. One is negative. The fact that it is possible and desirable to state the processes of an organized being in chemico-physical terms does not eliminate, but rather takes for granted whatever peculiar features living beings have. It does not imply that the distinguishing features of living and thinking beings are to be explained away by resolution into the features found in nonliving things. It is the *occurrence* of these peculiar features which it stated in physico-chemical terms. And, as we have already seen, the attempt to give an account of any occurrence involves the genuine and irreducible existence of the thing dealt with. A statement of the mechanism of vital and thinking creatures is a statement of *their* mechanism; an account of their production is an account of *their* production. To give such an account does not prove whether the existence in question is a good thing or a bad thing, but it proves nothing at all if it puts in doubt the specific existence of the subject matter investigated.

The positive point is that the evolution of living and thinking beings out of a state of things in which life and thought were not found is a fact which must be recognized in any metaphysical inquiry into the irreducible traits of the world. For evolution appears to be just one of the irreducible traits. In other words, it is a fact to be reckoned with in considering the traits of diversity, interaction, and change which have been enumerated as among the traits taken for granted in all scientific subject matter. If everything which is, is a changing thing, the evolution of life and mind indicates the nature of the changes of physico-chemical things and therefore something about those things. It indicates that as purely physical, they are still limited in their interactions; and that as they are brought into more and complex interactions they exhibit capacities not to be found in an exclusively mechanical world. To say, accordingly, that the existence of vital, intellectual, and social organization makes impossible a purely mechanistic metaphysics is to say something which the situation calls for. But it does not signify that the world "as a whole" is vital or sentient or intelligent. It is a remark of the same order as the statement that one is not adequately acquainted with water or iron until he has found it operating under a variety of different conditions, and hence a scientific doctrine which regards iron as essentially hard or water as essentially liquid is inadequate. Without a doctrine of evolution we might be able to say, not that matter *caused* life, but that matter under certain conditions of highly complicated and intensified interaction is living. With the doctrine of evolution, we can add to this statement that the interactions and changes of matter are themselves of a kind to bring about that complex and intensified interaction which is life. The doctrine of evolution implies that this holds good of any matter, irrespective of its date, for it is not the matter of 1915, as caused by matter that has now ceased to be, which lives. The matter which was active ten million years ago now lives: this is a feature of the matter of ten million years ago.

I am, however, getting beyond my main point. I am not concerned to develop a metaphysics; but simply to indicate one way of conceiving the problem of metaphysical inquiry as distinct from that of the special sciences, a way which settles upon the more ultimate traits of the world as defining its subject matter, but which frees these traits from confusion with ultimate origins and ultimate ends—that is, from questions of creation and eschatology. The chief significance of evolution with reference to such an inquiry seems to be to indicate that while metaphysics takes the world irrespective of any particular time, yet time itself, or genuine change in a specific direction, is itself one of the ultimate traits of the world irrespective of date.

ᴥᴥ XI ᴥᴥ

TIME AND INDIVIDUALITY[1]

This speculative essay has been ignored to the extent that it is not included in the standard bibliographies of Dewey. Yet it is one of the most striking illustrations of Dewey exploring the foundations of his philosophy and dealing with metaphysical issues. The natures of time, individuality, and potentiality are discussed and interrelated. Pursuing an insight which he shares with Bergson, James, and Whitehead, Dewey suggests that temporal quality and historical career are the marks of everything that exists and are the essence of their individuality. An historical career is a series of interactions whose uniqueness consists of the way in which the individual responds to encountered conditions. (Later Dewey used the technical term "transaction"; see Introduction, Part III.) Individuality, which is intimately bound up with temporal development, suggests a fresh approach to interpreting potentiality. "Potentialities are not fixed and intrinsic, but are a matter of an indefinite range of interactions in which the individual may engage." The web of ideas in this essay stretches out in a number of directions. "Individuality" has close affinities with "freedom" as discussed in "Philosophies of Freedom" and with the analysis of "selective interest" in "Context and Thought"; the remarks about the relation of science and art throw further light on "Having an Experience" and "Qualitative Thought." As one follows the intertwining of these ideas, which in their turn carry us to other basic concepts, a coherent and comprehensive philosophy of experience and nature emerges.

[1] *Time and Its Mysteries,* Series II (New York: 1940), pp. 85-109. This essay was originally presented as a lecture on April 21, 1938, at New York University. The lecture was given as part of a series entitled "Time and Its Mysteries," sponsored by the James Arthur Foundation.

THE GREEKS had a saying "Count no man happy till after his death." The adage was a way of calling attention to the uncertainties of life. No one knows what a year or even a day may bring forth. The healthy become ill; the rich poor; the mighty are cast down; fame changes to obloquy. Men live at the mercy of forces they cannot control. Belief in fortune and luck, good or evil, is one of the most widespread and persistent of human beliefs. Chance has been deified by many peoples. Fate has been set up as an overlord to whom even the Gods must bow. Belief in a Goddess of Luck is in ill repute among pious folk but their belief in providence is a tribute to the fact no individual controls his own destiny.

The uncertainty of life and one's final lot has always been associated with mutability, while unforeseen and uncontrollable change has been linked with time. Time is the tooth that gnaws; it is the destroyer; we are born only to die and every day brings us one day nearer death. This attitude is not confined to the ignorant and vulgar. It is the root of what is sometimes called the instinctive belief in immortality. Everything perishes in time but men are unable to believe that perishing is the last word. For centuries poets made the uncertainty which time brings with it the theme of their discourse—read Shakespeare's sonnets. Nothing stays; life is fleeting and all earthly things are transitory.

It was not then for metaphysical reasons that classic philosophy maintained that change, and consequently time, are marks of inferior reality, holding that true and ultimate reality is immutable and eternal. Human reasons, all too human, have given birth to the idea that over and beyond the lower realm of things that shift like the sands on the seashore there is the kingdom of the unchanging, of the complete, the perfect. The grounds for the belief are couched in the technical language of philosophy, but the cause for the grounds is the heart's desire for surcease from change, struggle, and uncertainty. The eternal and immutable is the consummation of mortal man's quest for certainty.

It is not strange then that philosophies which have been at odds on every other point have been one in the conviction that the ultimately real is fixed and unchanging, even though they have been as far apart as the poles in their ideas of its constitution. The idealist has found it in a realm of rational ideas; the materialist in the laws of matter. The mechanist pins his faith to eternal atoms and to unmoved and unmoving space. The teleologist finds that all change is subservient to fixed ends and final goals, which are the one steadfast thing in the universe, conferring upon changing things whatever meaning and value they possess. The typical realist attributes to unchanging essences a greater degree of reality than belongs to existences; the modern mathematical realist finds the stability his heart desires in the immunity of the realm of possibilities from vicissitude. Although classic rationalism looked askance at experience and empirical things because of their continual subjection to alteration, yet strangely enough traditional sensational empiricism relegated time to a secondary role. Sensations appeared and disappeared but in their own nature they were as fixed as were Newtonian atoms—of which indeed they were mental copies. Ideas were but weakened copies of sensory impressions and had no inherent forward power and application. The passage of time dimmed their vividness and caused their decay. Because of their subjection to the tooth of time, they were denied productive force.

In the late eighteenth and the greater part of the nineteenth centuries appeared the first marked cultural shift in the attitude taken toward change. Under the names of indefinite perfectability, progress, and evolution, the movement of things in the universe itself and of the universe as a whole began to take on a beneficent instead of a hateful aspect. Not every change was regarded as a sign of advance but the general trend of change, cosmic and social, was thought to be toward the better. Aside from the Christian idea of a millennium of good and bliss to be finally wrought by supernatural means, the Golden Age for the first time in history was placed in the future instead of at the beginning, and change and time were assigned a benevolent role.

Even if the new optimism was not adequately grounded, there were sufficient causes for its occurrence as there are for all great changes in intellectual climate. The rise of new science in the seventeenth century laid hold upon general culture in the next century. Its popular effect was not great, but its influence upon the intellectual elite, even upon those who were not themselves engaged in scientific inquiry, was prodigious. The enlightenment, the *éclaircissement*, the *Aufklärung*—names which in the three most advanced countries of Europe testified to the widespread belief that at last light had dawned, that dissipation of the darkness of ignorance, superstition, and bigotry was at hand, and the triumph of reason was assured—for reason was the counterpart in man of the laws of nature which science was disclosing. The reign of law in the natural world was to be followed by the reign of law in human affairs. A vista of the indefinite perfectibility of man was opened. It played a large part in that optimistic theory of automatic evolution which later found its classic formulation in the philosophy of Herbert Spencer. The faith may have been pathetic but it has its own nobility.

At last, time was thought to be working on the side of the good instead of as a destructive agent. Things were moving to an event which was divine, even if far off.

This new philosophy, however, was far from giving the temporal an inherent position and function in the constitution of things. Change was working on the side of man but only because of *fixed* laws which governed the changes that take place. There was hope in change just because the laws that govern it do not change. The locus of the immutable was shifted to scientific natural law, but the faith and hope of philosophers and intellectuals were still tied to the unchanging. The belief that "evolution" is identical with progress was

based upon trust in laws which, being fixed, worked automatically toward the final end of freedom, justice, and brother-
hood, the natural consequences of the reign of reason.

Not till the late nineteenth century was the doctrine of the
subordination of time and change seriously challenged. Bergson and William James, animated by different motives and
proceeding by different methods, then installed change at the
very heart of things. Bergson took his stand on the primacy
of life and consciousness, which are notoriously in a state of
flux. He assimilated that which is completely real in the
natural world to them, conceiving the static as that which life
leaves behind as a deposit as it moves on. From this point of
view he criticized mechanistic and teleological theories on
the ground that both are guilty of the same error, although
from opposite points. Fixed laws which govern change and
fixed ends toward which changes tend are both the products
of a backward look, one that ignores the forward movement of
life. They apply only to that which life has produced and has
then left behind in its ongoing vital creative course, a course
whose behavior and outcome are unpredictable both mechanically and from the standpoint of ends. The intellect is at home
in that which is fixed only because it is done and over with,
for intellect is itself just as much a deposit of past life as is the
matter to which it is congenial. Intuition alone articulates in
the forward thrust of life and alone lays hold of reality.

The animating purpose of James was, on the other hand,
primarily moral and artistic. It is expressed, in his phrase,
"block universe," employed as a term of adverse criticism.
Mechanism and idealism were abhorrent to him because they
both hold to a closed universe in which there is no room for
novelty and adventure. Both sacrifice individuality and all the
values, moral and aesthetic, which hang upon individuality,
for according to absolute idealism, as to mechanistic materialism, the individual is simply a part determined by the whole
of which he is a part. Only a philosophy of pluralism, of
genuine indetermination, and of change which is real and
intrinsic gives significance to individuality. It alone justifies

struggle in creative activity and gives opportunity for the emergence of the genuinely new.

It was reserved, however, for the present century to give birth to the out-and-out assertion in systematic form that reality *is* process, and that laws as well as things develop in the processes of unceasing change. The modern Heraclitean is Alfred North Whitehead, but he is Heraclitus with a change. The doctrine of the latter, while it held that all things flow like a river and that change is so continuous that a man cannot step into the same river even once (since it changes as he steps), nevertheless also held that there is a fixed order which controls the ebb and flow of the universal tide.

My theme, however, is not historical, nor is it to argue in behalf of any one of the various doctrines regarding time that have been advanced. The purpose of the history just roughly sketched is to indicate that the nature of time and change has now become in its own right a philosophical problem of the first importance. It is of time as a problem that I wish to speak. The aspect of the problem that will be considered is the connection of time with individuality, as the latter is exemplified in the living organism and especially in human beings.

Take the account of the life of any person, whether the account is a biography or an autobiography. The story begins with birth, a temporal incident; it extends to include the temporal existence of parents and ancestry. It does not end with death, for it takes in the influence upon subsequent events of the words and deeds of the one whose life is told. Everything recorded is an historical event; it is something temporal. The individual whose life history is told, be it Socrates or Nero, St. Francis or Abraham Lincoln, is an extensive event; or, if you prefer, it is a course of events each of which takes up into itself something of what went before and leads on to that which comes after. The skill, the art, of the biographer is displayed in his ability to discover and portray the subtle ways, hidden often from the individual himself, in which one event grows out of those which preceded and enters into those which follow. The human individual is himself a history, a career, and for this reason his biography can be related only as a temporal event. That which comes later explains the earlier quite as truly as the earlier explains the later. Take the individual Abraham Lincoln at one year, at five years, at ten years, at thirty years of age, and imagine everything later wiped out, no matter how minutely his life is recorded up to the date set. It is plain beyond the need of words that we then have not his biography but only a fragment of it, while the significance of that fragment is undisclosed. For he did not just exist in a time which externally surrounded him, but time was the heart of his existence.

Temporal seriality is the very essence, then, of the human individual. It is impossible for a biographer in writing, say the story of the first thirty years of the life of Lincoln, not to bear in mind his later career. Lincoln as an individual is a history; any particular event cut off from that history ceases to be a part of his life as an individual. As Lincoln is a particular development in time, so is every other human individual. Individuality is the uniqueness of the history, of the career, not something given once for all at the beginning which then proceeds to unroll as a ball of yarn may be unwound. Lincoln made history. But it is just as true that he made himself as an individual in the history he made.

I have been speaking about human individuality. Now an important part of the problem of time is that what is true of the human individual does not seem to be true of physical individuals. The common saying "as like as two peas" is a virtual denial to one kind of vegetable life of the kind of individuality that marks human beings. It is hard to conceive of the individuality of a given pea in terms of a unique history or career; such individuality as it appears to possess seems to be due in part to spatial separateness and in part to peculiarities that are externally caused. The same thing holds true of lower forms of animal life. Most persons would resent denial of some sort of unique individuality to their own dogs, but would be slow to attribute it to worms, clams, and bees. In-

eed, it seems to be an exclusive prerogative of the romantic
ovelist to find anything in the way of a unique career in
nimal lives in general.

When we come to inanimate elements, the prevailing view
as been that time and sequential change are entirely for-
ign to their nature. According to this view they do not have
areers; they simply change their relations in space. We have
nly to think of the classic conception of atoms. The New-
onian atom, for example, moved and was moved, thus chang-
ig its position in space, but it was unchangeable in its own
eing. What it was at the beginning or without any beginning
: is always and forever. Owing to the impact of other things
changes its direction and velocity of motion so that it comes
loser and further away from other things. But all this was
elieved to be external to its own substantial being. It had no
evelopment, no history, because it had no potentialities. In
:self it was like a God, the same yesterday, today, and for-
ver. Time did not enter into its being either to corrode or
> develop it. Nevertheless, as an ultimate element it was
ipposed to have some sort of individuality, to be itself and
ot something else. Time, in physical science, has been simply
measure of motion in space.

Now, this apparently complete unlikeness in kind between
ne human and the physical individual is a part of the prob-
em of time. Some philosophers have been content to note the
ifference and to make it the ground for affirming a sheer
ualism between man and other things, a ground for assign-
ig to man a spiritual being in contrast with material things.
)thers, fewer in numbers, have sought to explain away the
eeming disparity, holding that the apparent uniqueness of
uman individuality is specious, being in fact the effect of the
ast number of physical molecules, themselves complex, which
nake up his being, so that what looks like genuine temporal
hange or development is really but a function of the number
nd complexity of changes of constituent fixed elements. Of
ite, there have been a few daring souls who have held that
emporal quality and historical career are a mark of every-

thing, including atomic elements, to which individuality ma
be attributed.

I shall mention some of the reasons from the side of phys:
cal science that have led to this third idea. The first reason i
the growing recognition that scientific objects are purel
relational and have nothing to do with the intrinsic qualitie
of individual things and nothing to say about them. Th
meaning of this statement appears most clearly in the cas
of scientific laws. It is now a commonplace that a physical la'
states a correlation of changes or of ways and manners c
change. The law of gravitation, for example, states a relatio.
which holds between bodies with respect to distance and mas.
It needs no argument to show that distance is a relation. Mas
was long regarded as an inherent property of ultimate an
individual elements. But even the Newtonian conception wa
obliged to recognize that mass could be defined only in term
of inertia and that inertia could be defined only in terms, o
the one hand, of the resistance it offered to the impact c
other bodies, and, on the other hand, of its capacity to exe
cise impact upon them, impact being measured in terms c
motion with respect to acceleration. The idea that mass is a
inherent property which caused inertia and momentum wa
simply a holdover from an old metaphysical idea of force. A
far as the findings of science are concerned, independent c
the intrusion of metaphysical ideas, mass is inertia-momentu
and these are strictly measures and relations. The discover
that mass changes with velocity, a discovery made whe
minute bodies came under consideration, finally forced su:
render of the notion that mass is a fixed and inalienable po
session of ultimate elements or individuals, so that time :
now considered to be their fourth dimension.

It may be remarked incidentally that the recognition of th
relational character of scientific objects completely eliminat
an old metaphysical issue. One of the outstanding problem
created by the rise of modern science was due to the fact tha
scientific definitions and descriptions are framed in terms i
which qualities play no part. Qualities were wholly supe

uous. As long as the idea persisted (an inheritance from
Greek metaphysical science) that the business of knowledge is
to penetrate into the inner being of objects, the existence of
qualities like colors, sounds, etc., was embarrassing. The usual
way of dealing with them is to declare that they are merely
subjective, existing only in the consciousness of individual
knowers. Given the old idea that the purpose of knowledge
(represented at its best in science) is to penetrate into the
heart of reality and reveal its "true" nature, the conclusion
was a logical one. The discovery that the objects of scientific
knowledge are purely relational shows that the problem is an
artificial one. It was "solved" by the discovery that it needed
no solution, since fulfillment of the function and business of
science compels disregard of qualities. Using the older
language, it was seen that so-called primary qualities are no
more inherent properties of ultimate objects than are so-
called secondary qualities of odors, sounds, and colors, since
the former are also strictly relational; or, as Locke stated in
his moments of clear insight, are "retainers" of objects in
their connections with other things. The discovery of the
unscientific because of the empirically unverifiable and unnecessary character of absolute space, absolute motion, and
absolute time gave the final *coup de grâce* to the traditional
idea that solidity, mass, size, etc., are inherent possessions of
ultimate individuals.

The revolution in scientific ideas just mentioned is primarily logical. It is due to recognition that the very method
of physical science, with its primary standard units of mass,
space, and time, is concerned with measurement of relations
of change, not with individuals as such. This acknowledgment brought with it a further idea which, in spite of the
resistance made to it by adherents of older metaphysical views,
is making constant headway. This idea is that laws which
purport to be statements of what actually occurs are statistical
in character as distinct from so-called dynamic laws that are
abstract and mathematical, and disguised definitions. Recognition of the statistical nature of physical laws was first effected

in the case of gases when it became evident that generaliz
tions regarding the behavior of swarms of molecules were no
descriptions or predictions of the behavior of any individu
particle. A single molecule is not and cannot be a gas. It
consequently absurd to suppose that the scientific law is abou
the elementary constituents of a gas. It is a statement o
what happens when a very large number of such constituen
interact with one another under certain conditions.

Statistical statements are of the nature of probability formu
lations. No insurance company makes any prediction as to
what will happen to any given person in respect to death, o
to any building with respect to destruction by fire. Insuranc
is conducted upon the basis of observation that out of a larg
number of persons of a given age such and such a proportio
ate number will probably live one year more, another propo
tionate number two years, and so on, while premiums are ac
justed on the basis of these probability estimates. The validi
of the estimates depends, as in the case of a swarm of mol
cules, upon the existence of a sufficiently large number o
individuals, a knowledge which is a matter of the relativ
frequency of events of a certain kind to the total number o
events which occur. No statement is made about what wi
take place in the case of an *individual*. The application o
scientific formulations of the principle of probability statisti
ally determined is thus a logical corollary of the principle a
ready stated, that the subject matter of scientific findings
relational, not individual. It is for this reason that it is safe t
predict the ultimate triumph of the statistical doctrine.

The third scientific consideration is found in Heisenberg
principle of uncertainty or indeterminacy, which may be r
garded as a generalization of the ideas already stated. I
form, this principle seems to be limited in its applicatio
Classical science was based upon the belief that it is possib
to formulate both the position and the velocity at one tim
of any given particle. It followed that knowledge of the pos
tion and velocity of a given number of particles would enab
the future behavior of the whole collection to be accuratel

predicted. The principle of Heisenberg is that given the determination of position, its velocity can be stated only as of a certain order of probability, while if its velocity is determined the correlative factor of position can be stated only as of a certain order of probability. Both cannot be determined at once, from which it follows necessarily that the future of the whole collection cannot possibly be foretold except in terms of some order of probability.

Because of the fundamental place of the conceptions of position and velocity in physical science the principle is not limited in scope but is of the broadest possible significance. Given the classic conception, Laplace stated its logical outcome when he said "we may conceive the present state of the universe as the effect of its past and the cause of its future. An intellect who at any given instant knew all the forces of animate nature and the mutual positions of the beings who compose it . . . could condense into a single formula the movement both of the greatest body in [the] universe and of its lightest atom. Nothing would be uncertain to such an intellect, for the future, even as the past would be ever present before his eyes." No more sweeping statement of the complete irrelevancy of time to the physical world and of the complete unreality for individuals of time could well be uttered. But the principle of indeterminacy annihilates the premises from which the conclusion follows. The principle is thus a way of acknowledging the pertinency of real time to physical beings. The utmost possible regarding an individual is a statement as to some order of probability about the future. Heisenberg's principle has been seized upon as a basis for wild statements to the effect that the doctrine of arbitrary free will and totally uncaused activity are now scientifically substantiated. Its actual force and significance is generalization of the idea that the individual is a temporal career whose future cannot be *logically* deduced from its past.

As long as scientific knowledge was supposed to be concerned with individuals in their own intrinsic nature, there was no way to bridge the gap between the career of human individuals and that of physical individuals, save by holding that the seeming fundamental place of development and hence of time in the life histories of the former is only seeming or specious. The unescapable conclusion is that as human individuality can be understood only in terms of time as fundamental reality, so for physical individuals time is not simply a measure of predetermined changes in mutual positions, but is something that enters into their being. Laws do not "govern" the activity of individuals. They are a formulation of the frequency-distributions of the behavior of large numbers of individuals engaged in interactions with one another.

This statement does not mean that physical and human individuality are identical, nor that the things which appear to us to be nonliving have the distinguishing characteristic of organisms. The difference between the inanimate and the animate is not so easily wiped out. But it does show that there is no fixed gap between them. The conclusion which most naturally follows, without indulging in premature speculations, is that the principle of a developing career applies to all things in nature, as well as to human beings—that they are born, undergo qualitative changes, and finally die, giving place to other individuals. The idea of development applied to nature involves differences of forms and qualities as surely as it rules out absolute breaches of continuity. The differences between the amoeba and the human organism are genuinely there even if we accept the idea of organic evolution of species. Indeed, to deny the reality of the differences and their immense significance would be to deny the very idea of development. To wipe out differences because of denial of complete breaks and the need for intervention of some outside power is just as surely a way to deny development as is assertion of gaps which can be bridged only by the intervention of some supernatural force. It is then in terms of development, or if one prefers the more grandiose term, evolution, that I shall further discuss the problem of time.

The issue involved is perhaps the most fundamental one in

philosophy at the present time. Are the changes which go on in the world simply external redistributions, rearrangements in space of what previously existed, or are they genuine qualitative changes such as apparently take place in the physiological development of an organism, from the union of ovum and sperm to maturity, and as apparently take place in the personal life career of individuals? When the question is raised, certain misapprehensions must be first guarded against. Development and evolution have historically been eulogistically interpreted. They have been thought of as necessarily proceeding from the lower to the higher, from the relatively worse to the relatively better. But this property was read in from outside moral and theological preoccupations. The real issue is that stated above: Is what happens simply a spatial rearrangement of what existed previously or does it involve something qualitatively new? From this point of view, cancer is as genuinely a physiological development as is growth in vigor; criminals as well as heroes are a social development; the emergence of totalitarian states is a social evolution out of constitutional states independently of whether we like or approve them.

If we accept the intrinsic connection of time with individuality, they are not mere redistributions of what existed before. Since it is a *problem* I am presenting, I shall assume that genuine transformations occur, and consider its implications. First and negatively, the idea (which is often identified with the essential meaning of evolution) is excluded that development is a process of unfolding what was previously implicit or latent. Positively it is implied that potentiality is a category of existence, for development cannot occur unless an individual has powers or capacities that are not actualized at a given time. But it also means that these powers are not unfolded from within, but are called out through interaction with other things. While it is necessary to revive the category of potentiality as a characteristic of individuality, it has to be revived in a different form from that of its classic Aristotelian formulation. According to that view, potentialities are connected with a *fixed* end which the individual endeavors by its own nature or essence to actualize, although its success in actualization depended upon the co-operation of external things and hence might be thwarted by the "accidents" of its surroundings—as not every acorn becomes a tree and few if any acorns become the typical oak.

When the idea that development is due to some indwelling end which tends to control the series of changes passed through is abandoned, potentialities must be thought of in terms of consequences of interactions with other things. Hence potentialities cannot be *known* till *after* the interactions have occurred. There are at a given time unactualized potentialities in an individual because and in as far as there are in existence other things with which it has not as yet interacted. Potentialities of milk are known today, for example, that were not known a generation ago, because milk has been brought into interaction with things other than organisms, and hence now has other than furnishing nutriment consequence. It is now predicted that in the future human beings will be wearing clothes made of glass and that the clothes will be cleaned by throwing them into a hot furnace. Whether this particular prediction is fulfilled or not makes no difference to its value as an illustration. Every new scientific discovery leads to some mode of technology that did not previously exist. As things are brought by new procedures into new contacts and new interactions, new consequences are produced and the power to produce these new consequences is a recognized potentiality of the thing in question. The idea that potentialities are inherent and fixed by relation to a predetermined end was a product of a highly restricted state of technology. Because of this restriction, the only potentialities recognized were those consequences which were customary in the given state of culture and were accordingly taken to be "natural." When the only possible use of milk was as an article of food, it was "natural" to suppose that it had an inherent tendency to serve that particular end. With the use of milk as a plastic, and with no one able to tell what future consequences may be produced by new techniques which bring it into new inter-actions, the only reasonable conclusion is that potentialities are not fixed and intrinsic, but are a matter of an indefinite range of interactions in which an individual may engage.

Return for a moment to the human individual. It is im-possible to think of the historical career, which is the special individuality constituting Abraham Lincoln, apart from the particular conditions in which he lived. He did not create, for example, the conditions that formed the issues of states' rights and of slavery, the issues that influenced his develop-ment. What his being as an individual would have been without these interacting conditions it is idle to speculate upon. The conditions did not form him from without as wax is supposed to be shaped by external pressure. There is no such thing as interaction that is merely a one-way movement. There were many other persons living under much the same conditions whose careers were very different, because con-ditions acted upon them and were acted upon by them in different ways. Hence there is no account possible of Lincoln's life that does not portray him interacting day by day with special conditions, with his parents, his wife and children, his neighbors, his economic conditions, his school facilities, the incidents of his profession as a lawyer, and so on. The career which is his unique individuality is the series of interactions in which he was created to be what he was by the ways in which he responded to the occasions with which he was pre-sented. One cannot leave out either conditions as *oppor-tunities* nor yet unique ways of responding to them. An occasion is an opportunity only when it is an evocation of a specific event, while a response is not a necessary effect of a cause but is a way of using an occasion to render it a con-stituent of an ongoing unique history.

Individuality conceived as a temporal development involves uncertainty, indeterminacy, or contingency. Individuality is the source of whatever is unpredictable in the world. The indeterminate is not change in the sense of violation of law, nor laws state probable correlations of change and these probabilities exist no matter what the source of change may be. When a change occurs *after* it has occurred, it belongs to the observable world and is connected with other changes. The nomination of Lincoln for the presidency, his election, his Emancipation Proclamation, his assassination, after they took place can be shown to be related to other events; they can also be shown to have a certain connection with Lincoln's own past. But there was nothing in Lincoln's own life to cause by itself the conjunction of circumstances which brought about any one of these events. As far as he as an individual was concerned, the events were contingent, and as far as the conjunction of circumstances was concerned, his behavior at any given time in response to them was also contingent, or if you please fortuitous.

At critical junctures, his response could not be predicted either from his own past or from the nature of the circumstances, except as a probability. To say this is not arbitrarily to introduce mere chance into the world. It is to say that genuine individuality exists; that individuality is pregnant with new developments; that time is real. If we knew enough about Shakespeare's life we could doubtless show *after* Hamlet was produced how it is connected with other things. We could link it with sources; we could connect its mood with specific experiences of its author, and so on. But no one with the fullest knowledge of Shakespeare's past could have predicted the drama as it stands. If they could have done so, they would have been able to write it. Not even Shakespeare himself could have told in advance just what he was going to say—not if he was an individual, not a nodal point in the spatial redistribution of what already existed.

The mystery of time is thus the mystery of the existence of real individuals. It is a mystery because it is a mystery that anything which exists is just what it is. We are given to forgetting, with our insistence upon causation and upon the necessity of things happening as they do happen, that things exist as just what they qualitatively are. We can account for a change by relating it to other changes, but existences we have to accept for just what they are. Given a butterfly or an earthquake as an event, as a change, we can at least in theory find out and state its connection with other changes. But the individual butterfly or earthquake remains just the unique existence which it is. We forget in explaining its occurrence that it is only the *occurrence* that is explained, not the thing itself. We forget that in explaining the occurrence we are compelled to fall back on other individual things that have just the unique qualities they do have. Go as far back as we please in accounting for present conditions and we still come upon the mystery of things being just what they are.

Their occurrence, their manifestation, may be accounted for in terms of other occurrences, but their own quality of existence is final and opaque. The mystery is that the world is as it is—a mystery that is the source of all joy and all sorrow, of all hope and fear, and the source of development both creative and degenerative. The contingency of all into which time enters is the source of pathos, comedy, and tragedy. Genuine time, if it exists as anything else except the measure of motions in space, is all one with the existence of individuals as individuals, with the creative, with the occurrence of unpredictable novelties. Everything that can be said contrary to this conclusion is but a reminder that an individual may lose his individuality, for individuals become imprisoned in routine and fall to the level of mechanisms. Genuine time then ceases to be an integral element in their being. Our behavior becomes predictable because it is but an external rearrangement of what wert before.

In conclusion, I would like to point out two considerations that seem to me to follow, two morals, if you wish to give them that name. I said earlier that the traditional idea of progress and evolution was based upon belief that the fixed structure of the universe is such as automatically brings it about. This optimistic and fatalistic idea is now at a discount. It is easy in the present state of the world to deny all validity whatever to the idea of progress, since so much of the human world seems bent on demonstrating the truth of the old theological doctrine of the fall of man. But the real conclusion is that, while progress is not inevitable, it is up to men as individuals to bring it about. Change is going to occur anyway, and the problem is the control of change in a given direction. The direction, the quality of change, is a matter of individuality. Surrender of individuality by the many to some one who is taken to be a superindividual explains the retrograde movement of society. Dictatorships and totalitarian states, and belief in the inevitability of this or that result coming to pass are, strange as it may sound, ways of denying the reality of time and the creativeness of the individual. Freedom of thought and of expression are not mere rights to be claimed. They have their roots deep in the existence of individuals as developing careers in time. Their denial and abrogation is an abdication of individuality and a virtual rejection of time as opportunity.

The ground of democratic ideas and practices is faith in the potentialities of individuals, faith in the capacity for positive developments if proper conditions are provided. The weakness of the philosophy originally advanced to justify the democratic movement was that it took individuality to be something given ready-made; that is, in abstraction from time, instead of as a power to develop.

The other conclusion is that art is the complement of science. Science as I have said is concerned wholly with relations, not with individuals. Art, on the other hand, is not only the disclosure of the individuality of the artist but is also a manifestation of individuality as creative of the future, in an unprecedented response to conditions as they were in the past. Some artists in their vision of what might be but is not have been conscious rebels. But conscious protest and revolt is not the form which the labor of the artist in creation of the future must necessarily take. Discontent with things as they are is normally the expression of vision of what may be and is not, art in being the manifestation of individuality is this prophetic vision. To regiment artists, to make them servants of some particular cause does violence to the very springs of artistic creation. But it does more than that. It betrays the very cause of a better future it would serve, for in its subjection of the individuality of the artist it annihilates the source of that which is genuinely new. Were the regimentation successful, it would cause the future to be but a rearrangement of the past.

The artist in realizing his own individuality reveals potentialities hitherto unrealized. This revelation is the inspiration of other individuals to make the potentialities real, for it is not sheer revolt against things as they are which stirs human endeavor to its depths, but vision of what might be and is not. Subordination of the artists to any special cause no matter how worthy does violence not only to the artist but to the living source of a new and better future. Art is not the possession of the few who are recognized writers, painters, musicians; it is the authentic expression of any and all individuality. Those who have the gift of creative expression in unusually large measure disclose the meaning of the individuality of others to those others. In participating in the work of art, they become artists in their activity. They learn to know and honor individuality in whatever form it appears. The fountains of creative activity are discovered and released. The free individuality which is the source of art is also the final source of creative development in time.

NATURE IN EXPERIENCE [1]

When Dewey formulated his instrumentalism, he repudiated his early Hegelian belief that experience is ultimately taken up and encompassed in a system of knowledge. Experience includes far more than knowing situations, and the latter arise in response to conflicts within our experience. Knowing or inquiry is only one mode of the multifarious variety of experience. But while Dewey escaped the pitfall of idealism in which everything becomes a form of knowledge, it appeared as if he were to fall into a similar pitfall where everything becomes experience. One of the most serious problems of his later philosophy was to show that while nature enters into experiential transactions, experience is grounded in, and limited by, the more extensive range of natural transactions. At a symposium held at the 1939 meeting of the American Philosophical Association, Morris Cohen and William Ernest Hocking challenged Dewey on this and related issues. The following article is Dewey's reply to their criticisms. The entire symposium is an excellent example of lively philosophic dialectic. Dewey clarifies and defends his version of naturalism, which is sensitive to the unique qualities and patterns of behavior manifested by different types of natural transactions, but at the same time presupposes the continuity of nature and experience.[2]

THE TOPIC announced for this session is capable of two interpretations. When it was communicated to me I took it to mean that the subject for discussion was the relation between the theory of experience and the theory of nature. When the two papers we have just heard were sent

[1] *The Philosophical Review*, XLIX (1940), 244-58.

[2] See Morris Cohen, "Some Difficulties in Dewey's Anthropocentric Naturalism," and William Ernest Hocking, "Dewey's Concepts of Experience and Nature," *The Philosophical Review*, XLIX (1940). Dewey's reply is in this same volume.

to me I found that impression borne out in part. But it also became clear that the topic could be interpreted broadly so that anything I have written concerning either nature or experience is open for consideration. I had then to decide how should I plan my reply. I have adopted the first of the two topics. It has the advantage of enabling me to centralize what I have to say, since I should otherwise have to disperse what I have to say over a large variety of topics. It has the disadvantage that it may seem to show lack of respect for some quite important criticisms that are passed over, and perhaps that of accepting as sound the interpretations upon which the criticisms rest.

In this dilemma the finally decisive consideration was that the course which enables me to introduce more unity and organization serves also to focus attention upon a problem which is so central in philosophy that it must be met and dealt with by all schools. The theme of the Carus Lectures,[3] to which we are having the pleasure of listening, brings to our attention the importance of the category of perspectives, and this matter of perspectives is basic in the issue of the connection between nature and experience. I find that with respect to the hanging together of various problems and various hypotheses in a perspective determined by a definite point of view, I have a system. In so far I have to retract disparaging remarks I have made in the past about the need for system in philosophy.

The peculiar importance in philosophy of a point of view and of the perspective it institutes is enhanced by the fact that a fairly large number of alternative points of view have been worked out in the history of philosophy in terms of the ways in which the world looks from them; that is to say, in terms of the leading categories by which the things of the world are to be understood. The significations attached to words and ideas which recur in practically every system tend to become fixed till it seems as if no choice were left, save to give

[3] ["Toward a Perspective Realism," delivered by Evander Bradley McGilvary.]

the terms (and the problems to which they relate) the import sanctioned by some one or other past philosophic point of view. In the degree in which a philosophy involves a shift from older points of view and from what is seen in their perspectives, both its author and those to whom he addresses himself find themselves in difficulties. The former has to use words that have meanings fixed under conditions of more or less alien points of view and the latter have to engage in some kind of imaginative translation.

The bearing of this general remark upon the present theme has to do first of all with the word "experience" and the allied word "empiricism." There is a long tradition of empiricism in the story of philosophy; upon the whole the tradition is particularistic and nominalistic, if not overtly sensationalistic, in its logic and ontology. When empiricism has escaped from the limits thereby set it has, upon the whole, been through making human experience the broken but still usable ladder of ascent to an absolute experience, and there has been a flight to some form of cosmic idealism. Presentation of a view of experience which puts experience in connection with nature, with the cosmos, but which would nevertheless frame its view of experience on the ground of conclusions reached in the natural sciences, has trouble in finding ways of expressing itself which do not seem to lead into one or the other of these historically sanctioned alternative perspectives.

There is a circularity in the position taken regarding the connection of experience and nature. Upon one side, analysis and interpretation of nature is made dependent upon the conclusions of the natural sciences, especially upon biology, but upon a biology that is itself dependent upon physics and chemistry. But when I say "dependent" I mean that the intellectual instrumentalities, the organs, for understanding the new and distinctive material of experienced objects are provided by the natural sciences. I do *not* mean that the material of experienced things *qua* experienced must be translated into the terms of the material of the physical sciences;

[margin notes: Problem in terminology / Nature & Experience / Circularity (1) / Dependent methodological consideration]

not a reductionist naturalism

Circularity (2)

that view leads to a naturalism which denies distinctive significance to experience, thereby ending in the identification of naturalism with mechanistic materialism.

The other aspect of the circle is found in the fact that it is held that experience itself, even ordinary gross macroscopic experience, contains the materials and the processes and operations which, when they are rightly laid hold of and used, lead to the methods and conclusions of the natural sciences; namely, to the very conclusions that provide the means for forming a theory of experience. That this circle exists is not so much admitted as claimed. It is also claimed that the circle is not vicious; for instead of being logical it is existential and historic. That is to say, if we look at human history and especially at the historic development of the natural sciences, we find progress made from a crude experience in which beliefs about nature and natural events were very different from those now scientifically authorized to the latter. At the same time we find the latter now enable us to frame a theory of experience by which we can tell *how* this development out of gross experience into the highly refined conclusions of science has taken place.

I come now to certain topics and criticism to be dealt with on the basis of the idea of this circular relation. The most inclusive criticism of my friend Morris Cohen is suggested, I think, by the word 'anthropocentric' in the title of his paper; it is expressed in the saying that my absorption in human experience prevents me from formulating any adequate theory of nonhuman or physical nature. In short, it is held that the fact—which is not denied to be a fact—that experience involves a human element limits a philosophy that makes experience primary to human affairs as its sole material; hence it does not admit of propositions about such things as, say, the origin of life on earth or the events of geological ages preceding the advent of man and hence, of necessity, human experience.

Now there is a problem here which every empirical philosophy must meet; it can evade the challenge only to its own damage. Yet the problem is not confined to empiricism; the existence of experience is a fact, and it is fact that the organs of experience, the body, the nervous system, hands and eyes, muscles and senses, are means by which we have access to the nonhuman world. It would seem then as if the philosophy which denies that it is possible for experienced things and processes to form a road into the natural world must be controlled by an underlying postulate that there is a breach of continuity between nature and man and hence between nature and human experience. At all events, a fundamental question is raised. Is experience itself natural a doing or manifestation of nature? Or is it in some genuine sense extranatural, subnatural or supernatural, something superimposed and alien? At all events, this is the setting in which I shall place and interpret some of the more basic criticisms passed upon my views.

(1) There are traits, qualities, and relations found in things experienced, in the things that are typically and emphatically matters of human experience, which do not appear in the objects of physical science; namely, such things as immediate qualities, values, ends. Are such things inherently relevant and important for a philosophical theory of nature? I have held that philosophical empiricism must take the position that they are intrinsically pertinent. I have written (and Cohen has quoted): "It is as much a part of the real being of atoms that they give rise in time, under increasing complications of relationships, to qualities of blue and sweet, pain and beauty, as that they have, at a certain cross-section of time, extension, mass or weight." [4] Now whether this statement is correct or false, it is simply an illustration of what any theory must hold which sees things in the perspective determined by the point of view of the continuity of experience with nature.[5]

[4] [*Experience and Nature* (1925), pp. 109-10.]

[5] "Giving rise to" implies no particular theory as to causal determination, and the word "atom" is used illustratively. The point made would

From the point of view of a theory which sets up a breach of continuity it will be not so much false as nonsensical, egregiously absurd. I also write that domination of man by desire and reverie is as pertinent to a philosophical theory of nature as is mathematical physics. The point of this statement is also truistic, given the point of view of the continuity of experience with nature. It certainly is not countered by the statement that "For the understanding of the general processes of nature throughout time and space, the existence of human reverie and desire is surely not as illuminating as are considerations of mathematical physics".[6] For the whole point of the passage is that qualities of experienced things that are not the least bit illuminating for the understanding of nature in physical science are as important for a philosophy of nature as the thing most illuminating, namely mathematical physics —a view, as I have said, which any theory making experience continuous with nature is bound to hold.

This point gains more general philosophical significance because of the fact that qualities and values, which are not traits of the objects of natural science as these are now ascertained to be, were once completely fused with the material of what was taken to be science. The whole classic cosmology or theory of nature is framed in this sense. It is the progress of natural science itself that has destroyed this cosmology. As the history of modern philosophy proves, this destruction brought about that crisis which is represented by the bifurcation that is expressed in the opposition of subjective and objective, mind and matter, experience and nature. The problem involved is one which all philosophies alike must face. Any one view, such as the one I have set forth, can be intelligently criticized only from the standpoint of some alternative theory, while theories of bifurcation have their own difficulties and

Separation of philosophy & science

be the same if at some time in the future natural science abandoned the atomic theory and put something else in the place of atoms.

6 [Morris Cohen, "Some Difficulties in Dewey's Anthropocentric Naturalism," *op. cit.*, p. 201.]

troubles, as the history of modern thought abundantly proves.[7] Affirmation of the continuity of experience with nature has its difficulties. But they are not grasped nor the theory refuted by translating what it says into terms of a theory which assumes that the presence of the human factor in experience precludes getting from experience to the nonhuman or physical.

(2) The passage which has been cited about the "real being" of the atom contains an explicit contrast between nature as judged in a short-time span or "cross-section" and in a long temporal span—one long enough to cover the emergence of human beings and their experiences. In order to be understood, what I have said about genesis and function, about antecedents and consequences, has to be placed in the perspective suggested by this emphasis upon the need of formulating a theory of nature and of the connections of man *in* (not *to*) nature on the basis of a temporal continuum.

What is basically involved is that some changes, those for example which terminate in the things of human experience, form a *history,* or a set of changes marked by development or growth. The dichotomy of the old discussion as to whether antecedents or ends are of primary importance in forming a theory of nature is done away with when growth, development, history is taken to be primary. Genesis and ends are of equal importance, but their import is that of terms or boundaries which delimit a history, thereby rendering it capable of description. The sentence before the one about

[7] While Cohen, it seems to me, has somewhat overstated my opposition to Greek and medieval philosophy, it is just the fact of the enormous change that has taken place in the method and conclusions of natural science which is the ground of my insistence upon need for a radical change in the theory of nature and of knowledge. Upon this point, it seems to me that [it] is rather Cohen than myself who fails to attach sufficient importance to physical science in its relation to philosophy. Piety to classic thought is an admirable trait; but a revolution in the physical constituents of nature demands considerable change in cosmological theory, as change in the method of inquiry demands reconstruction *in* (though not *of*) logic.

the atom, reads, for example, as follows: "For knowledge, 'cause' and 'effect' alike have a partial and truncated being"; [8] the paragraph as a whole is devoted to criticizing the notion that causal conditions have a "reality" superior to that of outcomes or effects. It is argued that the prevalent view which attributes superior rank to them results from hypostatizing a *function:* the function of causal conditions as means of control (ultimately, the *sole* means of control) is converted into a direct ontological property. Moreover, the chapter of which the paragraph is a part is devoted to showing that while Existence as process and as history involves "ends," the change from ancient to modern science compels us to interpret ends relatively and pluralistically, because as limits of specifiable histories.

Of the many special points which follow from this basic element in my theory of the connection of experience with nature— as itself an historical outcome or "end," I shall here deal with only one. In what I have said about meanings my critic finds an undue importance attached to consequences; in what I say (in a discussion devoted to a special problem) about the background of Greek philosophy he finds an equally one-sided importance attached to genesis. That in discussion of one particular history the emphasis with respect to a particular problem falls upon results, and in another history discussed in respect to another particular problem, emphasis falls upon antecedents, involves no inconsistency. With respect to consequences in their connection with meaning and verification I have repeatedly and explicitly insisted upon the fact that there is no way of telling what the consequences are save by discovery of antecedents, so that the latter are necessary and yet are subordinate in function.[9]

(3) Another aspect of the perspective determined by the point of view expressed in the continuity of nature and ex-

---

8 [*Experience and Nature*, p. 109.]

9 My use of the compound word "genetic-functional" to describe what I regard as the proper method of philosophy is, then, directly linked to the position taken regarding the temporal continuum.

Theory — *practice*

science — *morals*

perience concerns the relation of theory and practical ends, particularly of physical science and morals. It is about this point, unless I am mistaken, that the fundamental criticisms of Cohen cluster, since the passages upon which the criticisms are based are interpreted in another perspective than that in which they are stated. The fact that I have, quite consistently and persistently, as far as I am aware, insisted that inquiry should follow the lead of its subject matter [10] and not be subordinated to any end or motive having an external source, is less important than the fact that any other view would be contradictory to my main theses regarding (i) the place of the natural sciences in the formation of the ends and values of practical life, and (ii) the importance of the experimental method of the natural sciences as the model for the sciences involving human practice, or the social and moral disciplines.

The view I have put forward about the nature of that to which the adjective "physical" applies is that, while it is arrived at by following out clews given in directly experimental matter, it constitutes the *conditions* upon which all the qualities and terminal values, the consummations, of experience, depend. Hence those things which are physical are the sole means that exist for control of values and qualities. To read anything extraneous into them, to tamper in any way with the integrity of the inquiry of which they are the product, would thus be to nullify the very function in terms of which the *physical* as such is defined, I have even gone so far as to

---

[10] I would call attention to one passage, found on pp. 67-68 of *The Quest for Certainty* (cf. p. 228). The text states the nature of the ambiguity in the word "theoretical" which is the source of misunderstanding, the confusion of the attitude of the *inquirer* with the nature of the *subject matter* inquired into. It is explicitly said that the former must be theoretical and cognitive, purged of personal desire and preference, marked by willingness to subordinate them to the lead of subject matter. But it is also said that only inquiry itself can determine whether or not *subject matter* contains practical conditions and qualities. To argue from the strictly theoretical character of the motives of the inquirer, from the necessity for "disinterested curiosity," to the nature of that investigated is a kind of "anthropocentrism" of which I should not wish to be guilty.

ascribe the backwardness of the human, the practical, sciences in part to the long period of backwardness of the physical sciences themselves and in part to the refusal of moralists and social scientists to utilize the physical, especially the biological, material that is at their disposal.

(4) These considerations bring me to my view regarding the nature and function of philosophy, a point which I think will be found crucial for the interpretation, and hence the criticism, of the passages upon which Cohen bases his view that I have pretty systematically subordinated inquiry, reflection, and science to extraneous practical ends. For speaking of *philosophy* (not of science) I have constantly insisted that since it contains value-considerations within itself, indispensable to its existence as philosophy—in distinction from science—it has a "practical," that is a *moral* function, and I have held that since this element is inherent, the failure of philosophies to recognize and make explicit its presence introduces undesirable properties into them, leading them on one side to make claims of being purely cognitive, which bring them into rivalry with science, and on the other side to neglect of the field in which they may be genuinely significant, that of possible guidance of human activity in the field of values.

The following passage is fairly typical of what I have said: "What would be its [philosophy's] office if it ceased to deal with the problem of reality and knowledge at large? In effect, its function would be to facilitate the fruitful interaction of our cognitive beliefs, our beliefs resting upon the most dependable methods of inquiry, with our practical beliefs about the values, the ends and purposes, that should control human action in the things of large and liberal human import." [11] Now whether this view of the nature of philosophic as distinct from distinctively scientific inquiry is correct or incorrect, the following points are so involved that the view cannot be understood without taking them into account: (i) It is an aspect of the general position of the experiential continuum constituted by the interaction of different modes of experi-

[11] *The Quest for Certainty*, pp. 36-37.

enced things, in this case of the scientific and the moral; (ii) it gives philosophy a subject matter distinct from the subject matter of science and yet inherently connected with the latter, namely, the bearing of the conclusions reached in science ("the most dependable methods of inquiry") upon the value-factors involved in human action, with criticism of current beliefs and institutions involving value-considerations, on the ground of the cognitive conclusions of science; (iii) there is no subordination of the results of knowledge to any precon-ceived scheme of values or predetermined practical ends (such as fixes the usual meaning of "reform"), but rather emphasis upon the reconstruction of existing ends and values in behalf of more generous and liberal human activities.

Now whether this view of philosophy is right or wrong (and my critic says nothing about what he takes to be the subject matter and function of philosophy in connection with, or dis-tinction from, that of science), if what is said about philos-ophy is taken to be said about science or about reflection in general, the meanings which result will be justly exposed to all the criticisms passed upon them.[12] It is perhaps significant that Cohen himself virtually recognizes the presence of the human and moral factor in philosophy as distinct from sci-ence. For the "resignation" which he finds to be the lesson taught by a just theory of nature is surely a human and moral factor; it remains such even if I have over-emphasized the

[12] It often happens in addition that what is said about a particular type of philosophic system, in a context which qualifies what is said, is taken by Cohen absolutely, without qualification. For example, if the reader will consult the passage (*The Influence of Darwin*, pp. 298-99) containing the words "luxury," "nuisance," etc., it will be seen that instead of referring to philosophy in general or even to a particular historical school or schools—much less to impartial inquiry—it is qualified by a succession of "ifs." And the passage which says (*Creative Intelligence*, p. 60) that phi-losophy is of account only if it affords guidance to action, occurs in a paragraph dealing with the grounds for the difference between the popu-lar and the professional reception of "pragmatism," not in a statement of my own view, although the idea that philosophy is love of wisdom as dis-tinct from love of knowledge and that "philosophy is the guide of life" is not peculiarly new nor peculiarly a product of pragmatism.

traits of courage and active responsibility, as I may have done in view of the fact that resignation and the purely consolatory office of philosophy have received more than enough emphasis in the historical tradition. But I have also pointed out that the classic or Catholic version of that tradition recognizes that this lesson of passive resignation is not final; that it has to be supplemented by a divine institution which undertakes the positive function of guidance, and that in so far the practical logic of the situation is with the Church rather than with traditional philosophy which is minus institutional support and aid. As far as I am concerned the issue is between a theory of experience in nature which renders experienced things and operations impotent, and a theory which would search for and utilize the things *in experience* that are capable of progressively providing the needed support and guidance.[13] Finally, while I am grateful and deeply appreciative of Cohen's approval of my personal Liberalism, I must add not only that this Liberalism is definitely rooted in the very philosophy to which he takes exception, but that any theory of activity in social and moral matters, liberal or otherwise, which is not grounded in a comprehensive philosophy seems to me to be only a projection of arbitrary personal preference.

I come now, rather belatedly, to the criticisms of my other friendly critic, Ernest Hocking. If I grasp aright the point of view from which his criticisms are made, it does not involve the postulate of separation of experience from nature that is found in Cohen's criticisms, but rather a point of departure similar to mine. In that respect, Cohen's paper involves a criticism of Hocking as well as of me, and reciprocally. The trouble with my views lies, then, according to Hocking, in the

13 Since readers cannot be expected to look up all quotations made from my writings, I will say that the sentence about the capacity of man to shape his own destiny is part of a passage about the atmosphere of the eighteenth-century thought which put forth the doctrine of the indefinite perfectibility of man. My own view is much more qualified. [The statement in question which Cohen quotes is: "Man is capable, if he will but exercise the required courage, intelligence and effort, of shaping his own fate." *Reconstruction in Philosophy* (New York: 1920), p. 49.]

The account I have given of experience, primarily in my failure to give its due place and weight to thought in relation to knowledge and to the world of reality. I am grateful to Hocking for his explicit recognition of the place given in my theory of knowledge to thought and theory, to his recognition that in my theory "the [scientific] process is intellectualized to the last limit." [14] His conclusion that, since I have done this, I am logically bound to go farther and take the position that "the more thought, the more reality," [15] thus has a relevancy to my position not possessed by criticisms based upon the notion that I have adopted the depreciatory view of thought, theory, and abstraction characteristic of traditional nominalistic empiricism.

(1) However, in criticizing sensational and particularistic empiricism and in insisting upon the indispensable role of thought and theory in the determination of scientific objects, I have not gone so far as to deny the equally indispensable role of observed material and the processes of observation. On the contrary, I have criticized traditional rationalism, not indeed for pointing out the necessary operational presence of thought, but for its failure to recognize the essential role of observation to bring into existence that material by which objects of thought are tested and validated—or the contrary— so as to be given something more than a hypothetical status. I quote from Hocking the following passage, speaking of such things as atoms and electrons: "Dewey will not say that I observe them, but only that I think them. I agree. But is the atom then less real than the chair?" [16] My view more completely stated is that *at present* atom and electron are objects of thought *rather* than of observation. But, instead of denying

[14] ["Dewey's Concepts of Experience and Nature," *op. cit.,* p. 233.]
[15] [*Op. cit.,* p. 238.]
[16] [Hocking's exact statement is: "But, if the object is a molecule in the wood of the chair, or an atom in the molecule, or an electron in the atom, Dewey will not say that I observe that, but only that I think it. I agree. But is the atom, then, less real than the chair which I observe?" *Op. cit.,* p. 237.]

the necessity of observed material, or even the possibility of observation of objects that are atomic in the scientific sense, I have held that the theoretical value of the atom consists in its ability, as a hypothesis or *thought,* to direct observations experimentally and to co-ordinate their results. The mere observation of something which if it were observed by a physicist would be an atom is not, however, observation of an atom as a *scientific object* unless and only in so far as it meets the requirements of definition which has been attained by a set of systematic inferences, that is, of the function to which the name thought is given. The place of differential equations in the formulation of the atom as a scientific theoretical and hypothetical object is undeniable. But the equations as far as atoms as *existences* are concerned (in distinction from their function in facilitating and directing further inferences) state conditions to be satisfied by any observed material if it is to be warrantably asserted to *be* atomic.

(2) The formulation of the conditions to be satisfied takes a form which prescribes operations that are to be performed in instituting and interpreting observations. This fact leads to consideration of what Hocking says about operations. If thought and its object *as* object of thought were as complete and final apart from any connection with observed things as Hocking assumes them to be, then the operational view of scientific objects would indeed hang idly and unsupported in the void. To place, as Hocking does, interest in the entities of differential equations in opposition to interest in operations is to overlook, it seems to me, the fundamental thesis of operationalism, namely that these entities, as far as physics, including mathematical physics, is concerned, *are* formulations of operations to be performed in obtaining specified observed materials and determining whether or not that material answers to or satisfies certain conditions imposed upon it if it is to merit the name of a certain scientific object, atom, electron, or whatever. As I have frequently said, a given scientific person may occupy himself exclusively with the mathematical aspect of the matter, and do so fruitfully as far as the historic

development of a science is concerned. But this fact taken by itself is not decisive about the actual place and function of the mathematical material.

(3) I come now to another criticism of Hocking's, connected with the "reality" part of his saying "the more thought, the more reality." My criticism of Hocking's criticism has up to this point concerned only the first part of his sentence. It amounts to saying that while he has not disrupted the continuity of experience with nature, he has, to my mind, broken off one aspect of experience, namely thought, from another aspect, that of observation. Further consequences of this artificial breach seem to me to be found in what he says about "reality." It is quite true, as he says, that one meaning of reality is the *"independent being [on] which other [being] depends";* [17] and he finds this independent being in "the content of true judgment," a saying which seems to me to express in an almost flagrantly emphatic way the isolation of one mode of experience and its material from other modes and *their* things. For he goes on to say that Nature, as the content of true judgment or the object of perfect thought in its capacity of measure of knowledge, is the independent reality of which experience is the dependent derivative.

Now reality is, I fear, more than a double-barrelled word. Its ambiguity and slipperiness extend beyond the two significations which Hocking mentions in such a way as to affect the interpretation of "independence" and "dependence" in the view taken by him. For there is a definitely pragmatic meaning of "dependence" and "derivation," which affects the meaning of that most dangerous of all philosophical words, "reality." The objects of knowledge, when once attained, exercise, as I have already said, the function of *control* over other materials. Hence the latter in so far depend for their status and value upon the object of knowledge. The idea of the ether was dropped when it ceased to exercise any office of control over investigations. The idea of quanta has increased its role because of its efficacy and fertility in control of in-

[17] *[Op. cit.,* p. 235.]

quiries. But this interpretation of dependence is strictly functional. Instead of first isolating the object of knowledge or judgment and then setting it up in its isolation as a measure of the "reality" of other things, it connects the scientific object, genetically and functionally, with other things without casting the invidious shadow of a lesser degree of reality upon the latter.

(4) This consideration brings me to the fourth point in Hocking's paper upon which I shall comment. It is of course true that I have emphasized the temporal continuity of inquiry, and in consequence the dependence of conclusions reached at a given time upon the methods and results of previous investigations, and their subjection to modification in subsequent inquiries. But, as far as I can see, the idea that this view indefinitely defers possession and enjoyment of stable objects to the end of an infinite progression applies rather to Hocking's position than to mine. That is, if I held that thought is the only valid approach to "Reality" and that the latter is the content of a perfect judgment, I should be troubled by the question of the worth, from the standpoint of Reality, of all my present conclusions.

But I do not see that the question arises within the perspective of my own point of view. For in the latter, instead of there being isolation of the material of knowledge, there is its continual interaction with the things of other forms of experience, and the worth (or "reality") of the former is to be judged on the basis of the control exercised by it over the things of noncognitive experiences and the increment of enriched meaning supplied to them. Even from the standpoint of knowledge by itself, inquiry produces such cumulative verification and stability that the prospect of future modification is an *added* value, just as in all other affairs of life those accomplishments that open up new prospects and new possibilities are enhanced, not depressed, by their power in this respect. But what is even more important is that, from the standpoint of the continuous interaction of the things of different modes of experience, the final test of the value of "contents of judgment" now attained is found not in their relation to the content of some final judgment, to be reached at the close of an infinite progression, but in what is done in the living present, what is done in giving enriched meaning to other things and in increasing our control over them.

In recurring to what I said at the outset about my choice of a theme, I wish to repeat that the limitation of my reply to criticisms passed upon my views only so far as they bear upon the problem of the connection of experience with nature is not intended to be evasive, nor does it evince lack of respect for criticisms I have not touched upon. I have not in the past been as unobservant or inattentive of criticisms as my good friend Ernest Hocking has humorously suggested. On the contrary, if my views have progressed either in clarity or in range, as I hope they have done, it is mainly because of what my critics have said and the thought I have given their criticisms. Given a point of view that determines a perspective and the nature and arrangement of things seen in that perspective, the point of view is, I suppose, the last thing to be seen. In fact it is never capable of being seen unless there is some change from the old point of view.

Criticisms are the means by which one is enabled to take, at least in imagination, a new point of view, and thus to re-see, literally to review and revise, what fell within one's earlier perspective. If I have succeeded today in making my views clearer to others than I have managed to do in my previous writings, it is because my critics have made their import clearer to myself. For that I am grateful to them, as I am deeply appreciative of the honor the Association and my friends Morris Cohen and Ernest Hocking have done me in giving time and thought to my writings.

Freedom: involves
① Choice
② Power
③ Reason

☙ XIII ❧

PHILOSOPHIES OF FREEDOM[1]

The treatment of freedom in this article is typical of
Dewey's approach to philosophic problems. First of all, *(1)*
there is a reconstructive criticism of dominant theories of
freedom in the history of civilization. Viewing these in their
cultural context, Dewey notes their limitations as well as
their positive insights. By focusing on the treatment of
freedom as choice, freedom as the power to act, and freedom
as effective reason, Dewey weaves together a philosophy of
freedom in which choice, power, and reason are linked together. "A choice which intelligently manifests individuality
enlarges the range of action, and this enlargement in turn
confers upon our desires greater insight and foresight, and
makes choice more intelligent." Secondly the approach to *(2)*
freedom illustrates Dewey's nonreductive naturalism which
is sensitive to both the continuity and the uniqueness of
the behavior of different natural transactions. Dewey accounts for choice by showing how it is continuous though
not reducible to less complex selective behavior. And not
only are genuine individuality of existences and causal
uniformity reconcilable, but the statement of scientific laws
presupposes the irreducible individuality of existences.
Thirdly, one can see the typical movement of Dewey's *(3)*
mature philosophizing. The discussion begins with the *a)*
specific problem of confusion about the meaning of "free- *b)*
dom," enlarges to a metaphysical analysis of choice as a
manifestation of selective behavior which is a "universal *c)*
trait of all things," and concludes with a brief discussion of
political and economic freedom, which "are required to
realize the potentiality of freedom each of us carries with
him in his structure."

[1] Originally published in *Freedom in the Modern World*, ed. Horace
Kallen (New York: 1928), pp. 236-71.

A RECENT BOOK on sovereignty concludes a survey of various theories on that subject with the following words: "The career of the notion of sovereignty illustrates the general characteristics of political thinking. The various forms of the notion have been apologies for causes rather than expressions of the disinterested love of knowledge. The notion has meant many things at different times; and the attacks upon it have sprung from widely [differing] sources and been directed toward a multiplicity of goals. The genesis of all political ideas is to be understood in terms of their utility rather than of their truth and falsity." [2] Perhaps the same thing may be said of moral notions; I do not think there is any doubt that freedom is a word applied to many things of varied plumage and that it owes much of its magic to association with a variety of different causes. It has assumed various forms as needs have varied; its "utility" has been its service in helping men deal with many predicaments.

Freedom & moral choice

Primary among the needs it has been employed to meet and the interests it has served to promote is the moral. A good deal is assumed in asserting that the center of this moral need and cause is the fact of choice. The desire to dignify choice, to account for its significance in human affairs, to magnify that significance by making it the center of man's moral struggles and achievements has been reflected in the idea of freedom. There is an inexpugnable feeling that choice *is* freedom and that man without choice is a puppet, and that man then has no acts which he can call his very own. Without genuine choice, choice that when expressed in action makes things different from what they otherwise would be, men are but passive vehicles through which external forces operate. This feeling is neither self-explanatory nor self-justificatory. But at least it contributes an element in the statement of the problem of freedom. Choice is one of the things that demands examination.

[2] *Sovereignty,* by Paul Ward, p. 167. [London: George Routledge & Sons, 1928.]

The theoretical formulation for the justification of choice
the heart of freedom became, however, involved at an early
ne with other interests; and they, rather than the unpreju-
ced examination of the fact of choice, determined the form
ken by a widely prevalent philosophy of freedom. Men are
ven to praise and blame; to reward and punishment. As
vilization matured, definite civil agencies were instituted
r "trying" men for modes of conduct so that if found guilty
ey might be punished. The fact of praise and blame, of civil
unishment, directed at men on account of their behavior,
gnifies that they are held liable or are deemed responsible.
he fact of punishment called attention, as men became more
quiring, to the ground of liability. Unless men were re-
onsible for their acts, it was unjust to punish them; if they
uld not help doing what they did, what was the justice in
olding them responsible for their acts, and blaming and
unishing them? Thus a certain philosophy of the nature of
oice as freedom developed as an apologia for an essentially
gal interest: liability to punishment. The outcome was the
octrine known as freedom of will: the notion that a power
lled will lies back of choice as its author, and is the ground
liability and the essence of freedom. This will has the
ower of indifferent choice; that is, it is equally free to choose
ne way or another unmoved by any desire or impulse, just
cause of a causal force residing in will itself. So established
d this way of viewing choice become, that it is still com-
only supposed that choice and the arbitrary freedom of will
e one and the same thing.[3]
It is then worth while to pause in our survey while we ex-
mine more closely the nature of choice in relation to this

[3] Doubt may be felt as to the assertion that this interpretation of free-
m developed in connection with the legal motif. The historic connect-
g link is found in the invasion of moral ideas by legal considerations
at grew up in the Roman Empire. The association was perpetuated by
e influence of Roman law and modes of moral thought, and even more
the incorporation of the latter in the theology and practices of the
ristian Church, the nurse of morals in Europe.

Choice + free will

alleged connection with free will, (free) here meaning u
motivated choice. Analysis does not have to probe to t
depths to discover two serious faults in the theory. It is a ma
a human being in the concrete, who is held responsible. If t
act does not proceed from the man, from the human being
his concrete make-up of habits, desires, and purposes, wl
should *he* be held liable and be-punished? Will appears as
force outside of the individual person as he actually is,
force which is the real ultimate cause of the act. *Its* freedo
to make a choice arbitrarily thus appears no ground for hol
ing the human being as a concrete person responsible for
choice. Whatever else is to be said or left unsaid, choice mu
have some closer connection with the actual make-up of d
position and character than this philosophy allows.

We may seem then to be in a hopeless dilemma. If t
man's nature, original and acquired, makes him do what
does, how does his action differ from that of a stone or tre
Have we not parted with any ground for responsibility? Wh
the question is looked at in the face of facts rather than in
dialectic of concepts it turns out not to have any terro.
Holding men to responsibility may make a decided differen
in their *future* behavior; holding a stone or tree to respon
bility is a meaningless performance; it has no consequence;
makes no difference. If we locate the ground of liability
future consequences rather than in antecedent causal con
tions, we moreover find ourselves in accord with actual pra
tice. Infants, idiots, the insane, those completely upset, are n
held to liability; the reason is that it is absurd—meaningless
to do so, for it has no effect on their further actions. A child
he grows older finds responsibilities thrust upon him. This
surely not because freedom of the will has suddenly been i
serted in him, but because his assumption of them is a nec
sary factor in his *further* growth and movement.

Something has been accomplished, I think, in transferri
the issue from the past to the future, from antecedents
consequences. Some animals, dogs and horses, have their f
ture conduct modified by the way they are treated. We ca

nagine a man whose conduct is changed by the way in which
e is treated, so that it becomes different from what it would
ave been, and yet like the dog or horse, the change may be
ue to purely external manipulation, as external as the strings
1at move a puppet. The whole story has not then been told.
here must be some practical participation from within to
1ake the change that is effected significant in relation to
hoice and freedom. From *within*—that fact rules out the
ppeal, so facilely made, to will as a cause. Just what is signi-
ed by that participation by the human being himself in a
hoice that makes it really a choice?

In answering this question, it is helpful to go, apparently at
ast, far afield. Preferential action in the sense of selective
ehavior is a universal trait of all things, atoms and molecules
s well as plants, animals, and man. Existences, universally as
ar as we can tell, are cold and indifferent in the presence of
ome things and react energetically in either a positive or
egative way to other things. These "preferences" or differ-
ntial responses of behavior, are due to their own constitution;
hey "express" the nature of the things in question. They
1ark a distinctive contribution to what takes place. In other
vords, while changes in one thing may be described on the
asis of changes that take place in other things, the *existence*
f things which make certain changes having a certain quality
nd direction occur cannot be so explained. Selective be-
avior is the evidence of at least a rudimentary individuality
r uniqueness in things. Such preferential action is not exactly
vhat makes choice in the case of human beings. But unless
here is involved in choice at least something continuous with
he action of other things in nature, we could impute genuine
eality to it only by isolating man from nature and thus treat-
ng him as in some sense a supra-natural being in the literal
ense. Choice is more than just selectivity in behavior but it is
t *least* that.

What is the more which is involved in choice? Again, we
nay take a circuitous course. As we ascend in the range of
omplexity from inanimate things to plants, and from plants

to animals and from other animals to man, we find an increa
ing variety of selective responses, due to the influence of li
history, or experiences already undergone. The manifestatio
of preferences becomes a "function" of an entire history. T
understand the action of a fellow man we have to know som
thing of the *course* of his life. A man is susceptible, sensitiv
to a vast variety of conditions, and undergoes varied and o
posed experiences—as lower animals do not. Consequently
man in the measure of the scope and variety of his past e
periences carries in his present capacity for selective response
large set of varied possibilities. That life history of which h
present preference is a function is complex. Hence the poss
bility of continuing diversification of behavior: in short, th
distinctive *educability* of men. This factor taken by itself do
not cover all that is included within the change of preferen
into genuine choice, but it has a bearing on that individu
participation and individual contribution that is involved i
choice as a mode of freedom. It is a large factor in our stron
sense that we are not pushed into action from behind as a
inanimate things. For that which is "behind" is so diversifie
in its variety and so intimately a part of the present self tha
preference becomes hesitant. Alternative preferences simu
taneously manifest themselves.

Choice, in the distinctively human sense, then presents itse
as one preference among and out of preferences; not in th
sense of one preference already made and stronger tha
others, but as the formation of a new preference out of a co
flict of preferences. If we can say upon what the formation
this new and determinate preference depends, we are close
finding that of which we are in search. Nor does the answe
seem far to seek nor hard to find. As observation and foresig
develop, there is ability to form signs and symbols that stan
for the interaction and movement of things, without involvir
us in their actual flux. Hence the new preference may refle
this operation of mind, especially the forecast of the cons
quences of acting upon the various competing preferences.
we sum up, pending such qualification of such confirmation

further inquiry may supply, we may say that a stone has its preferential selections set by a relatively fixed, a rigidly set, structure and that no anticipation of the results of acting one way or another enters into the matter. The reverse is true of human action. In so far as a variable life history and intelligent insight and foresight enter into it, choice signifies a capacity for deliberately changing preferences. The hypothesis that is suggested is that in these two traits we have before us the essential constituents of choice as freedom: the factor of individual participation.

Before that idea is further examined, it is, however, desirable to turn to another philosophy of freedom. For the discussion thus far has turned about the fact of choice alone. And such an exclusive emphasis may well render some readers impatient. It may seem to set forth an idea of freedom which is too individual, too "subjective." What has this affair to do with the freedom for which men have fought, bled, and died: freedom from oppression and despotism, freedom of institutions and laws? This question at once brings to mind a philosophy of freedom which shifts the issue from choice to action, action in an overt and public sense. This philosophy is sufficiently well presented for our purposes in the idea of John Locke, the author, one may say, of the philosophy of Liberalism in its classic sense. Freedom is *power to act* in accordance with choice. It is actual ability to carry desire and purpose into operation, to *execute* choices when they are made. Experience shows that certain laws and institutions prevent such operation and execution. This obstruction and interference constitutes what we call oppression, enslavement. Freedom, in fact, the freedom worth fighting for, is secured by abolition of these oppressive measures, tyrannical laws, and modes of government. It is liberation, emancipation; the possession and active manifestation of *rights,* the right to self-determination in action. To many minds, the emphasis which has been put upon the formation of choice in connection with freedom will appear an evasion, a trifling with metaphysical futilities, in comparison with this form of freedom, a desire for which

N.B.

has caused revolutions, overthrown dynasties, and which as it is attained supplies the measure of human progress in freedom.

Before, however, we examine further into this notion in its relation to the idea of choice already set forth, it will be well to consider another factor which blended with the political *motif* just mentioned in forming the classic philosophy of Liberalism. This other factor is the economic. Even in Locke the development of property, industry, and trade played a large part in creating the sense that existing institutions were oppressive, and that they should be altered to give men power to express their choices in action. About a century after Locke wrote, this implicit factor became explicit and dominant. In the later eighteenth century, attention shifted from power to execute choice to power to carry *wants* into effect, by means of free—that is, unimpeded—labor and exchange. The test of free institutions was the relation they bore to the unobstructed play of wants in industry and commerce and to the enjoyment of the fruits of labor. This notion blended with the earlier political idea to form the philosophy of Liberalism so influential in a large part of the nineteenth century. It led to the notion that all positive action of government is oppressive; that its maxim should be Hands Off; and that its action should be limited as far as possible to securing the freedom of behavior of one individual against interference proceeding from the exercise of similar freedom on the part of others; the theory of *laissez faire* and the limitation of government to legal and police functions.

In the popular mind, the same idea has grown up in a noneconomic form, and with the substitution of instincts or impulses for wants. This phase has the same psychological roots as the economic philosophy of freedom, and is a large part of the popular philosophy of "self-expression." In view of this community of intellectual basis and origin, there is irony in the fact that the most ardent adherents of the idea of "self-expression" as freedom in personal and domestic relations are quite often equally ardent opponents of the idea of a like freedom in the region of industry and commerce. In the latter realm, they are quite aware of the extent in which the "self-expression" of a few may impede, although manifested in strict accordance with law, the self-expression of others. The popular idea of personal freedom as consisting in "free" expression of impulses and desire—free in the sense of unrestricted by law, custom and the inhibitions of social disapprovals—suggests the fallacy inhering in the wider economic concept, suggests it in a more direct way than can readily be derived from the more technical economic concept.

Instincts and impulses, however they may be defined, are part of the "natural" constitution of man; a statement in which "natural" signifies "native," original. The theory assigns a certain intrinsic rightness in this original structure, rightness in the sense of conferring upon impulses a title to pass into direct action, except when they directly and evidently interfere with similar self-manifestation in others. The idea thus overlooks the part played by interaction with the surrounding medium, especially the social, in generating impulses and desires. These are supposed to inhere in the "nature" of the individual when that is taken in a primal state, uninfluenced by interaction with an environment. The latter is thus thought of as purely external to an individual, and as irrelevant to freedom except when it interferes with the operation of native instincts and impulses. A study of history would reveal that this notion, like its theoretically formulated congeners in economic and political Liberalism, is a "faint rumor" left on the air of morals and politics by disappearing theological dogmas, which held that "nature" is thoroughly good as it comes from the creative hand of God, and that evil is due to corruption through the artificial interference and oppression exercised by external or "social" conditions.

The point of this statement is that it suggests the essential fallacy in the elaborate political and economic theories of freedom entertained by classic Liberalism. They thought of individuals as endowed with an equipment of fixed and ready-made capacities, the operation of which if unobstructed by external restrictions would be freedom, and a freedom which would almost automatically solve political and economic problems. The difference between the theories is that one thought in terms of natural rights and the other in terms of natural wants as original and fixed. The difference is important with respect to special issues, but it is negligible with respect to the common premise as to the nature of freedom.

The Liberalistic movement in each of its phases accomplished much practically. Each was influential in supplying inspiration and direction to reforming endeavors that modified institutions, laws, and arrangements that *had* become oppressive. They effected a great and needed work of liberation. What were taken to be "natural" political rights and "natural" demands of human beings (natural being defined as inherent in an original and native fixed structure, moral or psychological) marked in fact the sense of new potentialities that were possessed only by limited classes because of changes in social life due to a number of causes. On the political side, there was the limited class that found its activities restricted by survivals of feudal institutions; on the economic side, there was the rise of a manufacturing and trading class that found its activities impeded and thwarted by the fact that these same institutions worked to protect property interests connected with land at the expense of property interests growing out of business and commerce. Since the members of the two classes were largely identical, and since they represented the new moving forces, while their opponents represented interests vested and instituted in a past that knew nothing of these forces, political and economic liberalism fused as time went on, and in their fusion performed a necessary work of emancipation.

But the course of historic events has sufficiently proved that they emancipated the *classes* whose special interests they represented, rather than human beings impartially. In fact, as the newly emancipated forces gained momentum, they actually imposed new burdens and subjected to new modes of oppression the mass of individuals who did not have a privileged economic status. It is impossible to justify this statement by an adequate assemblage of evidence. Fortunately it is not necessary to attempt the citation of relevant facts. Practically, every one admits that there is a new social problem, one that everywhere affects the issues of politics and laws; and that this problem, whether we call it the relation of capital to labor, or individualism versus socialism, or the emancipation of wage-earners, has an economic basis. The facts here are sufficient evidence that the ideals and hopes of the earlier liberal school have been frustrated by events; the universal emancipation and the universal harmony of interests they assumed are flagrantly contradicted by the course of events. The common criticism is that the liberal school was too "individualistic"; it would be equally pertinent to say that it was not "individualistic" enough. Its philosophy was such that it assisted the emancipation of individuals having a privileged antecedent status, but promoted no general liberation of all individuals.

The real objection to classic Liberalism does not then hinge upon concepts of "individual" and "society."

The real fallacy lies in the notion that individuals have such a native or original endowment of rights, powers, and wants that all that is required on the side of institutions and laws is to eliminate the obstructions they offer to the "free" play of the natural equipment of individuals. The removal of obstructions did have a liberating effect upon such individuals as were antecedently possessed of the means, intellectual and economic, to take advantage of the changed social conditions. But it left all others at the mercy of the new social conditions brought about by the freed powers of those advantageously situated. The notion that men are equally free to act if only the same legal arrangements apply equally to all—irrespective of differences in education, in command of capital, and the control of the social environment which is furnished by the institution of property—is a pure absurdity, as facts have demonstrated. Since actual, that is, effective,

Dewey's big thing

φ //

rights and demands are products of interactions, and are not found in the original and isolated constitution of human nature, whether moral or psychological, mere elimination of obstructions is not enough. The latter merely liberates force and ability as that happens to be distributed by past accidents of history. This "free" action operates disastrously as far as the many are concerned. The only possible conclusion, both intellectually and practically, is that the attainment of freedom conceived as power to act in accord with choice depends upon positive and constructive changes in social arrangements.

We now have two seemingly independent philosophies, one finding freedom in choice itself, and the other in power to *act* in accord with choice. Before we inquire whether the two philosophies must be left in a position of mutual independence, or whether they link together in a single conception, it will be well to consider another tract followed by another school of thinkers, who also in effect identify freedom with operative power in action. This other school had a clear consciousness of the dependence of this power to act upon social conditions, and attempted to avoid and correct the mistakes of the philosophy of classic Liberalism. It substituted a philosophy of institutions for a philosophy of an original moral or psychological structure of individuals. This course was first charted by Spinoza, the great thinker of the seventeenth century. Although the philosophy of Liberalism had not as yet taken form, his ideas afford in anticipation an extraordinarily effective means of criticizing it. To Spinoza freedom was power. The "natural" rights of an individual consist simply in freedom to do whatever he *can* do—an idea probably suggested by Hobbes. But what *can* he do? The answer to that question is evidently a matter of the amount of the power he actually possesses. The whole discussion turns on this point. The answer in effect is that man in his original estate possesses a very limited amount of power. Men as "natural," that is, as native beings are but parts, almost infinitesimally small fractions, of the whole of Nature to

Spinoza Freedom is Power

which they belong. In Spinoza's phraseology, they are "modes" not substances. As merely a part, the action of any part is limited on every hand by the action and counteraction of other parts. Even if there is power to initiate an act—a power inhering in any natural thing, inanimate as well as human—there is no power to carry it through; an action is immediately caught in an infinite and intricate network of *interactions*. If a man acts upon his private impulse, appetite or want and upon his private judgment about the aims and measures of conduct, he is just as much a subjected part of an infinitely complex whole as is a stock or stone. What he actually does is conditioned by equally blind and partial action of other parts of nature. Slavery, weakness, dependence, is the outcome, not freedom, power, and independence.

There is no freedom to be reached by this road. Man has however intellect, capacity of thought. He is a mode not only of physical existence but of mind. Man is free only as he has power, and he can possess power only as he acts in accord with the whole, being reinforced by its structure and momentum. But in being a mode of mind he has a capacity for understanding the order of the whole to which he belongs, so that through development and use of intellect he may become cognizant of the order and laws of the whole, and in so far align his action with it. In so far he shares the power of the whole and is free. Certain definite political implications follow from this identification of freedom with reason in operation. No individual can overcome his tendencies to act as a mere part in isolation. Theoretic insight into the constitution of the whole is neither complete nor firm; it gives way under the pressure of immediate circumstances. Nothing is of as much importance to a reasonable creature in sustaining effectively his actual—or forceful—reasonableness as another reasonable being. We are bound together as parts of a whole, and only as others are free, through enlightenment as to the nature of the whole and its included parts, can any one be free. Law, government, institutions, all social arrangements must be informed with a rationality that corresponds to the order of the whole, which is true Nature or God, to the end that power of unimpeded action can be found anywhere. It would be difficult to imagine a more complete challenge to the philosophy of Locke and the Liberalistic school. Not power but impotency, not independence but dependence, not freedom but subjection, is the natural estate of man—in the sense in which this school conceived "the natural." Law, however imperfect and poor, is at least a recognition of the universal, of the interconnection of parts, and hence operates as a schoolmaster to bring men to reason, power, and freedom. The worst government is better than none, for some recognition of law, of universal relationship, is an absolute prerequisite. Freedom is not obtained by mere abolition of law and institutions, but by the progressive saturation of all laws and institutions with greater and greater acknowledgment of the necessary laws governing the constitution of things.

It can hardly be said that Spinoza's philosophy either in its general form or in its social aspect had any immediate effect—unless it was to render Spinoza a figure of objurgation. But some two centuries later a phase of reaction against the philosophy of Liberalism and all the ideas and practices associated with it arose in Germany; and Spinoza's ideas were incorporated in deed in a new metaphysical scheme and took on new life and significance. This movement may be called institutional idealism, Hegel being selected as its representative. Hegel substituted a single substance, called Spirit, for the two-faced substance of Spinoza, and restated the order and law of the whole in terms of an evolutionary or unfolding development instead of in terms of relations conceived upon a geometrical pattern. This development is intrinsically timeless or logical, after the manner of dialectic as conceived by Hegel. But externally this inner logical development of a whole is manifested serially or temporally in history. Absolute spirit embodies itself, by a series of piecemeal steps, in law and institutions; they are objective reason, and an individual becomes rational and free by virtue of participation in the life of these institutions, since in that participation he absorbs their spirit and meaning. The institutions of property, criminals and civil law, the family and above all the national state are the instrumentalities of rationality in outward action and hence of freedom. History is the record of the development of freedom through development of institutions. The philosophy of history is the understanding of this record in terms of the progressive manifestation of the objective form of absolute mind. Here we have instead of an anticipatory criticism and challenge of the classic liberal notion of freedom, a deliberate reflective and reactionary one. Freedom is a growth, an attainment, not an original possession, and it is attained by idealization of institutions and law and the active participation of individuals in their loyal maintenance, not by their abolition or reduction in the interests of personal judgments and wants.

We now face what is admittedly the crucial difficulty in framing a philosophy of freedom: What is the connection or lack of connection between freedom defined in terms of choice and freedom defined in terms of power in action? Do the two ways of conceiving freedom have anything but the name in common? The difficulty is the greater because we have so little material to guide us in dealing with it. Each type of philosophy has been upon the whole developed with little consideration of the point of view of the other. Yet it would seem that there must be some connection. Choice would hardly be significant if it did not take effect in outward action, and if it did not, when expressed in deeds, make a difference in things. Action as power would hardly be prized if it were power like that of an avalanche or an earthquake. The power, the ability to command issues and consequences, that forms freedom must, it should seem, have some connection with that something in personality that is expressed in choice. At all events, the essential problem of freedom, it seems to me, is the problem of the relation of choice and unimpeded effective action to each other.

I shall first give the solution to this problem that commends itself to me, and then trust to the further discussion not indeed to prove it but to indicate the reasons for holding it. There is an intrinsic connection between choice as freedom and power of action as freedom. A choice which intelligently manifests individuality enlarges the range of action, and this enlargement in turn confers upon our desires greater insight and foresight, and makes choice more intelligent. There is a circle, but an enlarging circle, or, if you please, a widening spiral. This statement is of course only a formula. We may perhaps supply it with meaning by first considering the matter negatively. Take for example an act following from a blind preference, from an impulse not reflected upon. It will be a matter of luck if the resulting action does not get the one who acts into conflict with surrounding conditions. Conditions go against the realization of his preference; they cut across it, obstruct it, deflect its course, get him into new and perhaps more serious entanglements. Luck may be on his side. Circumstances may happen to be propitious or he may be endowed with native force that enables him to brush aside obstructions and sweep away resistances. He thus gets a certain freedom, judged from the side of power-to-do. But this result is a matter of favor, of grace, of luck; it is not due to anything in himself. Sooner or later he is likely to find his deeds at odds with conditions; an accidental success may only reinforce a foolhardy impulsiveness that renders a man's future subjection the more probable. Enduringly lucky persons are exceptions.

Suppose, on the other hand, our hero's act exhibits a choice expressing a preference formed after consideration of consequences, an intelligent preference. Consequences depend upon an interaction of what he starts to perform with his environment, so he must take the latter into account. No one can foresee all consequences because no one can be aware of all the conditions that enter into their production. Every person builds better or worse than he knows. Good fortune or the favorable co-operation of environment is still necessary. Even with his best thought, a man's proposed course of action may be defeated. But in as far as his act is truly a manifestation of intelligent choice, he learns something: as in a scientific experiment an inquirer may learn through his experimentation, his intelligently directed action, quite as much or even more from a failure than from a success. He finds out at least a little as to what was the matter with his prior choice. He can choose better and *do* better next time; "better choice" meaning a more reflective one, and "better doing" meaning one better co-ordinated with the conditions that are involved in realizing purpose. Such control or power is never complete; luck or fortune, the propitious support of circumstances not foreseeable is always involved. But at least such a person forms the habit of choosing and acting with conscious regard to the grain of circumstance, the run of affairs. And what is more to the point, such a man becomes able to turn frustration and failure to account in his further choices and purposes. Everything in so far serves his purpose—to be an intelligent human being. This gain in power or freedom can be nullified by no amount of external defeats.

N.B.

In a phrase just used, it was implied that intelligent choice may operate on different levels or in different areas. A man may, so to speak, specialize in intelligent choices in the region of economic or political affairs; he may be shrewd, politic, within the limit of these conditions, and in so far attain power in action or be free. Moralists have always held that such success is not success, such power not power, such freedom not freedom, in the ultimate sense.

One does not need to enter upon hortatory moralization in order to employ this contention of the great moral teachers for the sake of eliciting two points. The first is that there are various areas of freedom, because there is a plural diversity of conditions in our environment; and choice, intelligent choice, may select the special area formed by one special set of conditions—familial and domestic, industrial, pecuniary, political, charitable, scientific, ecclesiastic, artistic, etc. I do not mean, of course, that these areas are sharply delimited or that there is not something artificial in their segregation. But within limits, conditions are such that specialized types of choice and kinds of power or freedom develop. The second (and this is the one emphasized by moral teachers in drawing a line between true and false power and freedom), is that there *may* be—these moral idealists insist there *is*—one area in which freedom and power are always attainable by any one, no matter how much he may be blocked in other fields. This of course is the area they call *moral* in a distinctive sense. To put it roughly but more concretely: Any one can be kind, helpful to others, just and temperate in his choices, and in so far be sure of achievement and power in action. It would take more rashness than I possess to assert that there is not an observation of reality in this insight of the great teachers of the race. But without taking up that point, one may venture with confidence upon a hypothetical statement. If and in as far as this idea is correct, there is one way in which the force of fortunate circumstance and lucky original endowment is reduced in comparison with the force of the factor supplied by personal individuality itself. Success, power, freedom in *special* fields is in a maximum degree relatively at the mercy of external conditions. But against kindness and justice there is no law: that is, no counteracting grain of things nor run of affairs. With respect to such choices, there may be freedom and power, no matter what the frustrations and failures in other modes of action. Such is the virtual claim of moral prophets.

A.   An illustration drawn from the denial of the idea that there is an intimate connection of the two modes of freedom, namely, intelligent choice and power in action, may aid in clearing up the idea. The attitude and acts of other persons is of course one of the most important parts of the conditions involved in bringing the manifestation of preference to impotency or to power in action. Take the case of a child in a family where the environment formed by others is such as to humor all his choices. It is made easy for him to do what he pleases. He meets a minimum of resistance; upon the whole others co-operate with him in bringing his preferences to fulfillment. Within this region he seems to have free power of action. By description he is unimpeded, even aided. But it is obvious that as far as he is concerned, this is a matter of luck. He is "free" merely because his surrounding conditions happen to be of the kind they are, a mere happening or accident as far as his make-up and his preferences are concerned. It is evident in such a case that there is *no growth* in the intelligent exercise of preferences. There is rather a conversion of blind impulse into regular habits. Hence his attained freedom is such only in appearance: it disappears as he moves into other social conditions.

Now consider the opposite case. A child is balked, inhibited, interfered with, and nagged pretty continuously in the manifestation of his spontaneous preferences. He is constantly "disciplined" by circumstances adverse to his preferences—as discipline is not infrequently conceived. Does it follow then that he develops in "inner" freedom, in thoughtful preference and purpose? The question answers itself. Rather is some pathological condition the outcome. "Discipline" is indeed necessary as a preliminary to any freedom that is more than unrestrained outward power. But our dominant conception of discipline is a travesty; there is only one genuine discipline, namely, that which takes effect in producing habits of observation and judgment that insure intelligent desires. In short, while men do not think about and gain freedom in conduct unless they run during action against conditions that resist their original impulses, the secret of education consists in having that blend of check and favor which influences thought and foresight, and that takes effect in outward action through this modification of disposition and outlook.

I have borrowed the illustration from the life of a child at home or in school, because the problem is familiar and easily recognizable in those settings. But there is no difference when we consider the adult in industrial, political, and ecclesiastic life. When social conditions are such as to prepare a prosperous career for a man's spontaneous preferences in advance, when things are made easy by institutions and by habits of admiration and approval, there is precisely the same kind of outward freedom, of relatively unimpeded action, as in the case of the spoiled child. But there is hardly more of freedom on the side of varied and flexible capacity of choice; preferences are restricted to the one line laid down, and in the end the individual becomes the slave of his successes. Others, vastly more in number, are in the state of the "disciplined" child. There is hard sledding for their spontaneous preferences; the grain of the environment, especially of existing economic arrangements, runs against them. But the check, the inhibition, to the immediate operation of their native preferences no more confers on them the quality of intelligent choice than it does with the child who never gets a fair chance to try himself out. There is only a crushing that results in apathy and indifference; a deflection into evasion and deceit; a compensatory over-responsiveness to such occasions as permit untrained preferences to run riot—and all the other consequences which the literature of mental and moral pathology has made familiar.

I hope these illustrations may at least have rendered reasonably clear what is intended by our formula; by the idea that freedom consists in a trend of conduct that causes choices to be more diversified and flexible, more plastic and more cognizant of their own meaning, while it enlarges their range of unimpeded operation. There is an important implication in this idea of freedom. The orthodox theory of freedom of the will and the classic theory of Liberalism both define freedom on the basis of something antecedently given, something already possessed. Unlike in contents as are the imputation of unmotivated liberty of choice and of natural rights and native wants, the two ideas have an important element in common. They both seek for freedom in something already there, given in advance. Our idea compels us on the other hand to seek for freedom in something which comes to be, in a certain kind of growth; in consequences rather than in antecedents. We are free not because of what we statically are, but in as far as we are becoming different from what we have been. Reference to another philosophy of freedom, that

Kant

causal law

of Immanuel Kant, who is placed chronologically in the generation preceding that of Hegel and institutional idealism, may aid in developing this idea. If we ignore the cumbrous technicalities of Kant, we may take him as one who was impressed by the rise of natural science and the role played in science by the idea of causation, this being defined as a necessary, universal, or invariant connection of phenomena. Kant saw that in all consistency this principle applies to human phenomena as well as to physical; it is a law of all phenomena. Such a chain of linked phenomena left no room for freedom. But Kant believed in duty, and duty postulates freedom. Hence in his moral being, man is not a phenomenon but a member of a realm of noumena to which as things-in-themselves free causality may be ascribed. It is with the problem rather than the solution we are concerned. How one and the same act can be, naturalistically speaking, causally determined while transcendentally speaking it is free from any such determination is so high a mystery that I shall pass it by.

But the *problem* as Kant stated it has the form in which it weighs most heavily on contemporary consciousness. The idea of a reign of law, of the inclusion of all events under law, has become almost omnipresent. No freedom seems to be left save by alleging that man is somehow supranatural in his make-up—an idea of which Kant's noumenal and transcendental man is hardly more than a translation into a more impressive phraseology.

This way of stating the problem of freedom makes overt, explicit, the assumption that either freedom is something antecedently possessed or else it is nothing at all. The idea is so current that it seems hopeless to question its value. But suppose that the origin of every thought I have had and every word I have uttered is in some sense causally determined, so that if anybody knew enough he could explain the origin of each thought and each word just as the scientific inquirer ideally hopes to explain what happens physically. Suppose also—the argument is hypothetical and so imagination may be permitted to run riot—that my words had the effect of rendering the future choices of some one of my hearers more thoughtful; more cognizant of possible alternatives, and thereby rendering his future choices more varied, flexible, and apt. Would the fact of antecedent causality deprive those future preferences of their actual quality? Would it take away their reality and that of their operation in producing their distinctive effects? There is no superstition more benumbing, I think, than the current notion that things are not what they are, and do not do what they are seen to do, because these things have themselves come into being in a causal way. Water is what it *does* rather than what it is caused by. The same is true of the fact of intelligent choice. A philosophy which looks for freedom in antecedents and one which looks for it in consequences, in a developing course of action, in becoming rather than in static being, will have very different notions about it.

Yet we cannot separate power to become from consideration of what already and antecedently is. Capacity to become different, even though we define freedom by it, must be a present capacity, something in some sense present. At this point of the inquiry, the fact that all existences whatever possess selectivity in action recurs with new import. It may sound absurd to speak of electrons and atoms exhibiting preference, still more perhaps to attribute bias to them. But the absurdity is wholly a matter of the words used. The essential point is that they have a certain opaque and irreducible individuality which shows itself in what they do; in the fact that they behave in certain ways and not in others. In the description of causal sequences, we still have to start with and from existences, things that are individually and uniquely just what they are. The fact that we can state changes which occur by certain uniformities and regularities does not eliminate this original element of individuality, of preference and bias. On the contrary, the statement of laws presupposes just this capacity. We cannot escape this fact by an attempt to treat each thing as an effect of other things. That merely pushes individuality back into those other things. Since we have to admit indi-

viduality no matter how far we carry the chase, we might as
well forego the labor and start with the unescapable fact.

In short, anything that is has something unique in itself,
and this unique something enters into what it does. Science
does not concern itself with the individualities of things. It
is concerned with their *relations*. A law or statement of uniformity like that of the so-called causal sequence tells us
nothing about a thing inherently; it tells us only about an
invariant relation sustained in the behavior of that thing with
that of other things. That this fact implies contingency as an
ultimate and irreducible trait of existence is something too
complicated to go into here. But evidence could be stated from
many contemporary philosophers of science, not writing with
any thought of freedom in mind, but simply as interpreters
of the methods and conclusions of science, to the effect that
the laws leave out of account the inner being of things, and
deal only with their relations with other things. Indeed, if
this were the place and if I only knew enough, it could be
shown, I think, that the great change now going on in the
physical sciences, is connected with this idea. Older formulas
were in effect guilty of confusion. They took knowledge of
the relations that things bear to one another as if it were
knowledge of the things themselves. Many of the corrections
that are now being introduced into physical theories are due
to recognition of this confusion.

The point needs an elaboration that cannot here be given
if its full import for the idea and fact of freedom is to be
clearly perceived. But the connection is there and its general
nature may be seen. The fact that all things show bias, preference or selectivity of reaction, while not itself freedom, is
an indispensable condition of any human freedom. The present tendency among scientific men is to think of laws as statistical in nature—that is, as statements of an "average" found
in the behavior of an enormous number of things, no two of
which are exactly alike. If this line of thought be followed
out, it implies that the existence of laws or uniformities and
regularities among natural phenomena, human acts included,

does not in the least exclude the item of choice as a distinctive fact having its own distinctive consequences. No law does away with individuality of existence, having its own particular way of operating; for a law is concerned with relations and hence presupposes the being and operation of individuals. If choice is found to be a distinctive act, having distinctive consequences, then no appeal to the authority of scientific law can militate in any way against its reality. The problem reduces itself to one of fact. Just what *is* intelligent choice and just what does it effect in human life? I cannot ask you to re-traverse the ground already gone over. But I do claim that the considerations already adduced reveal that what men actually cherish under the name of freedom is that power of varied and flexible growth, of change of disposition and character, that springs from intelligent choice, so there is a sound basis for the common-sense practical belief in freedom, although theories in justification of this belief have often taken an erroneous and even absurd form.

We may indeed go further than we have gone. Not only is the presence of uniform relations of change no bar to the reality of freedom, but these are, *when known,* aids to the development of that freedom. Take the suppositions case already mentioned. That my ideas have causes signifies that their *rise,* their *origin* (not their nature), is a change connected with other changes. If I only knew the connection, my power over obtaining the ideas I want would be that much increased. The same thing holds good of any effect my idea may have upon the ideas and choices of some one else. Knowledge of the conditions under which a choice *arises* is the same as potential ability to guide the formation of choices intelligently. This does not eliminate the distinctive quality of choice; choice is still choice. But it is now an intelligent choice instead of a dumb and stupid one, and thereby the probability of its leading to freedom in unimpeded action is increased.

This fact explains the strategic position occupied in our social and political life by the issue of freedom of thought and freedom of speech. It is unnecessary to dwell by way of

Dewey's Position N.B.

either laudation or exhortation upon the importance of this freedom. If the position already taken—namely, that freedom resides in the development of preferences into intelligent choices—is sound, there is an explanation of the central character of this particular sort of freedom. It has been assumed, in accord with the whole theory of Liberalism, that all that is necessary to secure freedom of thought and expression is removal of external impediments: take away artificial obstructions and thought will operate. This notion involves all the errors of individualistic psychology. Thought is taken to be a native capacity or faculty; all it needs to operate is an outer chance. Thinking, however, is the most difficult occupation in which man engages. If the other arts have to be acquired through ordered apprenticeship, the power to think requires even more conscious and consecutive attention. No more than any other art is it developed internally. It requires favorable objective conditions, just as the art of painting requires paint, brushes, and canvas. The most important problem in freedom of thinking is whether social conditions obstruct the development of judgment and insight or effectively promote it. We take for granted the necessity of special opportunity and prolonged education to secure ability to think in a special calling, like mathematics. But we appear to assume that ability to think effectively in social, political, and moral matters is a gift of God, and that the gift operates by a kind of spontaneous combustion. Few would perhaps defend this doctrine thus boldly stated; but upon the whole we act as if that were true. Even our deliberate education, our schools, are conducted so as to indoctrinate certain beliefs rather than to promote habits of thought. If that is true of them, what is not true of the other social institutions as to their effect upon thought?

This state of things accounts, to my mind, for the current indifference to what is the very heart of actual freedom: freedom of thought. It is considered to be enough to have certain legal guarantees of its possibility. Encroachment upon even the nominal legal guarantees appears to arouse less and less resentment. Indeed, since the mere absence of legal restrictions may take effect only in stimulating the expression of half-baked and foolish ideas, and since the effect of their expression may be idle or harmful, popular sentiment seems to be growing less and less adverse to the exercise of even overt censorships. A genuine energetic interest in the cause of human freedom will manifest itself in a jealous and unremitting care for the influence of social institutions upon the attitudes of curiosity, inquiry, weighing and testing of evidence. I shall begin to believe that we care more for freedom than we do for imposing our own beliefs upon others in order to subject them to our will, when I see that the main purpose of our schools and other institutions is to develop powers of unremitting and discriminating observation and judgment.

The other point is similar. It has often been assumed that freedom of speech, oral and written, is independent of freedom of thought, and that you cannot take the latter away in any case, since it goes on inside of minds where it cannot be got at. No idea could be more mistaken. Expression of ideas in communication is one of the indispensable conditions of the awakening of thought not only in others, but in ourselves. If ideas when aroused cannot be communicated they either fade away or become warped and morbid. The open air of public discussion and communication is an indispensable condition of the birth of ideas and knowledge and of other growth into health and vigor.

I sum up by saying that the possibility of freedom is deeply grounded in our very beings. It is one with our individuality, our being uniquely what we are and not imitators and parasites of others. But like all other possibilities, this possibility has to be actualized; and, like all others, it can only be actualized through interaction with objective conditions. The question of political and economic freedom is not an addendum or afterthought, much less a deviation or excrescence, in the problem of personal freedom. For the conditions that form political and economic liberty are required in order to realize the potentiality of freedom each of us carries with him in his very structure. Constant and uniform relations in change and a knowledge of them in "laws," are not a hindrance to freedom, but a necessary factor in coming to be effectively that which we have the capacity to grow into. Social conditions interact with the preferences of an individual (that *are* his individuality) in a way favorable to actualizing freedom only when they develop intelligence, not abstract knowledge and abstract thought, but power of vision and reflection. For these take effect in making preference, desire, and purpose more flexible, alert, and resolute. Freedom has too long been thought of as an indeterminate power operating in a closed and ended world. In its reality, freedom is a resolute will operating in a world in some respects indeterminate, because open and moving toward a new future.

INDEX